Trade with Passion and Purpose

Spiritual, Psychological, and Philosophical Keys to Becoming a Top Trader

MARK WHISTLER

BICENTENNIAL

1807

WILEY

2007

BICENTENNIAL

John Wiley & Sons, Inc.

Published by John Wiley & Sons, Inc., Hoboken, New Jersey.
Published simultaneously in Canada.

Wiley Bicentennial Logo: Richard J. Pacifico.

For general information on our other products and services or for technical support, please contact our Customer Care Department within the United States at (800) 762-2974, outside the United States at (317) 572-3993 or fax (317) 572-4002.

Wiley also publishes its books in a variety of electronic formats. Some content that appears in print may not be available in electronic books. For more information about Wiley products, visit our web site at www.wiley.com.

Library of Congress Cataloging-in-Publication Data:

Whistler, Mark.
   Trade with passion and purpose : spiritual, psychological, and philosophical keys to becoming a top trader / Mark Whistler.
      p.   cm. – (Wiley trading series)
   Includes bibliographical references and index.
   ISBN 978-0-470-03908-3 (cloth)
    1. Investments – Psychological aspects.   2. Investments – Moral and ethical aspects.
3. Stocks – Religious aspects.   4. Stocks – Moral and ethical aspects.   I. Title.
HG4515.15.W48 2007
332.63'22 – dc22

                                            200603463

Printed in the United States of America.

10 9 8 7 6 5 4 3 2 1

To the memory of Christy Myers and the continued strength of Joe Myers. After fighting cancer for eight years, the world sadly lost Christy in the spring of 2006. If ever there were a woman who was so wonderfully amazing, compassionate, loving, optimistic, and brilliant, Christy was she. Christy and Joe have taught me that no matter what happens in this life, true love conquers all. They've taught me to never stop living life to its fullest each and every day, and to never give up on someone you love. I've never met two more genuine, loving, and sincere people in my life.

Truly, thank you . . . and I love you.

To Cece Anna Lee. In the middle of the mania of this book, you patiently read, and reread, and reread this manuscript after my endless nights of writing. You are my best friend and the most incredible artist I've ever known. You're a beautiful woman and a brilliant editor too! I only hope that someday I am able to support you in the same way.

I love you.

Contents

Acknowledgments

To Karen and Mike Eck and my nephew who is due about the same time that this book will come out: I am so excited for the new addition to your family, and to be the best uncle I can be!

To Sandy Whistler and Ed Juhan: When the world was crumbling, you were there for me at every step. I owe all that I am to you. I love you and thank you for being so incredibly wonderful.

To Kevin Commins, Emilie Herman, and Laura Walsh of John Wiley & Sons: Without you, this book would have never been possible. You are such genuinely good people; I am so grateful for everything that you have done. I'm not sure how to thank you enough! Also, thank you Mary Daniello for your patience.

To Mike Ward, Julia Guth, Karim Rahemtulla, Steve McDonald, and all of my new friends and mentors at The Oxford Club, Mt. Vernon Options Club, and Agora Publishing: I am so thankful for all of you. And, Mike, as my writing gets a little better day by day, I know I owe so much of this to you. Thank you.

To the memory of my godmother, Diane Hall, Eric Hasjford, Sue Landis, and Joan Rodda. These wonderful people all left a footprint in my life, and they are all sorely missed.

Thank you to Bill Wright, Bob Williams, Bobby Juhan, Brad Evans, Del Rio, Dr. Royce Peterman, Hugh McCullogh, Joe Ritchie, Kevin Cuddie, Matt McCall, Mike and Wendy Huff, Mike Palumbo, Paul, Laurren and Alexis Whistler, Rev. Dr. Michael Eckelcamp, Ryan and Jenny Dempster, Sara Jacobson, Steven King, Sue Myers, Vic Frierson, Wayne Ellis, Leigh Stevens, Dr. Lois Conn, Alex Williams, Colleen Monahan, Levi Wardell, Jim Turner, Danielle Morino, and Pamela van Giessen . . . you all helped make this book happen.

Thank you Perry Henderson for being a friend, mentor, and spiritual guide when I needed you most.

Thank you Francois Safieddine for still believing in me, even when my trading was falling through the floor.

And thank you Ed Gunts for the beautiful rowhome while I was finishing this book.

To Reuben the cat: You've taught me that no meal, and not one single moment to share love, should ever be overlooked. You, sir, are so very, very brilliant. And yes, I know you can read this . . . I find your paw prints all over my manuscripts all the time.

MARK WHISTLER

Introduction

It's the possibility of having a dream
come true that makes life interesting.
—Pablo Coelho, *The Alchemist*

Everyone knows that trading is a dirty, cutthroat business. It brings out our dark side. People do it for one reason only: to make money. But this book breaks the myth that trading is a soul-less act. The key to being a successful trader is not how hungry you are, or how much you know about the markets, or even how much of an edge you have over the other guy. The key, as you'll see, is forged from personal strength and emotional intelligence. The key to being an incredible trader comes from a well-rounded sense of psychology and spirituality. It emerges from a quality of being from within. It's a concept that you won't find in most trading or investing books.

Understanding ourselves, our emotions, our drives, and the way we interact with life and trading are critical to developing a purpose-center, which is a deep accepting of ourselves and our direction in life (something you will read more about in Chapter 1). You can't make all your dreams come true without knowing who you are and why you're doing what you're doing. And, if you're going to trade, it means little if you are doing it without passion and a purpose-center. I'm asking you to take control of your trading life right now... at this very moment. Your future is in this very second, and with every word written here; and by taking immediate action, you will be the most incredible trader that you can possibly dream.

Unfortunately in reality, much of Hollywood's take on the stereotypical Gordon Gecko–type trader is probably pretty accurate. Many in the financial markets are very, very, mean and greedy people. But there are those who aren't. And when you meet one of them, you know you are standing in the presence of true brilliance. And, thankfully, throughout my career, I've been fortunate to meet some of these amazing people, who have taught me how to steer clear of the avaricious megalomaniacal monsters that often covet the worlds of finance and trading.

Life is tough, and trading is too... there's no doubt about it. But regardless of the difficulties we face, any of our dreams can come to fruition, no matter how old we are, or where we're at in our lives. We simply have to dig within ourselves to find all the answers, because they're already in there.

I'm going to take you on a journey of self-discovery and inspiration. Think of it as a psychological boot camp that will hone your skills as a trader.

- You'll read interviews with incredible traders, a professional athlete, two doctors, and two men who have overcome amazing adversity, all showing that you have the same core abilities that they had to become successful.
- You'll learn the importance of understanding stress and how to work with it, affirmations, and visualizations, and you'll learn how to relax.
- You'll learn about fear, how to recognize it, and how to defeat it as well. What's more, we'll develop direct understanding of your trading future through a trading plan and risk plan designed to help you value the most important person of all: you!
- Finally, we're going to uncover the inevitable market truth of change and the veracity of intuition, all the while finding a sense of gratitude that will enable you to be the best you can possibly be. Without this honed psychological tool bag, you can only be mediocre trader at best.

BELIEVING IN OURSELVES

Sometimes believing in ourselves in the middle of a chaotic trading career seems like a losing proposition. Here's the thing about the markets: All the financial education in the entire world will never help any of us make a single dime in the market, unless we understand why markets really move. And there's only one reason why they do: Markets move up or down *only* because traders and investors *believe* they should be buying or selling at that time. It's ridiculously simple, I know. But stick with me for a moment.

In trading, "It is what it is." And what it is, is a collective mind-set of fear and greed. You've heard it before . . . it's the old market cliché that's been passed on for many, many years. But clichés are true for a reason.

Amazingly, so many of us think that there's some cloak-and-dagger number, or magical algorithm to the financial markets and life. But here's the big secret: *there is*. It's you . . . and me. It's our own emotional understanding, united with our knowledge and effort that is the secret to prosperity. This is the enigmatic key that dogs so many of us. The mystical algorithm of success in life (and in the markets) is simply our understanding of human emotions, coupled with a solid understanding of ourselves. With our past experiences, the information at hand, and our expectations of the future, nothing can stop us from plugging into the markets. *Anyone* can do it.

It's almost impossible for any of us to make any decision without any emotion whatsoever. It's just not how humans are programmed. From the very beginning, most of us are wired to feel, and there's nothing we can do to totally shut out our personalities from the moments at hand. However, if we dig deep into understanding why we do what we do, and then work on trying to keep ourselves balanced during emotionally stressful moments, we have the possibility of making the most of every second, and every trade that crosses our paths.

Like a Zen master, we have the ability to make calm, purpose-centered decisions in the markets and in life . . . and make all our wildest dreams come true. Our dreams are the foundation of every ounce of hope in this world. Our dreams give us hope. And, I put my entire self behind these words: Hope is one of the most beautiful things in this entire world.

No one can destroy all hope. Very, very wretched people and horrendously difficult situations can stamp out hope temporarily, *but hope will always return.* While it's true that many of our dreams are slightly different, we all still hope that our dreams will come true. Hope is the key to the rhythm of success. Within hope is every single dream—of everything wonderful and brilliant. And for many of us, making our dreams come true is why we trade everyday . . . because in the financial markets, we have a shot at making all of our dreams a reality.

> *All men dream but not equally. Those who dream by night in the dusty recesses of their minds wake in the day to find that it was vanity; but the dreamers of the day are dangerous men, for they may act their dream with open eyes to make it possible.*
> —T.E. Lawrence

I've been investing for almost 10 years and have been trading professionally for the past 8 . . . since just before the markets began to tumble in 1999. Boy, do I ever have timing! However, the lessons I've learned about the markets and about life are immeasurable. Perhaps it's only because I've been lucky enough to have timed my professional career with one of the most volatile and unforgiving markets of the past century. Thankfully though, when times got tough, I never gave up, and because of that, I gained enormous insights into how and why we succeed as traders. What it comes down to is all the fundamental, technical, or mathematical trading brilliance in the world won't save us unless we have a strong grasp of our emotions. The market is unforgiving, and if you overstep the most important part of trading—you!—your account is dead in the water. I know because I've been there, more than once. But I've personally seen that as I've come to better understand my own emotions, and understand that I need to keep myself calm while the entire market is a storm, my wealth continues to grow day by day.

If you're going through hell, keep going.
—Sir Winston Churchill

In this book, I believe I've identified what separates superstar traders from the crowd. I've discovered strategies of self that most investment books never mention. Most importantly, I discovered the single most important success factor: If you dig deep with an internal sense of confidence, you'll find you can't lose. You have all the tools you need within your own heart.

Some of you reading this book might be doing so because the market's been kicking you around a little. And, truthfully, it seems like most traders and investors don't usually begin to look into market psychology until they're bruised by a few dings. It's simply in our nature that we don't really look for answers until we get beat up a few times. Funny enough, life is the exact same way . . . most people don't turn to introspective books or help from others until something's gone terribly wrong. Conversely, if you're one of the few proactively seeking to improve themselves, and if you're one of the insightful, congratulations! But, if you're trying to turn over a few new stones—in light of some recently tough times—give yourself a pat on the back as well. It takes guts, and more importantly, *honesty* to look inward. I applaud you for taking this road. Every losing trade, every wrong call, every miscalculated market correction, and every mistaken detail in research that leads to misfortune is just another opportunity for success. Every time we err, we have a chance to blossom bigger, brighter, and more brilliant than ever.

Not taking time for introspective self-evaluation can often lead to further breakdown of self-worth. Denying ourselves the proper time for intense honesty and acceptance in the midst of any challenge simply discounts any possible reconciliation and future hope. After all, if a lesson is not evaluated and learned, history is doomed to repeat itself . . . over and over. Consequently, those who have not learned from the past are doomed to a life much like that of the mythological Greek figure Sisyphus, who spends eternity pushing a boulder up a hill, only to see it roll back down every time he gets to the top. Such is the life of a trader! But unlike Sisyphus, we can reach the top . . . and see our boulders stay there. But it takes time, guts, the desire to ask ourselves some hard questions, and then relentless determination to take action.

I've pointlessly rolled the same boulder up the same hill so many times that I lost count. Every time that boulder rolled to the bottom, I was crushed. But still, I did it again and again. I learned that the first time the boulder rolls down is the worst. That hurt can break every ounce of spirit. *But every time after, whenever the boulder rolls down again, it hurts less and less.*

And then that hurt changes. You discover that the hurt is completely within yourself, something self-created, until you ask yourself:

"Why am I rolling the same boulder up again and again?" It's our own lack of self-understanding that's doing the wounding. So why do we keep rolling the boulder up the hill, when we absolutely know it will roll back down, over and over? Is it blind faith? Is it empty hope? Is it just bad luck?

Nope. We push that boulder up time and time again, because we haven't resolved something within ourselves, . . . something which needs to change. The boulder and the hill aren't the problem; it's our approach to the situation (in trading or life) that's the problem. We've somehow missed the point that if we don't change something, the same thing will continue endlessly. And let me tell you, as we get a little older, the boulder constantly gets more difficult to push up that same damn hill.

But hopefully we finally get smart. After becoming completely exhausted from the never-changing outcome, we eventually stop and ask, "If I roll it up one more time, how am I going to make it stick?"

When we get to the point of asking this question, it is the point where everything changes. That's where this book begins. It's the turning point; *your* turning point. No longer will you roll that boulder up pointlessly. This book will show you the secrets to making that boulder stay at the top. It will stay once you make a total change in your perception, and it will be as real, illuminating, and satisfying as a winning portfolio. As one of my most respected friends, Denver Parks, says, "Yield not; within yourself every change is possible. Yield not; within yourself is every answer."

With Mr. Parks's words in mind, take a moment to read the poem, "Brilliant Hope" by Joppa JaMocha:

Dreams will never fade
And our destiny is never truly made
And even when the night is brisk with frost
There is no reason to ever be afraid
Because trust can never be lost

Never give up . . . even if all seems gone
. . . And see that which we truly love
Forever stand tall and strong . . .
Real truth comes from within our hearts
Knowing our passions can never fall apart

We quietly reflect on all of time
Wishing for everything to unwind
It's true . . . life can change on a dime
And when we least expect to touch the sky
We do so in the blink of an eye

The ship of self can float adrift
Can the fate of this man ever shift?
Drifting from shore with broken rope
The whole of soul feels lost and missed
But in the end, there's only brilliant hope.

Looking inward to evaluate ourselves can make all the difference in the world to help us become successful traders, and, as I've already mentioned, to help us find the rhythm of success. But taking the road less traveled requires an open mind, unequivocal unbiased honesty, self-evaluation, and then unrelenting effort—all of which you will read about in this book. These are the lessons of one hell of a tough trading career . . . and the rocky road of life.

I've searched high and low for every bit of psychological, historical, philosophical, and spiritual information that relates to those of us who are constantly striving for something greater as people, investors, and traders. And I've done my best to keep things unbiased, especially with the spiritual stuff. Honestly, I would be *very* surprised if some readers aren't already asking why there's "spiritual mumbo jumbo" in here in the first place. Good question. Here's why: No matter what, you believe in something. I don't care if you're Buddhist, Christian, atheist, or whatever. In the end you believe in something. For atheists, believing in nothing is still believing in the something of nothingness. At the end of the day, though, the questions we ask the universe about our existence—if even at the very least—define a little bit about who and what we are. We all ask. Not one of us hasn't at one time or another. With this insight in mind, please understand that I believe *all* things spiritual have important lessons to help us on our journey, if even only on an intellectual level.

Lastly, please remember that hope is the most important thing in the world. And when we go through very tough times, hope is born of suffering. During times of intense difficulty and anguish, we have opportunities to grow as people. Thus I say to every losing trade, every wrong call, every miscalculated market correction, and every mistaken detail in research that leads to misfortune . . . bring it on! And, bring it on again and again, because every time we err, we have a chance to become bigger, brighter, and better than ever!

All of the Answers Are Already Within

Part I of *Trade with Passion and Purpose* looks at basic psychological concepts in an effort to understand the framework behind why we make the decisions that we do. At times you may wonder how the concepts actually apply to trading in the stock market, but it's important to keep reading. Experienced traders know that success in the markets is less about what's happening with stocks and more about what's happening inside of each individual to influence their decisions to buy or sell. It's easy to assume that our financial and trading knowledge is what will make us successful or not. However, our book knowledge is not what will make us successful traders. Instead, it is our understanding of our self and our ability to handle stress, fear, and anxiety that will help us to be the best we can be in the world of trading.

At the end of the day, buying and selling are decisions built on emotions. As much as we try to logically reason through everything, the fact is that emotions are a major part of every trader's day. And if we don't understand *why* we are making the decisions we are, then all the logic piled on top will never make a difference. Imagine being an auto mechanic without really ever understanding how an engine works. You might be able to fix the occasional small problem, but when it comes to rebuilding the whole thing, you might as well forget it. But if you've taken the time to understand all of the principles, you won't just be able to rebuild an engine, you might also be able to make the engine even better.

Thus, while you're reading Part I of the book, remember that the markets are about emotions, not just numbers. If we take the time to look at our personal principles of self, we will know how we are *emotionally* reacting to the movements of the markets. And by looking into self, we will learn not only to trade with passion and purpose, but also by instinct and intuition.

All of the concepts in Part I have to do with you, not the markets. You are the most important part of the market, because you are the only one pushing the buy and sell button. It's easy to overlook this point and only look outside of ourselves for market factors that present trading opportunities. However, truly profitable trading does not come from the market, it comes from us, distinguishing when opportunity has presented itself and then pulling the trigger. Successful trading is built on a solid sense of personal psychology and emotions, not numbers.

CHAPTER 1

Finding Your Purpose-Center

The greatest revolution of our generation is the discovery that human beings, by changing the inner attitudes of their minds, can change the outer aspects of their lives.

—William James

Deep in your heart, you have all the answers. You already know the answers to questions like: Do I love my life? Do I really love trading? Can I really make it? Do I have the dedication? Do I really want to be doing this? If you dig deeply and honestly, you'll find a clear, firm *purpose-centered* voice that will guide you through the chaos.

Looking deep within and inquiring whether you are truly open to change is the first step toward taking your life to the next level. Have you ever tried to study for an exam in a course that you absolutely hated? It's almost impossible. If your heart isn't in it, generally you'll be lucky to pull off an average grade. But we don't just want to be average; we want to live *passionately with purpose* to find true happiness.

THE GROUNDWORK

We *want* to be successful. But what is success? The answer is different for everyone. For some, success is $500 a month, enough to live humbly and paint the days away. For others, it means becoming the next Warren Buffett. Success is a deeply personal feeling, and achieving success isn't easy, especially if your yardstick is tied to making money in the markets.

So where do we begin? First and foremost, we must make a conscious commitment to persevere, even when things are tough. This admonition sounds simple, but is often overlooked. To be successful in the markets, we have to make the initial conscious commitment to be the best we can be and to love every moment of what we're doing. Write down a statement of commitment and display it to where you can see it. It's critical to keep reminding yourself, "I am a trader, and I've already made the conscious commitment to being the best trader I can possibly be. I equally understand there are going to be some very tough times ahead, but when they come, I will remain calm and weather the storm." Use language that feels true for you, but writing out something similar is the first step to clarifying your commitment to trading with passion and purpose. The only person who can make a difference in your bottom line is you. And, we often forget that we are in control of our trading destiny. We cannot rely on hope or luck; we need to rely only on the conscious decisions we make every day.

The key to making these decisions rationally is to make the conscious commitment to becoming the best traders we can be. Part of this commitment comes from finding our purpose-center, so we know why we are doing what we are doing. Once we've completed this step and made the conscious commitment to being the best we can be, we're ready to take the additional steps to lay the groundwork for our success. The next section in this chapter helps us find our purpose-center by taking the time to outline our mission statements.

Once we have a deep understanding of why we are doing what we are doing, we can then look into the framework of our beliefs and discover why we make the trading decisions that we do. Specifically, you'll read about this concept in terms of Morita therapy and dogma. Morita therapy helps us remain in the moment, while understanding dogma helps us transcend the beliefs that hold us down, all of which will help us live and trade with a purpose-center, in the zone. I would like to reiterate that while reading Part I, you may wonder, "What does this have to do with trading?" Understanding your mission statement and being able to stay "in the moment" has everything to do with trading. There are countless books out there on trading strategies, but none will do you an iota of good if you do not have a solid understanding of your own psyche. Trading is emotional, a fact that's easy to overlook. But as the most important key to success, it is something that we simply cannot afford to schlep aside.

CLARIFYING YOUR PURPOSE-CENTER THROUGH THE MISSION STATEMENT

As with anything else in life, to be effective traders, we need to be passionate about what we are doing. In the world of trading, passion can be our lifeline to profitability. More important, we must have a clear purpose of who we are, what we believe in, and what we are attempting to do. We must understand the macro picture of ourselves. So many of us wander around from day to day never knowing what our purpose is. And while some may never find their true purpose in life, we can at least *try* to understand what it is that we are seeking from a calm, rational stance, particularly in the markets. If we don't have some idea as to why we are trying to accomplish what we are, we will simply wander aimlessly from thing to thing, until we finally cave in or, by luck, find the one thing that fits. While this wandering course may ultimately prove successful, the journey is that much more difficult and confusing.

Finding our bigger purpose in life is certainly something that each of us must undertake on our own. Everyone's purpose is unique. My aim is to help you uncover your life and investing purposes by looking at the bigger picture of who you are, your desires, and the motivations behind your wishes. This discovery is essential to becoming great traders.

To begin clarifying your purpose in the market (and life), take a moment to write down why you are trading in the first place, what you want out of trading, and what you hope to achieve. This is what I wrote:

My trading purpose is to make money, and I am trading because I love trading. Moreover, I am trading so that I can financially liberate myself to pursue my other passions: painting, writing, helping others, my spiritual journey, and my family. I am a trader because I love the excitement of it. I am trading for a living because I want to make $50 million dollars before I am 40. I believe that in the markets, anything is possible, and I believe I can do it.

You might be asking yourself: Why is any of this necessary? My argument is this: The primary step in ensuring our success is knowing precisely why we're doing what we're doing. The road to success is stressful. When everything is crumbling and I ask myself, "What's the point?" because I've written out my mission statement and clarified my purpose-center (which you just read), I will have an *answer*. That answer is my purpose-center, and because I have taken the time to write it out, I will overcome the self-defeating lack of self-assuredness that the other guys around me are probably going through, and I will instantly have given myself the psychological edge of having a clear understanding within myself of *why* I am doing what I am doing. It's one less question to rattle around in my head when I need to be clear to make accurate decisions.

When the heat turns on in the market (and life), we can often ask ourselves, "What's the point?" I ask myself this negative question particularly often after a sting of losing trades. But when I do, I remind myself of what I have already written out in my purpose-center mission statement, and then in the back of my mind I say, "Oh yeah, now I remember."

Let me give you an example. In October of 2006, I felt the markets were significantly overbought and that a reversal would soon appear. Through my research, I noticed that there was plenty of room to run on the upside over the long term, but for the present moment, the major indexes had run up way too fast. I believed that a significant pullback would appear, bringing the indexes back to a normal level, where buying could then resume.

Acting on this belief, I began taking put positions on almost everything I could find. Within a week of Halloween, I had built option positions exceeding 1,600 put contracts, or 160,000 shares. But I was early, and before I knew it, my options had lost over $60,000 in premium, due to time decay, and the market's traveling higher. I felt very frustrated, angry, and, most of all, just plain wrong. Every night, I would pore over charts, earnings releases, and economic data. And at about midnight, when I turned off the lights, I felt the same way... that the markets were overbought in the short-term.

Then each day I'd try to trade my way out of the market moving higher, while my P&L continued to grow more and more red. Countless times I asked myself, "If I'm so good, why am I losing so bad? What's the point? No one can beat the markets." And then, somewhere inside of me, a little voice would say, "I am trading for a living because I love it; that's the point. And if it was easy, everyone would be doing it."

I hung in there, and in the first week of the November, most of my positions traded exactly in the direction I'd hoped, and I kicked butt. But these gains didn't come without a price; I've never been so stressed out in my entire life, and it was all I could do to simply keep it together. But I learned that knowing our purpose-center works... especially when times get really, really tough. This isn't just talk. What I'm covering in this book are things that have helped me make a ton of money. Simply examining my psyche and knowing my purpose-center saved me from closing my positions when the walls were caving in.

It's as simple as this: In writing down a trading mission statement, we provide ourselves with a clear idea of why we're doing what we're doing.

You might have noticed that my trading purpose overlaps into some of my life's purposes as well. And, I think for many, we will find that as we turn over one stone of purpose on a micro level (like trading), we will find another stone of our macro life purposes. Knowing why we are doing what we are will give us that much better chance of moving through our trades with precise direction. If we haven't honestly clarified why we're trading in the first place, when things start to get really rough, there's a pretty good chance (read: almost certain) that we will begin to question everything.

If we know our purpose-center, every moment is a new beginning in which we can change everything that is. It's the place where, no matter how disappointed we feel, we will remember our dreams and find hope again. If we know our purpose-center, our dreams are that much closer to becoming a reality.

I cannot stress how important it is to *write down your mission statement (purpose-center)*. You might think doing so is corny, but it's not. It's good housekeeping and is as vital as writing down your goals often. Unless you just get lucky, you will *never* make it in the world of trading if you don't have some idea of how and why. I've seen thousands of traders blow up and fade out because they never made the solid commitment to plan how they are going to succeed based on *why* they were trading in the first place. They flounder, they dwindle, they're gone before you know it. Don't be one of them.

Writing down your mission statement and knowing your purpose-center is not the same as creating a trading plan. The two activities overlap, but they are not the same. The mission statement clarifies *why* you are doing what you are doing; the trading plan lays out *how* you're going to get there, and it is vital to being a successful trader as well. Chapter 17 covers the trading plan.

It's easy to struggle with the mission statement, as it means that we have to know ourselves on an intimate level, while embracing and accepting all of our faults, strengths, and characteristics of self that make us who we are. If we find that we are not centered, perhaps it is because we haven't quite found an understanding of ourselves. And, with so many outside distractions, if we are not centered, we can easily become pawns in the larger game of life, allowing ourselves to be tossed about by its changing and chaotic winds. With this concept in mind, over the next section we investigate and test our purpose-centeredness from the standpoint of Morita therapy and dogma. Some of the ideas may surprise you! In Chapter 3, you then take these concepts one step further, putting them in the context of ego and esteem.

For now though, we focus solely on the purpose-center of our balanced self. The following concepts are very important in day-to-day life and the world of trading, and can help you narrow your mission statement as well.

MORITA THERAPY AND DOGMA

Founded in Japan by Dr. Shoma Morita in the late 1800s and early 1900s, Morita therapy combines principles of psychotherapy with hints of Zen Buddhism. Morita was forming his ideas in Asia at the same time as Sigmund Freud and Carl Jung were working in Europe. For the context of this discussion, we do not delve into Freud, though we cover a slight bit of Jung and the collective unconscious, which you will read more about in Chapter 9.

Dr. Morita attempted to bring each person into the "now" by making the subject cognitively aware of what reality was presenting at that particular moment in time.[1] Dr. Morita believed that unless we understand and are aware of what is happening in the reality around us, we cannot understand what needs to be done. If we cannot or do not want to see the reality unfolding in front of our very eyes, we just won't have the perceptive ability to create change . . . or simply handle the events at hand. His theory further contends that we have to understand what we can and cannot control, and not try to fix everything. Those things that are beyond our control must be comprehended in an undetached manner and then accepted. We must understand the moment, but not overanalyze every second that crosses our path.

Morita therapy finds some similarity to the Serenity Prayer of Alcoholics Anonymous, which says, "God, grant me the serenity to accept the things I cannot change, the courage to change the things I can, and the wisdom to know the difference." (Oddly enough, some roots of Alcoholics Anonymous can be traced back to Carl Jung through one of his patients, Rowland H., who eventually passed his ideas along to Ebby Thatcher, a friend of A.A. cofounder, Bill Wilson.) The point is that we must have the courage to change the things that we can, and to let go of the things that we can't. You've heard the statement "It is what it is." What this statement is saying is that "it" is done, and that by accepting "it," we receptively bring ourselves into the moment at hand. We are not pretending "it" is something different than the reality that it is. When we admit the truth of the situation to ourselves, we validate our feelings and ourselves as people. And we are accepting the reality of the moment at hand.

It's important to understand that by accepting the moment at hand, and letting go of the things we cannot control doesn't mean that we mindlessly forget what has happened or ignore the future. It means that we understand that we can analyze the past and the future, but we accept the present and make a conscious decision to remain completely in "it." When we don't feel emotionally comfortable with something, one of the easiest things for us to do is check out. We basically build a comfy little wall of apathy, resentment, anger, or some other defensive emotion so that we don't have to really examine the emotion at hand. It's a game we all play with ourselves, especially when we are faced with the possibility that we are wrong. Some people do this by blaming other people for the problems in their life, a bad trade they just made, or the complete devastation of their portfolio. No one likes to admit they were in control of the things that caused the walls to crumble.

In Morita therapy, when we develop this bad habit (which tends to lead to anxiety), we must take one step at a time to correct the problem. Part of the healing process in Morita therapy is living in a state of *arugamama*, which means accepting our feelings or thoughts without trying to change them. When we actively involve Morita therapy in our purpose-center, we are accepting ourselves for all that we are. Moreover, when we have a losing trade and, instead of trying to blame it on some facet of the market, accept that we made the wrong decision and accept the grief, pain, and sense of loss that accompanies the losing trade, we free ourselves. In doing so, we are able to move beyond the moment at hand.[2]

Think about what you have just read in terms of dogma. Dogma is a principle, doctrine, or belief that is upheld regardless of truth.[3] It's important to note that my referring to dogma here is not done from the standpoint of religion. Instead, I am referring to dogma and dogmatism as upholding beliefs only to conform to what we have been conditioned to know on social and business levels. The problem is that when we abide by the dogmatic principles of what we've been conditioned to believe, we fail to see the truth of the situation. In other words, our attachment to dogma dangerously blinds us from seeing, experiencing, and understanding multiple facets of any situation. From the standpoint of Morita therapy, unchecked dogma only keeps us from becoming purpose-centered people, because we wind up seeing reality with a rigid, one-sided lens. Moreover, if we do not see the present in a clear sense, we cannot know what to do in trivial and difficult situations, except stick to whatever idiosyncratic line of thinking we've subconsciously, or consciously, accepted as reality.

Thus, in our journey to find our purpose-center we must be in the moment, shedding the potentially dogmatic principles that are restricting us from ourselves and a clear sense of reality. Morita therapy holds that we must transcend our feelings and emotions to find our purpose-center. But we can only do so by accepting our feelings and emotions. We must understand the dogma of ourselves and the dogma of the market around us. In doing so, our sense of self evolves into a new paradigm of centered awareness that allows us to move beyond conventionally upheld imaginary beliefs. If we do not take the time to accept the emotions that are the true cause of our discomfort, we can create a credulous reality that will only keep us from the moment. To overcome this destructive way of life, we must simply acknowledge and accept our feelings in order to move beyond them and remain centered. We must break the defensive dogma of self that keeps us from accepting ourselves and the reality of the situation at hand. Through this acceptance, we bring ourselves in the moment. And to be successful traders, this is a principle that we must attempt to embrace. Otherwise we will never be able to remain purpose-centered within ourselves, the moment at hand, and the markets we are trading in.

In the Western world of psychology, we are often taught that we should learn to control our emotions. This viewpoint holds that by controlling our emotions, we can overcome ourselves. But we're only human, you and me. We have emotions, and when investing, we often have a flood of them.

Through Morita therapy, we need to understand that our feelings are uncontrollable; we can't just stuff them down or pretend that they're not happening. We can't just control them and make them go away. In Morita therapy we're not trying to modify our emotions or push them aside; we're simply accepting them. When we accept what we are feeling, we can take new action without pretending that the emotion we were just feeling doesn't exist. We accept the emotion and thus transcend it. We are not trying to make the bad emotion go away, we're just saying, "it is what it is," and opening ourselves up to new emotions.

Accepting our emotions when they surface creates a state of nonsuffering. What's more, when we accept our emotions, we often are able to let them go, which also brings us out of a state of "me." Anger is an emotion based on "me." Sadness is an emotion based on "me." Hope is an emotion based on something that will happen in the future. While hope is an emotion that has much to do "me," it is not an emotion that is completely preoccupied with ourselves. It is an emotion that relies on a positive event in the future. When we accept our negative emotions (like anger from a losing trade), we leave our pity-pot, step into the moment, and look for the next great trade. Accepting our emotions is an act of personal balance. And this is why Morita therapy is called "the psychology of action." We're not just sitting around analyzing why we're mad at the trade we just made; we're saying to ourselves, "I'm mad at myself, I made a bad decision, and I accept that I made that decision. It's okay to be mad at myself, and I'm going to try to make a better trading decision the next time."

If we're going to be great, we have to take action, not sit around and analyze why we're sad, mad, or frustrated. We do need to understand that there are some emotions that need to be examined—like fear—but in the end, the only way to overcome the emotion is to accept it. (Chapter 6 covers fear in more detail.) If we're afraid of something, we can't just face it without first accepting it. If we do, we won't know how to let go of it, because we have never really accepted it as a valid emotion in the first place. From a general stance of social conditioning (seen in much Western psychology), if you fall off a bike, mostly we're taught to get back up and do it again. Don't think about it, just do it. And that's fine; it is taking action, after all. But even after you get back on the bike, you'll still have that fear in the back of your mind. It won't be until you ride it over and over that you build confidence. But if you say, "I'm afraid to ride that bike again, and I just accept the fear as fear, and recognize that it is fear. But I'm going to try to do it again," when you do get back on the bike, you have a greater chance of being purged from the fear for good because you know what it is, and have recognized it. And you might be more courageous about riding the bike sooner because you know why you're not courageous. You're courageous because you were feeling fearful, and your actions have overcome the fear. It's important to point out that we didn't overanalyze why we were fearful of riding the bike; we just accepted that we were.

From another viewpoint, by accepting our emotions, such as elation when a huge trade moves in our direction, we recenter ourselves so as not to make a foolish decision in the future without thinking. Accepting our successes as an emotion keeps our ego in check...something you'll read more about in Chapter 16 on self-destruction.

The bottom line is that to accept our emotions, we must break down the dogma of self and the world around us to have a clear sense of personal understanding. When we challenge dogma, we strengthen our purpose-center.

PURPOSE-CENTER AS SELF-AWARENESS IN STYLE

Ponder the word *proprioception* for a moment. What this funny word means is to have a sense of self. I stumbled on this word, when reading about tango. When dancing the tango, "to become experts in shared movement, we need to learn how to extend ourselves through our partner's body—an extension that is continually changing shape, balance, axis, and position."[4] Think of the stock market as your dance partner. When you move with the market, you have to understand that so many factors are constantly shifting. To have a solid sense of self and avoid falling on your face, you need to really pay attention to your space, your movements, the music. Without a sense of self in the greater picture, we are hopelessly moving erratically, while continually stepping on the toes of the market around us.

In trading, many are not purpose-centered because they have not found the truth within themselves, but also have not found where they stand in the market that surrounds them. Many generally assume that there are hard-and-fast rules to trading and that a particular style of trading will return constant profits. And when they hear about a style of trading that works well for another (usually hype), they chase after it like hounds on the hunt. But there is a fundamental breakdown in doing so. When we simply apply the so-called rules of the game that have been developed by someone else without taking ourselves into the equation, we forget that *we are the most important part of the equation.* What I'm referring to is the false belief that there can ever be a set of hard rules of trading that exclude human emotion. So many people rely on the idea that there's an infallible system of trading that will always work for them. It's dogma all over again, and one that can inevitably lead to an unpleasant surprise.

Let me paint a brief picture of what I'm talking about. A tennis player can master all the rules of the game. She can have a mechanically sound swing that returns the ball time and time again. However, she may also find that when in competition, she is running ragged all over the court. And then she loses the game. When she stops to ask what went wrong, she might stumble on the idea that she's simply not playing "her game." Perhaps she failed to consider that depending on what she thinks as her saving grace—be it that same mechanical swing or some other strength—it did not allow her to play as aggressively as she could or be the best tennis player possible. She is relying so much on the fundamentals of the game that she forgets to consider the changes in her environment, or even within herself. Once she finds her purpose-center she can then refine the mechanics of the game to best suit her abilities and play in harmony with the ever-changing moment. Understanding the mechanics of the game is vital, but understanding how we each can best utilize the mechanics is even more important.

Some of the best traders know all the rules, but they play with a purpose-centered, personalized style of trading that puts money into their pockets on a regular basis. They have found out how to live in the reality of the moment, with their own style, while understanding that there are never dogmatic hard rules to every situation. Their purpose-center informs their every move. Self-awareness through purpose-center is the combination of knowledge and an actualized sense of style. Purpose-center is moving beyond simply protecting ourselves from our feelings by restricting ourselves to the fundamentals of the game. When we have a solid sense of self and purpose-center, we are living in the moment and seeing all of reality clearly.

See, the market is a really tricky place, and often the game shifts on a regular basis. I've seen many instances of a company reporting blowout earnings, only to then see the stock tank. All fundamental logic said the stock should have gone up. But it didn't. Someone somewhere had a huge position and decided to dump it because the earnings (even though they beat Wall Street), didn't quite fit the bill. Fundamental rules would have said to hold the stock after earnings, but the reality of the situation was more like "get rid of it," otherwise you're going to be stuck in a loser. In developing our sense of style while still understanding the fundamentals, we may have had a better chance of seeing the moment, situation, and sell off more clearly. The market is tricky, and the mechanics *always* change.

Now let's apply this concept of purpose-center in the practical sense. When you quiet yourself, how do you perform the best when the heat is on? Listen closely to yourself. Picture yourself right now where you do all your trading. Where are you? How are you breathing? What do your shoulders feel like? Pay attention to what's going on inside your mind and body. Now acknowledge the emotions that begin to surface when the bids in your portfolio's position start to dry up. In your mind's eye—and be very honest with yourself—are you performing to your highest level without emotion? What do you do next? Can you identify how you feel? Are any of your actions/decisions based on protecting your emotional well-being? Do you break down because you were trading something that you felt uncomfortable with? Do you discover you were trading a particular market that is above your risk tolerance? The point is that when we find out what we are comfortable with and what appeals most to us—what *feels* absolutely right—we have taken a crucial step to finding our purpose-center. Even more important, if we can calmly look at ourselves when everything starts to fall apart and our emotions form a violent tornado within, we are given a precious and vital opportunity to finally overcome the destructive habit of never seeing the situation clearly. It's often said that you have to know all the rules before you can break them. And this is too often all too true. But when we have a solid sense of self and know our purpose-center, we develop our own style while also being able to still see all situations clearly. We are well balanced from within, because we can live in the moment while still hanging on the infrastructure of self that is our style. In essence, we know the so-called rules of the market, but because we also know the rules of ourselves, we can break the rules of the market . . . and create the trading success we dream of.

We all know—internally—when we are off balance. We know when we are doing something that makes us feel off-kilter. In trading, if you feel off-kilter, you are not trading in the purpose-center of you, and most likely the emotion of the situation will command the outcome. If you are a technician, and you decide to buy a stock because the price-earnings ratio is low, will you know where to close the trade if the stock begins to tumble? What I'm saying is that if you are a technical analyst, why did you allow fundamentals to get you into the trade? In contrast, you may be a fundamental analyst, holding a stock that you believe is a great value. If the stock breaks below the 200-day moving average, and you close it based on the aforementioned technical event, will you be kicking yourself when Wall Street realizes the stock *is* a good value and buys it up?

But, there's more to this story. Sometimes we find a method of style that appeals to us, and by getting attached to this method, somehow forget to recognize the other important facets of knowledge that are so vitally important to our success. Remember our tennis player with the mechanical swing? In essence, when we mistakenly determine that the strict fundamentals of the game are our purpose-center, we are really creating a falsely dogmatic situation that will only set us up for failure. The key is to remain open to all possibilities. Again, only by knowing all the rules will we ever be able to break them.

THE DOGMA OF STYLE

Purpose-centeredness with Morita theory holds the idea that if you believe you are a fundamental or technical analyst in the first place is a dogmatic situation setting you up for failure. Our eagerness to find that "it," that ultimate *methode du jour* that we can claim as our very own style, will result in negative emotions when things start to break down. We will find ourselves even more frustrated, not only with the situation at hand, but with ourselves due to our overidentification with the method that's not working. Worse, if there's no realization that our trading knowledge is faulty, we wind up overlooking, repressing, or denying the emotions that surface in tandem, instead of acknowledging them and seeing the situation clearly. The essence of who you are, knowing how you prefer to trade, and listening to what *you* are telling you, is only as good as your ability to live in the moment, even if the reality of the situation presents something you are uncomfortable with, don't know, don't understand, or simply can't comprehend. You can be both a fundamental and technical trader—there are no rules to what you can or can't do—but you just need to know yourself and make the commitment to look at the reality of every situation for what it is, even if it is beyond your comfort level. What's more, you must make the conscious commitment to not overidentify with one style of trading. You can create your own style, but not taking the time to look at all the information out there will only lead to ruin. Even more important, once you do develop *your* style, it's important to still keep one eye open for new ideas in the market. I've heard many fundamental traders scoff at technical analysis and vice versa, and when I do, I think to myself, "You're only hindering yourself by *not* taking the time to learn new things." The markets are about emotions, and, sometimes, the greater public is selling because of a technical event, not a fundamental one. It would be a shame to not be able to see the situation clearly simply because our chosen style prevented us from learning all that we could.

In bringing this back to our conversation about Morita therapy, our purpose-center, and dogma, to become successful investors we must first find ourselves, do the work necessary to understand the market, and then loosely assemble our stylistic methods (being careful not to create a rigid sense of dogma) by which we expect to profit. And we must also never shut the door on accepting new realities or learning new things if we are to remain in the reality of the moment. Only then—through learning, discipline, commitment, and learning even more—will our trading lives truly be set free. Our purpose-center can help us stay on this path, while constantly reminding us to stay clear of creating false dogma.

When someone scoffs at an idea, chances are it's because they don't really understand it. All the great inventions in this world would have *never* happened unless someone went out on a limb and tried something new. It's the same for your purpose-center and trading style; you can create something *totally new*. You just have to know yourself and the rules of the game first. Learn the rules of the game, and then break them.

Once we discover our purpose-center in the market, or in our personal lives, we are able to find a sense of self that allows each of us to be the best we can be, within the context of ourselves. In short, by understanding our purpose-center, we can then take advantage of our strengths to develop our personal trading style, but, even more so, we will be able to see where our weaknesses are as well. And knowing what we are not good at is just as important as knowing what we do very well.

Here's something that will help further develop your purpose-center and commence destroying dogma: Take inventory of yourself and what you know. Begin by writing out on a sheet of paper all the things you know about trading and investing. Write down what you know about fundamental and technical analysis, economics, trading rules, trading platforms, your money management plan, commodities, foreign markets, and so on. By doing so, you will see (on paper) the inventory of your trading life. Then you will be able to see what you are lacking as well. Next, where you find that you don't know something, ask yourself why you haven't taken the time to learn. Chances are you have not studied the missing items yet because some dogmatic aspect that you believe to be true has kept you from learning everything you can.

Then start picking items from the list and begin learning about them. When you are done working through the list, go back and write out your mission statement again. Chances are that with your new knowledge, it may change a little. Because you know more, your approach to the market and why you are doing what you are doing might have changed. Your new sense of style may change your mission.

Remember, though, that if you're not good at a particular style of trading but you really want to trade that way, it doesn't mean you can't do it. You can; you just have to work a little harder than the next guy to be the best. If you've clarified in your mission statement that you want to trade a particular way, while also stating that you know you struggle with that style, but make the commitment to yourself to be the best, then nothing can stop you. Take Spud Webb for example, who has an amazing story of overcoming odds.

When the infamous basketball player Spud Webb was in junior high school, the coach told him to "sit in the stands" because of his small stature. At the time, he was only 4′11″. The summer before his senior year, he worked tirelessly to achieve a 42″ vertical jump to dunk a basketball. That's almost four feet! But it didn't come easy, and he had to work hard every day to do it. Webb eventually grew to 5′7″, which is nearly laughable when considering playing in the pros. But he did. He played 814 games with the Atlanta Hawks and the Sacramento Kings, and he won the 1986 Slam Dunk contest.

What we learn from Spud's story is that if you want it bad enough, you can get it. You just have to decide what it is that you want, and then work your tail off to make it happen. And, more important, don't ever laugh at someone else if you think they can't do something, or you think they're not doing it the right way . . . they might just make you eat your words someday. When we know our purpose-center, recognize the dogma we want to crush, and remain in the moment, *nothing* can stop us.

SUMMARY

Over the course of this chapter we've covered a brief understanding of our purpose-center from the aspect of Morita theory, which tells us that to be the most effective traders we can be, we have to know why we're doing what we're doing, and we have to remain in the moment. Moreover, when we learn the rules of the game, we can develop our own sense of style, but we have to be very careful not to let this style impede us from knowing what's true or impair our ability to learn new things and see the situation from a clear, unbiased standpoint. And we have to be able to accept our emotions for what they are, while understanding that there's a fine line between acceptance and overanalysis. Lastly, we must at least try to understand our purpose-center though a mission statement, which is what will help us clarify why we're doing what we're doing in the first place. Knowing our mission statement will help keep us together when things get rough.

We've built a solid foundation so far and now we're going to add to it by examining our awareness of the moment, while hearing from the closing pitcher for the Chicago Cubs. What you read in Chapter 2 will bring together everything we've covered so far.

The Time Is Now

Victory becomes, to some degree, a state of mind. Knowing ourselves superior to the anxieties, troubles, and worries which obsess us, we are superior to them.

—Basil King

The time is now, and it will always be now. The urgency of our awareness is absolutely essential to our longevity and capacity to live the life we've always dreamt of... and to fully be the trader or investor we know we can be. This moment will never come back. Absolutely no trade you make, words you ever speak, things you do, or seconds you spend with another person will come back either.

The world is turning so amazingly fast that with every rotation and every second that passes by, so are our dreams. But there's no sorrow in yesterday, because if we put all of ourselves into what we are doing in the present, we will make the most of every precious second that is. And even if we've had some failures, even if we've had some setbacks, even if we've completely fallen down and lost everything, we will have learned something new—that we are cognizant of in the future—and we will have the introspective awareness to stay the course and move mountains. And the next time we are faced with a challenge, there's no stopping us either, because we will have experience, patience, knowledge, and esteem on our side. With all of this in mind, throughout this chapter we investigate why the necessity of staying in the moment with a calm and clear mind is so vitally important. This chapter is meant to help us as traders stay focused when we need it most—when we're sitting on massively profitable trades, or the floor just started to cave in—the moments when everything feels like a mess, and we feel paralyzed. What's more, the chapter contains an interview with Chicago Cubs closing pitcher Ryan Dempster, who sheds dramatic light on the importance of remaining in the moment.

IN THE MOMENT

With all that you've read so far, perhaps you're wondering why it's coming from a trader of all people? Here's the skinny—because my dreams are so important to me, I've been willing to risk so much to see them come true, and, subsequently, I've lost a ton, several times over, on the way. I know personal and financial bottoms. And I mean more than one. But I also know that every time I had to leave the floor in dismal straits after a trading tornado, and every time I've ever had any regrets in life whatsoever, I also couldn't help but notice that somewhere in the back of my mind, I know that I experienced something great. When we have a deeper understanding of what's happening around us, and our reaction to the events at hand, we are able to see the entire universe as a moving code of emotions and numbers. When we have experience, good or bad, we are able to use it again in the future, staying in the moment.

I once heard someone say, "The toughest part of making it to the top is getting through the crowd at the bottom." I really agree. And the kicker is that making it through the crowd is even more difficult if we cannot hear or recognize the wisdom that our purpose-centered self is telling us . . . to help make the best decision at every turn.

We have to train ourselves to not only understand *all* of our emotions in life and trading, but discover how to completely merge with our irrational emotive self . . . and then completely separate ourselves from the situation, while being completely *in* the situation, all the time, knowing our purpose of why we're doing what we are doing. I know that was a mouthful, but it is what it is. And what it is, is intuitively analyzing everything happening at hand in the market (or life), reflecting on what we know to be true (experience and knowledge), accepting the emotions that we are feeling in any moment, and then turning all of our attention to the present moment.

To illustrate what I'm talking about, here's a brief story: A few years ago, I was sitting with prospective trader, a young guy just out of college. Within five minutes of meeting him, he blurted out, "I can trade circles around any market maker!" Of course I raised an eyebrow, and as he caught me taking a sip of coffee, I almost spit it all over my monitor in surprised reflex. But, in all fairness, the guy was playing the part of a hotshot trader, and to play my part too, I just nodded in awestruck amazement, as I struggled to swallow.

We sat at my desk watching order flow blaze by in the QQQQs (Nasdaq Composite tracking stock) for a while when I said to him, "Okay, show me what you can do. I want you to tell me when to buy the Qs ... right here today ... I don't care how much you risk, and I don't care how much you lose, and I don't care when you make the trade ... just do it before the end of the day today. You tell me when you want to enter and I'll fire out the order." He glanced at me with a slight bit of suspicion, before quickly diverting all of his attention to the time and sales window where the time, size, and price of the trades flash by. Not wanting him to feel too much pressure, I swiftly mentioned that I was serious about him making the next trade, but to "not take it too serious and just follow his instincts."

I also mentioned that he had nothing to worry about, because if he were horrendously wrong, I would quickly close the position and cut the losses. Additionally, I let him know that I wasn't worried about the outcome; that it wouldn't matter if the trade made money or not, but that I just wanted to see his trading instincts in action, with real money. Obviously, this was a high-pressure situation for him, and I was trying to let him know not to sweat it too much. I assured him one more time that there would be no fallout, money was not a concern, and to just "trust his instincts."

We sat there in silence for about 30 minutes. I've never seen a person look at the screens so intently in my entire life; I couldn't figure out how he wasn't blinking. At one moment, I remember looking over at him, and the veins on the side of his head looked as if they were about to burst. Because I was seriously worried about him, I decided to move the cup of coffee that was sitting in front of him over a little, just in case he passed out and slumped forward. Nervously looking around, I considered calling the challenge off, when suddenly, like a foghorn, he let out, "Now man, now." Staring at me with a look in his eyes, like he'd just seen Bigfoot, the self-declared market maker trader-a-rounder said, "Long now! The market's going up!"

I replied, "Great, what kinda size you want?"

Obviously this was a wrench in the works, and he looked instantly puzzled, but sort of asked and stated, "Ten grand?!"

"Ten thousand bucks or shares?" I had a feeling it would mess with him a little, so I just had to ask. But this is where it gets good; he raised one eyebrow, and then two, and then in a firm voice that sounded something like a wounded chicken, he chirped, "Ten thousand shares." I knew that what he was really initially thinking was $10,000 bucks, and he probably knew that I knew, but seeing as how I had upped the ante with the shares comment, he felt he had to accept.

Anyway, I think at the time, the QQQQs were trading at about $30 per share (the tracking stock of the Nasdaq 100), so his 10,000 shares meant putting $300,000.00 in the trade. I could tell he did the math quickly (a good sign), and then realized that $10,000 would have only been a meager 333 shares, equating to substantially less potential loss exposure. (To this day I still won't ever know if it was really what he meant, or if he just felt compelled to take the bigger bet because of typical machismo trader crud.) Regardless, I fired out the order, and turning to him spouted, "You're on. Cool, this is great. We're gonna be rich!"

Mr. Wall Street looked at me like we had just hijacked a train, and then quickly darted his eyes back to the trade that he thought his entire future depended on.

I paused for a moment to reflect on the situation—and actually felt really bad because he'd completely taken the bait. But then I stumbled on the thought that I could use another cup of coffee.

After about three minutes (while the trade was going in his favor), I said, "Hold out your hand." Again, the weird look, but he cautiously held out his palm. Grabbing his wrist, with my fingers on his pulse, I looked to my left and asked the trader next to us to count to 15. We sat in an awfully awkward silence for a quarter of a minute. I released his hand and said, "120." Then, I held out my wrist and said, "Take my pulse." Another strange look followed, but he grabbed my wrist nonetheless. I said, "Got my pulse?" He nodded, and I asked the trader next to us to count to 15 again. When he finished, I asked for the count, which was 60.

Quietly, I inquired, "How much money do you want to make from this trade?"

And the poor guy replied with a blank look, a shoulder shrug, and then an unsure, "One grand?"

And then I asked, "What do you want out of life?"

He replied, "What?"

The whole situation was clearly taking a toll on him, but I piped in with, "Hmmm . . . just asking, forget about it though; but hey, look, we're already up over a grand! I have to ask though, why are you so nervous, a guy who can trade with the best market markers in the world, should be cool as a cucumber."

I think at that moment he had a huge epiphany, and replied in a low voice, "I don't know?!"

I'm pretty sure he was really thinking about punching me in the nose.

Of course I recommended the guy for the trading desk, but the point was that we both knew that at the very moment when I put him on the spot, he didn't know what size (how many shares) he wanted to trade or how much he wanted to make in the trade. What's more, he really had no idea why he was on the trading floor in the first place. My bet is that after just graduating from college, he decided trading was where he could make a ton of money really fast. That's usually the case. And, just 'cause I'm a nice guy and was worried he would have a heart attack, I never asked what his stop was.

The point to all of this, however, is that we're all so concerned about when to "get in" that we never even stop to consider the reality of the situation. See, in all of our lives we're so concerned about missing the market going up (or if you're like me, even missing anything at all in life), that we never really look at the most important things—like what's really happening, what the moment really is, how far the market will rally after we get in, or where we will get out should everything fall apart . . . or why we're even there in the first place, for that matter. And some of us never consider what our risk should be given the current conditions. In the case of the young trader, he never even asked to look at anything else, like other stocks in the Nasdaq Composite, broader market news, or other news that might directly impact the major indexes. He was so concerned about getting there quickly that he let the *emotion* of the moment prevent him from seeing the *reality* of the moment.

Putting it in different terms, we're all in such a rush all the time that we forget that traffic can come unexpectedly to a screeching halt sometimes. And if we aren't awake or prepared for a potential out-of-the-blue gridlock, we're most likely going have a big, fat wreck sooner or later. It is so vital to remain in the moment, in the now, but to do so effectively we have to remain in a calm state of awareness. If we're just "trying to get in," we're not living in the moment at hand; we're simply just trying to get "there." And we can't get there without being here first. I once heard someone say that if you have a foot in yesterday and a foot in tomorrow, you go the bathroom all over today.

The second point here is that while my trading account was at risk, I wasn't the one with an accelerated heart rate. Of course some of the situation was due to his worrying over the entire interview and the bizarre situation at hand, but even with this in mind, I ask you to ponder whether you've ever noticed yourself with sweaty palms after entering a trade. When we find ourselves so nervous that we get sweaty and jittery, we are not living in the moment and more than likely our emotions are getting the best of us. Fact is, when we are feeling uneasy about a trade, it's probably because we're so worried about the outcome that we can't even handle what's happening right there in front of us. Instead we are living in the adrenaline-induced fear, anxiety, or elation of the situation. It's so easy to become controlled by our emotions when we are not purpose-centered or seeing the situation clearly. And going by what we just covered in Chapter 1, if the young trader had more of a purpose-center based on why he was there in the first place, he probably wouldn't have been so uneasy with the entire situation. He did make the right decision, but surely his blood pressure was feeling the effects of the entire trade. I later asked him if he'd considered his emotions while making the trade, and he said that he'd "never even considered considering." There are times when our emotions will sneak up on us, and we won't notice . . . but if we do, just accepting them can cool the situation down a notch and help us make the best decision possible in the moment at hand. What's more, if we have a clear understanding of why we're doing what we're doing, it makes our emotions of the moment that much more easily recognized.

The one thing I've observed in my attempt at understanding success in trading is that seasoned traders, or investors, are generally less apt to make emotional decisions based on the moment. Why? Because they've been around the block once or twice and are most likely only entering a trade because many things are aligned, including a favorable stop-loss (indicating a great risk-to-reward ratio for the trade) and clear understanding of the entire reality at hand. These guys not only know their purpose-center, but also have a plan. There's no reason to worry because the outcome has already been intuitively perceived, even before it happens. And even when things begin to come unglued, their clear sense of now will enable them to make the right decisions. These guys live in the moment; keeping their emotions in check by accepting them, they always make an effort to see the situation clearly. At some point, these champions acknowledge their emotions at such a high level, that they have moved beyond making irrational emotional decisions. Moreover, these guys also move with the situation and never hold only to a dogmatic set of beliefs that will keep them from profitability. They move organically with the trade at hand and do not let their emotions hold them back from seeing the next buying or selling opportunity coming. Successful traders are aware of everything happening around them and live in the moment, while also perceiving the greater whole of events occurring in the market. In Buddhism, this state of being is known as "mindfulness," the practice of consciously knowing our thoughts and actions in the moment.

This ability to make amazing decisions in the middle of a market storm only comes after we have purpose-centered ourselves from within. We must have unreserved faith that what we know comes from an unshakeable purpose-center. What's more, when we achieve this level of intuitive excellence, we are confidently open to new paradigms of the market and emotional or knowledge-based ideas that can help us see more clearly. Finally, when we achieve this state of understanding, we have the unconscious ability to execute in the situation—being fully cognizant of the state of affairs, while being completely emotionally detached from the moment at hand. We are trading, as they say, in the zone.

> *The* dharma *is such that it cannot be attained by* groping *or searching about. In the realm of seeing, knowledge perishes. At the moment of attaining, mind is surpassed.*
>   —Dogen, "Moon in a Dewdrop"

When we are trading in the zone, it takes a lot to move us off center, and, hence, we perceive all things equally. In this elevated place of consciousness, we are able to make the most rational decisions possible because through all of our psyche, experience, self-awareness, esteem, hope, and ambition, we are able to stay purpose-centered in the middle of a tornado.

Conceptually, achieving purpose-centeredness and staying in the moment are simple; however, in practice, they are much, much harder. With this in mind, there's one guy who really knows his purpose-center and definitely knows about staying in the moment. Chicago Cubs closing pitcher Ryan Dempster has worked very hard to achieve his highest level of accomplishment, and it shows. With his incredible track record, the things he has to say are definitely worth taking note of.

THROUGH RYAN DEMPSTER'S EYES

Ryan Dempster is a perfect example of hard work producing incredible results. The 2000 All-Star closer for the Chicago Cubs was only 21 when he first signed with the Florida Marlins. Several years later, in 2003, Ryan underwent the infamous Tommy John surgery to repair his elbow. At this point in Ryan's career, many doubted he would rise to the top again, and some were even betting that he would just fade away. Overcoming all pressure, Dempster went on to achieve 33 saves during the 2005 season, earning the best save percentage in the league that year.

* * *

MW: Ryan, thanks for taking time out of your busy schedule for this interview. As you know, this entire book is about becoming the best we can be on an emotional, spiritual, psychological, and philosophical level. And it sounds like you are a really purpose-centered guy, so hopefully you can share some of your insights with us. First, can you open up a little about some of the pressure you face on a regular basis as a closing pitcher?

RD: I think it's probably the most pressure-filled job out there. The entire game lies in your hands. You can go out there with a two-run lead in the top of the ninth, and then all of a sudden, the bases are loaded with only one out—talk about pressure. You're expected to do the same job whether you have the lead or are behind. Especially as a closer, if you go out there and give up two runs in one inning, it might be enough to lose the game. It's the most pressure I've ever experienced. If you fail one time, the whole world looks down on you. But I love the pressure of having the entire game in your hands, having the bases loaded and two outs, maybe it fuels me on the inside. Maybe my entire life has been like that. I think as far as pressure goes, in professional sports you're on TV, live, in front of 40 zillion people. And then there are all the people behind you, which you don't want to let down.

What separates the men from the boys, though, is understanding how we look at failing and succeeding. I don't want to fail; I don't even want to give up a run. I fear not pulling through for the entire team. The guys who have a fear of success, though, are the ones who can really keep themselves down

MW: So how do you overcome things like that?

RD: I learned a ton from Harvey Dorfman's book, *The Mental Game of Baseball* [Diamond Communications, 2002]. I've learned that I can't get caught up in thinking outside the play at hand. *The bottom line is the only thing you can control is the one pitch you can throw at a time.* You can't control the previous pitch, or three in the future. I can only control the ball in my hand at that moment.

In your mind you have to simplify the task at hand . . . the pitch at hand. I could have the bases loaded with one out, but I have to stop thinking about the double play and only concentrate on the pitch at hand. As far as relief pitchers go, so many guys are in the habit of thinking about three outs to end the game . . . but they add so much pressure. You can only control one pitch at a time.

MW: Looking back into recent history, you had to overcome all mental and physical odds to recover from your elbow surgery. How did you do it mentally and physically, and what advice would you give someone who is also facing (metaphorically) a Tommy John surgery in his or her financial lives?

RD: I looked at the surgery as a challenge. To give you a little background first, where I came from in life, there are no other major league players who are from my little town. I took a ferry ride 80 minutes every day to make this dream come true. Keeping this in my mind, I told myself if I'm going to have surgery, and I'm going to have it fixed, I need to do everything I can to come back. What's the point of having something fixed if you're not going to make the most of the outcome? I made the conscious decision to dedicate myself 100 percent. It was monotonous doing the same exercises every day, but I never took any moment for granted. I focused on the moment at hand and pushed as hard as I could. When people were saying I was done at 26, I came back—because I worked so hard to make it happen. It was motivational to accept this challenge. Life isn't always as smooth as we want, there are always bumps in the road, but we have to accept the challenges that face us and rise to the occasion.

MW: Wow, that's amazing! Can you give us another example of how you put yourself completely in the moment?

RD: Last year I had a game in Pittsburgh, the bases were loaded with one out...I executed my pitch; I was thinking, *all I have to do is get a ground ball.* I knew the pitch I wanted to throw, because I also knew our shortstop was Neifi Perez. Just a few minutes before I threw the pitch, Neifi came over the mound and said, "Hey, you see this, this is made of gold [holding up his glove], if you get him to hit to me, I'll turn a double play." So I threw the pitch, and Neifi turned the double play. Talk about amazing.

MW: It sounds like you stopped in the moment and made the pitch fit the reality at hand. Weren't your emotions really getting the best of you, though? How do you keep your emotions in check?

RD: The best part about being a closer is that your having success directly correlates with the team doing well. You see the results of your actions right away. You can't have a great year as a closer and not have the team doing well. And it's about achievement; not just me, but, rather, the whole team. One of the biggest motivators is the fact that I was a starting pitcher, and I had my wins blown for me. So now I also concentrate on coming through for the starting pitcher. I want to pull through for the guy who started the game.

MW: On the mound surely your emotions have to be running a million miles an hour. What are some of the techniques you use to calm yourself down and remain completely in the moment...to see the reality of the situation at hand?

RD: Breathing. As a young guy when things were intense, I tried to work faster and quicker, and hurry to get it over with. Now I take a step off the mound and practice breathing techniques. It works; you'd be surprised how much it relaxes you. I think to myself that I've been in the situation before; I'm good enough to get my guys out, now I just need to relax. You always have to realize that.

Young guys come up to the big leagues, and it's such an elite level—they're facing the superstars. I see the young guys think they need to be better. But they don't need to be better, they just need to be themselves and execute their pitch. They need to trust in themselves and only think about the pitch at hand.

MW: But what if the moment is totally overwhelming?

RD: It's easy to collapse and give up, but if you don't do it, don't doubt, and believe in what you can do, you won't lose focus. It's at those moments that you have let everything go, quiet out the crowd that's going bananas, and take a deep breath.

Then ask yourself, what do I have to do to succeed here? If I do what I have to do at this very moment, and I trust myself, my chances of succeeding are better than anything else. You can't say "can't." Think of what you can do. Think about only the things that you can control.

MW: Being in so many high-pressure situations to perform your best when the heat is on, what are some additional words of wisdom you would give to others trying to cope with intense stress, whether on a pitcher's mound or while investing?

RD: I think the biggest thing you have to realize is that if you're in the most intense situation in the entire world, no matter what it is, you have to trust that you have all the knowledge and you've done the repetitions.

MW: In your opinion, what's the difference between remaining calm and being aggressive? What I mean is, on the mound, are you trying to remain calm and stay centered, or are you aggressively thinking about winning?

RD: Aggressive under control. It's a fine line; you have to be under control—but with a killer instinct at the same time. One thing people always forget as a pitcher is that aggressive doesn't mean fastball—aggressive is a slider, breaking ball, anything you plan under control. If you're not aggressive you won't succeed. However, when you look at a guy like Greg Maddox, he throws 83–90 miles an hour . . . not the fastest, but he aggressively goes after the batters. Life is just like that too! You hear about a major company making an acquisition, when you see something you want, you go after it with aggressiveness, but with smarts.

People always think "What if?" But there are no what if's. You can ask me "what if" I don't work hard enough, that's cool, but don't ask me, "What if it doesn't work out?" because if I train my hardest, work my hardest, and dedicate every inch of myself, it *will* work out.

MW: Do you use any of the techniques to calm (or prepare yourself) for the mound in any other areas of your life?

RD: I don't get worked up over a lot of things. When things are out of your control, don't sweat it. In the grand scheme of life, ask yourself, did this really affect my day?

MW: In your experience, is there one particular way of thinking that defeats us in high-pressure situations?

RD: Doubt. Let it go. Never doubt that you can do the job. The minute you put an ounce of doubt in yourself, you're done. If I doubt I can do my job, and the batter does not doubt he can do his, I've immediately handicapped myself. I see guys out here that doubt the amazing; they doubt that they can make every play happen.

You have the tools, the knowledge, and if you trust the experience you've gained, and you go out there to control what you can control, the outcome will most likely be favorable. And remember, nobody's perfect. Part of the fun of life is to have failures and learn from those failures. More often than not, with this in mind, you're going to succeed. If you look in the mirror the morning after something went against you, and you can honestly say, "I did everything to prepare, and I did my best," . . . then you have no reason for regrets.

SUMMARY

There are several very important points to look back on here. First, we have to know our purpose-center in order to be able to remain in the moment. Also, remaining in the moment is effective only so long as we can break the dogma of doubt. But we must also understand that the reality of the moment, and staying completely in the moment, is the only way we will achieve great success. Ryan pointed out that we must believe in ourselves, and believe in what we know. And he pointed out several times that we must stay in the moment. Dempster said, "You have the tools, the knowledge, and if you trust the experience you've gained, and you go out there to control what you can control, the outcome will most likely be favorable."

With this viewpoint, just like Morita therapy, we have to understand that some circumstances are beyond our control. Staying aware of the variables contributing to those circumstances, while knowing that we have done our necessary homework, will enable us to be the best we can possibly be in the moment at hand. In terms of trading, you can't control a market sell-off. However, you can control your pitch and timing, which, in the case of the trader, is the trade that's open (or about to be opened) at that moment. By being completely in the moment and consciously aware of everything happening around us, the outcome will be, as Ryan put it, "most likely favorable." What's more, if you've done all of your homework, including tackling the mental aspects of trading, even if you lose, you can never look back and be upset with yourself. In fact, you will use the experience to better yourself in the future. In the first chapter, I gave an example where I had opened a ton of put positions in 2006, betting that the market would roll over. At the pinnacle of my pain, when I was about to close everything, I remember thinking, "You know, I should have opened up some cheap out-of-the-money index calls a month ago, just to hedge my risk." And at this point, even when I was worried that I was about to take some huge losses, I realized that no matter what happened, I had learned something about my own trading. And at the same time, simply by not beating myself up about what I had not done and realizing that no matter what, I had learned something great about myself, I was able to pull myself back into the moment and focus on my positions. What's more, I also reminded myself of my purpose-center . . . that I trade for a living because I love it, which helped take some of the pressure off. All of the above helped me stay in the moment. I did add a few long positions "just in case," but fortunately the market rolled over, and I walked away with some massive wins. (Keep in mind that I am a very aggressive short-term trader, as the major indices finished the year at highs.)

* * *

To recap the first two chapters, we've uncovered the necessity of being "in" the moment, while also understanding that we must know "why" we are doing what we are doing. In Chapter 3, we will look a little further into ourselves and attempt to uncover the sense of "self" that makes us tick the way we do. We're going to look directly at our egos and self-esteem, two things that we must have a great understanding of to be great in life, and in trading.

> *Nothing profits more than self-esteem, grounded on what is just and right.*
>
> —John Milton

CHAPTER 3

Self-Honesty and Self-Esteem

M uch like life, when examining investing, we have to understand how we are approaching the matter at hand. And when approaching our personal and financial lives, our foundation (intellectual, instinctual, spiritual, and psychological) will be the root of our success. In the previous chapters we've covered knowing our mission statement, attempting to live in the moment, breaking dogma, and understanding personal style, why our purpose-center is so important to look into, and our awareness of the reality around us. Now we're going to put these concepts into the construct of self in an attempt to understand our ego, esteem, and pride. First though, this chapter requires a brief introduction, followed by a few words on self-honesty. In the end, this chapter serves to develop an overall understanding of the things we would probably chat about in a psychiatrist's office, from the comfort of his or her couch.

While the first two chapters were fairly Eastern-philosophy minded, this chapter looks at Western concepts. I initially planned to make this the first chapter of the book, but decided that it must come after examining our mission statement, purpose-center, the destruction of dogma, and the importance of now. Here's why: If we dissect our sense of esteem without first knowing what our mission statement and purpose-center are, it's like taking apart an engine without knowing what kind of engine it is that we're trying to fix. I'm not saying anything's broken in the first place; for many, there's already a solid sense of self. But we can't get under the hood and start taking stuff off the motor unless we understand the type of motor it is in the first place. And with our mission statements already written out, we have identified the brand of the engine. For example, if you remember my mission statement in Chapter 1, I wrote:

> *My trading purpose is to make money, and I am trading because I love trading. Moreover, I am trading so that I can financially liberate myself to pursue my other passions: painting, writing, helping others, my spiritual journey, and my family. I am a trader because I love the excitement of it. I am trading for a living because I want to make $50 million dollars before I am 40. I believe that in the markets, anything is possible, and I believe I can do it.*

With this statement I have identified the brand of my engine—I know why I want what I want in trading. Now I can examine the construct of self that will determine whether I make the engine run smoothly, that is, my sense of self.

THE FOUNDATION OF SELF

Our understanding of the essence of ourselves, arguably, determines whether we sink or swim when times get tough. And in this world, there are bound to be tough times that will test the fabric of our sense of self. With this logic, it's fairly easy to see why we must at least try to understand what makes us who we are if we're going to emotionally persevere in the markets ahead.

I would like to illustrate with a brief story. A short while ago, I had the epiphany that I am an excellent trader, that I could easily trade forex on the side (even though I had never traded currencies live) and write about my grand success. A friend of mine was already trading and showed me where to open a small online account with $500.00—receiving 200 to 1 leverage, meaning that my $500 would allow me to invest $100,000.00 in the open market. Of course, being the diligent investor I am, I traded in a so-called demo account for two weeks prior to going live. My demo account—trading play money—quickly grew almost 60 percent within the first two weeks. Thus I decided I was ready to trade real cash. My trading plan was to use nothing but technical analysis and stop-losses. I thought, "Just cut the losers and let the winners run, remove all emotion."

While I do have a fair bit of advanced currency trading knowledge, I had never actually traded them live. The results in my account showed exactly that—my $500.00 was worth $53.00 at the end of a week and a half. Ouch!

My excellent money management skills weren't enough to salvage the poor entry points I chose.

The forex lesson cost me a few bucks, but it was worth it because I learned some new things about myself. First, you can never trade in a market where you don't have a solid foundation of understanding and knowledge. Or, most of the time at least, you'll get killed if you're trying to trade in a market that you know nothing about. I was not purpose-centered in understanding why I was doing what I was, other than I thought I could make some extra big bucks, quick.

I had some currency market knowledge, but when it came to actually trading with real money, I found myself wrong more often than not. My ego was the culprit in trading a live account, with real money, long before I should have. I was not approaching the decision from a stance of center; I was egotistically thinking that I knew it all, including how currency trading works.

The second and most important lesson was that I was trading a market without understanding why I was really there in the first place. Trading currencies was not really an essence of myself, or my preferred trading. Again, I was not purpose-centered in any sense of myself to fully understand everything happening with my trades. I was trading currencies because I wanted to make some quick cash in a market that I viewed as easy to trade and speculative enough to fill my coffers with a boatload of greenbacks. Don't get me wrong. I'm already trading currencies again, but unless there's enough passion motivating me to work extremely hard to build my currency market knowledge, I will never be purpose-centered enough to trade profitably. When my trades started falling apart, I started making excuses. What's more, when I asked myself why the heck I was trading currencies in the first place, I discovered that I honestly did not have a decent answer other than wanting to make big bucks quick. I know that as I trade currencies again, I need to be purpose-centered; otherwise my account will repeat the same losses . . . over and over and over.

The third point here is that trading a demo forex account for two weeks and then opening a live account in an attempt to make a few speedy bucks was a breezy, casual, and cocky way to think and trade. I wasn't living in the reality of the moment; I was living with a cheap pipe dream that I could make big cash with little effort. Trying to succeed from that viewpoint is about the same as going to Vegas intent on making easy money. In contrast, our purpose-centeredness is not a flashy ego-feed that we can take lightly or dismiss on the spur of the moment. It takes time to uncover and requires deep soul searching and honesty. Once we find it, everything falls into place, and that purpose-center becomes the foundation and spine in all our trading. Without it we can easily find ourselves lost and confused anytime the pressure is on.

HONESTY

Self-honesty is difficult to achieve, no matter who you are. Unfortunately, denial allows us to protect ourselves from the cold reality of our personal shortcomings. But the main foundation of any good trader sits upon unbridled self-honesty. Thus we need to address the important role honesty has in achieving excellence before we can examine how we tick. I once heard, "The definition of insanity is doing the same thing over and over, expecting a different result each time." And if you remember the story of Sisyphus in the Introduction, he would agree with that definition. With this in mind, I know many traders who are completely insane. Day in and day out, I see them doing the same thing, over and over . . . even though it never seems to work. They constantly bark that they are "doing all the right things, but the market is yanking them around." They think the market is wrong. But it's not. If you lose a trade, *you* were wrong. Period. And if you're wrong over and over and over, perhaps you're stuck. It's okay to be stuck, but you have to get honest to become unstuck. It takes a huge dose of self-honesty to recognize that, for whatever reason, what we are attempting simply isn't working for us. Self-honesty is a process—it doesn't just happen.

Sometimes it's very hard to distinguish our denial from stubborn persistence. We can get caught up in thinking that if we just work harder and longer, what we're attempting to do will eventually work out. And while this may be true in some cases, like the example of Spud Webb, more often than not, it's Sisyphus all over again. Sure we can tell ourselves we're not as foolish as Sisyphus, but our egos are 100 percent vested in our habits, and we're not going to let go without a fight! Honesty means more than being willing to see where we've made mistakes. It requires courage to admit that we still believe and want something that ultimately betrays or hurts us. It requires stepping outside our egos long enough to see where and when we might have misperceived, misunderstood, or completely misjudged that which we thought was foolproof. Before we're willing to risk changing directions, a painful unpeeling from our attachment to no-win situations has to occur. When something stops working for incredible traders, and they're honest enough to admit it, they will switch positions or trading styles. Those who are caught in the confines of denial just continue doing the same thing, again and again, with the same horrible results.

There's a big difference between hard work against difficult odds to achieve and sticking to something that just isn't working. And for each of us, recognizing this difference is only something that we can answer from within, after examining everything that is. We don't want to quit when things get rough, but we don't want to stand in front of a loaded gun either, just because we're too tough to get out of the way. It takes some serious soul searching to make honest decisions. And, in this area, there's almost no way

I can tell you how to become honest with yourself. One suggestion is to sit down and write out an inventory of everything you believe about yourself and the market, which I discussed in Chapter 1. What's important, though, is that you have to *want* to do it yourself, and have to have the courage to look deep within. It's hard, I know. I've spent many periods in my life stuck in the ruts of losses only because I couldn't find the honesty in myself to make bold changes. Self-honesty is something that each of us must find on our own. If you're stuck in a string of losses and can't figure out what's wrong, here's how we can set up some diagnostic tools in an attempt to uncover the moments of unconscious ego-based smokescreens that keep us from seeing things clearly.

First, we can look at the reality of what's happening for warning signs that something's wrong. In trading, some of the signs that we are having trouble being honest with ourselves include stagnant P&Ls, losing P&Ls over a period of time, ensuing apathy, moodiness, and anger. Simply put, when our lives are out balance and we aren't being completely honest with ourselves, the troublesome results usually show up in our bottom lines. So ask yourself, are there areas of your life or trading that are producing negative emotions? And here's where you really have to dig deep! If you can sincerely answer yes, you are on your way towards change. If you can sincerely answer no, I'm probably not telling you anything you don't already know.

Second, by leaning into the discomfort of the situation, we can sometimes see if we're having trouble being honest with ourselves. The Buddhist nun Pema Chodron wrote a wonderful book on embracing all the things most people want to run away from, *When Things Fall Apart, Heart Advice for Difficult Times*. In it, she says, "We might think, as we become more open, that it's going to take bigger catastrophes for us to reach our limit. The interesting thing is that, as we open up more and more, it's the big ones that immediately wake us up and the little things that catch us off guard. However, no matter what the size, color or shape is, the point is to lean toward the discomfort of life and see it clearly rather than to protect ourselves from it."[1]

If we can take the step of letting go of our cherished habits that no longer serve us and be really honest with ourselves, we can transcend the murky haze of the self-created illusions that have trapped us. What's more, by allowing ourselves to see our problems clearly, we lean completely into the issue that is tearing at our hearts or our trading. Recall in Chapter 1 where we covered accepting our emotions to live in the moment. By accepting our emotions, like anger, we *have* to lean into the pain. If I'm mad at a trade that just crushed my P&L for the day, and I blame the market, I'm not really leaning into the discomfort. I'm blaming something other than my own decisions in an effort to pad myself from the honesty of the situation.

However, if I accept that I screwed up, and accept that my anger is really directed at myself for fudging the moment, I am able to let go of the pain. This acceptance is not only a very honest way to live with our emotions, but it is also very emotionally intelligent.

Later (in Chapter 9) we'll look at how emotional identification and emotional intelligence ties into our approaches to life and trading, but for now I want to stress how getting to honesty is a process, and it's not always easy. Without intense self-honesty, we will never be able to fully see ourselves, or any trade clearly. Simply having the desire to be honest with oneself is only the first step in leaning into the discomfort of the moment at hand so we can disengage from whatever keeps us from becoming well rounded, purpose-centered people. But then acting on the desire is the true evolution to real self-honesty. We can't just say we are honest with ourselves; we must actually do the footwork.

The funny thing is that it's easy to create a false sense of honesty and basically lie to ourselves. We can say, "So my trading sucks lately. Geez, now aren't I being honest with myself?" And then give ourselves a big pat on the back for all of our wonderful honesty. But are we really being honest? Are we taking responsibility for our decisions? Do we care about the long-term effect of those decisions? No, we are simply protecting our feelings by being cynical spoiled brats, and more than likely regressing to some sort of childhood behavior. True honesty is saying, "My trading has been very bad lately, I accept that I am out of balance, I accept that I am angry with myself, and that, at some level, I'm afraid to make another trade; I don't want any more losses. I need to examine all possible conflicts that may be causing the problem." In the best-selling book *Who Moved My Cheese*, the authors write, "[You have] to admit that the biggest inhibitor to change lies within yourself, and that nothing gets better until *you* change."[2] But change within ourselves cannot occur until we are willing to see our participation in everything that happens to us. If we look hard and honestly about where we are, we'll see it's always us in the driver's seat.

Being completely honest with ourselves will help begin the diagnostic stage of finding and acknowledging the problem within. And in doing so, we have a chance to free ourselves from the internal issues that keep us down. How does this work? In the book *Mars and Venus Starting Over: A Practical Guide for Finding Love Again After a Painful Breakup, Divorce, or the Loss of a Loved One* (I know it must seem odd to refer to this book in a book about trading), the author mentions that one of the most important facets of healing after a broken heart (which could be synonymous with many losing days in the market) is to simply acknowledge our emotions (i.e., emotional identification). When we find ourselves losing money over a long period of time, we must acknowledge our emotions of frustration and anger, while also honestly admitting to ourselves that something is out of whack in our trading. By admitting that there is a problem, you have accepted the situation at hand and are on your way to finding a solution. What's more, you've enabled yourself to acknowledge the emotions stirring within you, and in doing so it is that much easier to release them. You have leaned into your discomfort, and thus you are rewarded with the wonderful release of the negative feelings you were harboring. You are the positive recipient of your own honesty.

Once we are completely honest with ourselves, and concede to the issue, we are, however, left with the cold reality of having to deal with the problem or trade at hand. And this reality is partially why many traders have such a hard time admitting to themselves that they were wrong in the first place, even if leaning into the discomfort would remedy the problem. By directly facing, even embracing, whatever is plaguing us, we are forced to truthfully see how we've erred. Many investors and traders will lie to themselves indefinitely, leaving a losing position open until an account is completely devastated. Have you ever read *Rogue Trader*, the story of Nick Leeson, who single-handedly upended Barings Bank with liabilities totaling close to $1.3 billion? Mr. Leeson's unchecked gambling (read: lack of self-honesty) brought an entire bank to its knees![3]

As flawed human beings, we have a tendency to fib to ourselves on a daily basis. And as traders, it's arguable that we do so even more often. Some of the fibs we tell ourselves as traders are:

- The losing position wasn't my fault, the market moved against me.
- The trade was right—I followed all the rules and they just took the market down after I bought the stock.
- I just have bad luck; I always buy the top, or sell the bottom.
- I won't sell yet; eventually the stock has to go up.
- Bigger size equals bigger profits.
- I don't have to close the losing position yet—I can just average down to lower my cost basis.
- Because I made so much money in that one trade yesterday, I'm going to be rich, and I can take on more risk today.
- If the market is down often, it means I can't make much money.
- The only reason why I'm not profitable is because I'm not trading a large enough size yet.
- I've had too many winners in a row; I should have a big loser now.

If we let our psyches run feral, the possibility of complete devastation in our accounts can easily become all too real. Ask yourself, "Did I lose money when the bubble burst of 1999?" Answer honestly! I don't know anyone who didn't. And actually, I don't know anyone who didn't lose too much, simply because a million excuses prevented them from closing beaten down positions. People's excuses included "My broker will tell me when it's time to get out"; "It's fundamentally sound, I'll wait for the next bounce"; "that guy on TV said the market would come back"; "I can't take the loss here"; . . . yada . . . yada . . . yada. The most inherent problem is simply the lack of honesty with ourselves. We're only human, and being honest is often all too painful.

I lost almost a quarter of a million dollars in 1999 by sticking my head in the sand like an ostrich. My excuse was that of good old-fashioned denial. Deep down I knew that if I ever took my head out of the sand, I would have to deal with the fact that I was losing money, and that if I'd simply had a stop-loss order in effect, I would have been saved. I was *hoping*, and not being *honest* with myself.

There is no salvation for those who lie to themselves, and, thus, self-honesty is always the best policy. Oh, and just in case you're wondering, my investment in 1999 never came back, but somehow the catastrophic loss helped open my eyes to the desperate need for self-honesty in trading . . . for one of the first times.

Sun Tzu said in *The Art of War*, "When fire breaks out inside an enemy's camp, respond at once with an attack from without."[4] When our accounts are on fire, we must step outside of ourselves, find honesty, and then quickly bolt into action before our internal duress causes a complete breakdown. When we are losing money and we are not able to be honest enough with ourselves to correct the problem, we are our own enemy. There's a fire going on inside the camp of us, and if we don't respond quickly, the market will . . . and eventually our trading accounts will be all zeros. In understanding our foundation of self-honesty, we must then look within ourselves to comprehend the fundamental psychology behind our sense of self. I mean taking out the scalpel and dissecting everything. We must do this because trading is as much about personal esteem and ego as financial formulas or analysis. Without a deep understanding of ourselves, we can hardly expect to persevere in both good and bad times, or truly be honest with ourselves. And if we cannot be honest with ourselves, we will not be able to find our purpose-centeredness and remain in the moment when trading. Self-honesty is a prerequisite to analyzing our own operating systems and understanding how and why we think and feel the way we do.

Before we move on to specific self-psychology, I want to stress the importance of understanding self-honesty one last time. In the book *Manias, Panics, and Crashes*, by Charles P. Kindleberger, the author asserts, "Financial distress for an economy also has a prospective rather than an actual significance and implies financial adjustments or disturbances ahead. It is a lull before a possible storm, rather than the havoc in its wake."[5]

With this in mind, it's important to note that we shouldn't wait to start being honest with ourselves only when things fall apart, or as a final reactionary solvent to a problem. To build long-term personal and financial wealth, self-honesty must be utilized proactively to prevent storms, not extinguish fires and rebuild accounts. By being proactively transparent in our personal honesty, all of our psychological being will prosper. With complete personal honesty, we will be able to see our ego versus our esteem and, in the end, form a significant sense of pride.

EGO VERSUS ESTEEM

I'm amazed how often I see ego and esteem play such vital roles in the world of trading. It seems at every turn, the two are battling it out, much like fear and greed. And because of this, to find a solid purpose-center and sense of pride, we must examine our ego and esteem to understand the underpinnings of who we are and why we make the decisions we do. It sounds like "just psychology" and not trading, but I can assure you that ego and esteem have everything to do with the financial markets. And by examining our egos and esteem, we will also have that much greater ability to be honest with ourselves, something sorely needed when we are going through a rough patch of trading.

Ego

When discussing the ego, it's almost impossible to not talk about Sigmund Freud, who advanced his theories about the ego in *The Ego and the Id* in 1923. Without going into too much detail, Freud maintains the ego is based on the id, super-ego, and the external world. For more concise explanation of the ego, though, I would like to reference Nathaniel Branden's book, *Honoring the Self*. Branden states, "Ego (the Latin word for 'I') is the unifying center of consciousness, the irreducible core of self-awareness—that which generates and sustains a sense of self, of personal identity. Our ego is not our thoughts, but that which thinks; not our judgments, but that which judges; not our feelings, but that which recognizes feelings; the ultimate witness within; the ultimate context in which all of our narrower selves or sub-personalities exist."[6]

Thus, from my perspective, we see why traders and investors alike have such *big* egos. Egos are not our thoughts or feelings themselves, but an instigator of such. When making amazing trades, we feel unstoppable, and our egos promote the feelings of our successes. However, the ego is far different than self-esteem, which is why egos can be so dangerous. Market and ego go hand in hand; however, the markets and self-esteem do not. I've learned that too much ego in the market is a sure warning sign that personal development and financial education have both failed to occur, and losses will ensue. Why? Self-esteem is the fundamental of ego, and without a strong self-esteem, ego is false and will *not* hold up when the walls begin to crumble. Egos dissolve like butter when the oven gets hot. Simply put, large egos live in glass houses, and to be successful traders, we must build our self-esteem houses out of bamboo. Bamboo? Yes, it's very strong, bends in the wind, and hardly ever snaps. Bricks tumble, concrete erodes, steel rusts; but bamboo grows season after season, bending in the most traumatic conditions, only to grow again and again, year after year. Only by working on our self-esteem will we be able to build a solid sense of ego that will weather the test of time in trading.

ESTEEM

> *Along with success comes a reputation for wisdom.*
> —Euripides

Self-esteem is defined as:[7]
   Pride in oneself; self-respect.

1. A feeling of pride in yourself [syn: self-pride]
2. the quality of being worthy of esteem or respect; "it was beneath his dignity to cheat"; "showed his true dignity when under pressure".

Referencing Branden again, he states,

> *Self-esteem, we have seen, is the integrated sum of self-confidence and self-respect. Our need for self-esteem is our need to know that the choices we exercise are appropriate to reality, appropriate to our life and well-being. It is our need to know that we have made ourselves competent to live. Since reality continuously confronts us with alternatives, since we must choose our goals and actions, since we are constantly obliged to make decisions concerning our interactions with the environment, our sense of efficacy and security requires the conviction that we are right in our method of choosing and of making decisions; right in our characteristic manner of using our consciousness; right in principle appropriate to reality.[8]*

Are you beginning to see why self-esteem and ego play such a vital part in trading? If we lack self-esteem, we cannot possibly imagine ourselves to have the proper ego to trade well. In effect, self-doubt is the product of low self-esteem—and often a falsely inflated ego—riddling a trader with losses until the issue is resolved.

However, the destruction of ego, and repair of self-esteem, is not something that can happen overnight. You cannot read these words and say, "Oh, I get it . . . now that I understand a little more about my self esteem, I can build a solid sense of ego, and trade better." Nope, it just doesn't work that way, but I sure wish it would. As I sit here writing this book, I'm still working on these principles. It's a constant conscious battle of self-will to be good. One morning I was having breakfast with a mentor, Hugh McCulloh when he said, "People with egos want to *look* good, not *be* good." And he was so right. Positive self-esteem comes from the pursuit of *being* good, not just looking good.

> *Try not to become a man of success but a man of value.*
>
> —Albert Einstein

I hate to admit this, but in my early years of trading, there were times when I think I was walking with a big ego. I was making money and not only thought I knew it all, but that I was the best trader in town. I had my rear handed to me by the market. I wasn't good; I was average at best. It wasn't until I was forced to eat some *huge* losses that I began building my knowledge on self-esteem, not ego. Though I did want to be good at trading, I was also equally concerned about looking good. And it was only through the losses that I was able to finally take an honest look inside to see that I was not as good as I thought. At the end of the day, solid self-esteem in trading is only built on hard work, not on a few big winners.

Once we've developed a solid sense of self-esteem, we can also have a healthy sense of ego and pride in our accomplishments. And in doing so, we develop a sense of self-efficacy, which "is belief in one's capacity to succeed at tasks."[9]

When we work very hard at being the best we can be, we transcend simple esteem and ego and develop a circular relationship between ego, esteem, and efficacy, all of which turn into pride.

PRIDE

Pride is the cyclical relationship of self-respect through positive self-esteem. If we have a solid sense of purpose-center based on self-honesty and hard work, we feel infinitely capable of undertaking great tasks. We feel self-efficacy, self-respect, and esteem. In the application of trading, when we have pride in our research, and ourselves, we will be able to rise to the occasion when the market moves against us, keep a cool head, and make the right decisions. The inevitable conclusion of everything we've covered so far in the chapter is that when we work hard to be very honest with ourselves and then actually act on our self-honesty, we are able to develop a sense of pride, which can help us overcome any challenge in the market.

In trading, pride comes from a mixture of diligent research, intuition, unbridled self-honesty, and, of course, execution. If you've worked hard, and a trade works out according to plan, or you are able to stop a loser and move onto a winning position, you will have pride in your market actions. Knowing that you can handle the most difficult of situations will then promote a healthy self-esteem, self-efficacy, and, of course, a vibrantly healthy ego. The crux, though, is to understand that *really* good traders are not usually the loud cocky megalomaniacs that run amuck on trading floors. Really good traders usually have a calmness about them that reeks of strong self-esteem and ego, but they never actually flagrantly flaunt it. This is because their history has given them such pride that they know they can handle any situation . . . and they've been humbled a few times.

With this in mind, I would like to come back to something Chicago Cubs closer Ryan Dempster said in Chapter 2, "People always think 'What if?' But there are no what if's. You can ask me 'what if' I don't work hard enough, that's cool, but don't ask me what if it doesn't work out, because if I train my hardest, work my hardest, and dedicate every inch of myself, it will work out."

Here we see where a solid sense of esteem, built on hard work creates a significant sense of pride. Ryan Dempster is not a guy with ego; rather, he is an elite athlete with a solid sense of self-esteem, self-efficacy, and self-confidence, all translating into his ability to win game after game. And with each win, Ryan can rest easy with a sense of pride that all of this hard work has paid off.

SUMMARY

As traders, we can achieve any level of success that we've ever dreamed, but only if we really understand what makes us *be* good, rather than just trying to *look* good.

Earlier in the chapter, I mentioned that we have to know what type of engine is under the hood if we are ever going to fix it. And that's where we are now. Take a few moments and in your personal inventory write down how you operate . . . are you driven on ego or esteem? Self-honesty here is critical. Do you have pride in your trading? Is the pride built on wins that you may have just gotten lucky on, or are you truly prideful in your knowledge, based on a healthy sense of esteem? What's more, do you feel that your trading knowledge and skills give you the sense of efficacy that you can handle any situation? If you shrugged at any of these questions, it's time to get honest. It's something that takes time, but if you go through this chapter again, it may be easier to see.

This chapter is a template of psychological self-examination that will help you be a more purpose-centered trader in the future, operating from a sense of esteem and efficacy. What's more, if you have a moment when you feel your ego creeping up on you, simply having read this chapter and being able to recognize it may be enough to stop you from making a cocky decision after a string of wins, something every trader has trouble with. After reading this chapter, I hope you take the time to look inward, because there are some important clues to becoming an even better trader right there in your ego and esteem. But you have to take a good long look.

* * *

Sometimes, it's not until we are greatly humbled by something in life, or the market, that we are finally able to really be honest with ourselves. In trading, I've seen it time and time again with new traders, and had to learn the lesson of humbleness myself. But, when we do learn the lesson of humbleness, we can begin to use it to further our sense of esteem and efficacy. Over the next two chapters we will begin talking about humbleness (Chapter 4) and forgiveness (Chapter 5), something we desperately need as traders. While I initially thought the discussion of humbleness should come before Chapter 3, I finally decided that it's better to crack open ego before talking about humbleness. After all, that's the way it usually works in the real world of traders . . . it's not until their ego is cracked open a few times that they truly begin to understand how important humbleness really is.

CHAPTER 4

The Balance of Humbleness

To entirely build a solid foundation self and to remain purpose-centered, we must accept humbleness as a positive aspect of change. This characteristic allow us to honestly look deep into ourselves, thus bringing us back into, or keeping us in, the moment. I would like to state that when we are humbled, we are also (at times) in a state a humility. In essence, the terms are redundant, but it's important to note that if you catch yourself feeling humiliated by a trade, you are feeling humble, which is a good thing.

THE IMPORTANCE OF HUMBLENESS

Humbleness isn't just a trait of those who have fallen, it's a characteristic of the great, of those who are purpose-centered without ego. However, when humbleness appears after a disaster, it brings a kind of pain, but in retrospect we find that during times of anguish when we are broken, we learn to laugh at ourselves, learn to love ourselves for our faults, and learn to look at the rest of the world with an open and graceful heart. Humbleness is one of the most important stones in the foundation of self (and trading) that should be solidly planted within all of our hearts. It requires a certain amount of vulnerability, which can only happen if we are courageous enough to accept that we are merely human. When we are vulnerable, we are open to enormous changes and even greater success.

> *He who is humble is confident and wise. He who*
> *brags is insecure and lacking.*
> —Lisa Edmondson

One aspect of humbleness that many of us find so hard to deal with is simply finding the courage in ourselves to accept that we have goofed up, fallen down, or completely blown up. We can never truly find ourselves accepting of humbleness unless we have the courage to admit we were wrong in the first place.

Humbleness is the exact opposite of arrogance. When we are humble, we constantly open ourselves to learning new things and to being the best we can be. Being humble doesn't mean that we don't have pride, a healthy sense of esteem, or ego; it just means that we are wise enough to see that we can never stop growing, learning, or accepting that we don't know it all.

Humbleness is a feature of greatness.

I think that some (especially on trading floors) can often confuse humbleness with meekness or a lack of self-confidence. However, it is the exact opposite of such a lack or weakness. Humbleness requires the courage to recognize our inner weaknesses as well as our strengths, and to be able to accept ourselves in every situation, even if it's a bad one.

With this description in mind, it's important to remember that part of being humble is remembering that it's okay to ask for help. Life and trading are not easy, and sometimes we just can't do it alone. Thus, if you find yourself in dire straits, or just going through a rough period, remember that humbly asking for help is actually a sign of courage.

And, when we enlist the help of others, we can often find that we are able to begin making the incredible changes that were previously hidden just under our noses. You're about to read inspiring interviews with supertraders Mike Palumbo and Kevin Cuddie that hit on just this point.

MIKE PALUMBO—WORDS OF WISDOM FROM A SUPERTRADER

Several years ago, I had the opportunity to sit on the trading desk for Third Millennium Trading in Chicago, where I met Mike Palumbo. Mike was an adopted child who grew up on the Northwest side of Chicago. After graduating from Northwestern with a master's degree in business at the age of 23, Mike went to work for Susquehanna Investment Group as a clerk. It only took him six months to move from clerk to trader, a record-setting achievement in the history of the firm. Despite Mike's incredible knack for trading, the firm only paid Mike a little over 10 percent of his profits. Seeking to earn more money, Mike went to work for a man named John Stafford, who allowed Mike to keep over 50 percent of every dollar he earned. After saving roughly $250,000, Mike started Third Millennium Trading with a partner who, unfortunately, left the firm in 1998 during a very tough period for the U.S. stock market and for the company. Third Millennium struggled through the rest of 1998, but began its rise to greatness in 1999.

When the dust settled, Mike's initial start-up capital of $250,000 had grown to more than $120 million dollars. The firm now has four partners in all, and employs approximately 20 people as office staff, prop and floor traders, market makers, and quantitative analysts. It is currently eyeing the next stage of evolution—becoming a hedge fund. Mike is the ultimate trading success story.

In 2005, Mike shared his five secrets to trading success with Victoria Weinberg of *TraderMonthly* magazine, which were published in March of 2005 in the article, "Big-Picture Player."[1]

Rule #1: Know When to Be Greedy—and When to Be Scared

This is the fundamental underpinning of everything that separates men from the boys in the trading arena. If you've done the legwork and you're in it to win, do so—double down for bigger profits rather than settle for the smaller pot. Don't just be satisfied with not losing—win big. On the other hand, if you're hoping that your lucky boxer shorts turned inside out are going to save you when a dicey position starts to look worse, get out before it gets ugly. "That's the delicate balance of arrogance and humility that separates the great traders from the pack," Palumbo says. "Many traders have the arrogance part down cold, but not the humility."

Rule #2: Always Look at the Big Picture

"The times I've made the most money have been when I've foreseen macroeconomic events," Palumbo says. Regardless of what you trade or where, the world's economic and political forces affect you every day. Better to steer clear if factors that are even tangentially linked to your position are turning negative. "With everything connected in one way or another," Palumbo adds, "it's essential to know what's happening."

Rule #3: Know the Difference Between a Good Bet and a Pipe Dream

Trading and poker have similarities, but there's a huge difference between having a strong trade and a situation in which a miracle is essential. Too many traders rely too heavily on Lady Luck to boost their fortunes.

Rule #4: Limit the Times You Play Out a Weak Hand

This goes right in tandem with rule three. It's great to learn from your mistakes, but not if doing so is wiping you out. Controlling your destiny as much as you possibly can is critical.

Rule #5: Be Realistic in Your Assessment of the Worst-Case Scenario

This is possibly the hardest of the five rules to grasp and practice. Even the best traders don't really want to think about the worst possible outcome, yet doing so can make or break a trade. It's better to prepare for the worst possibilities than to be blindsided. "It's tough to imagine what will happen if you're completely wrong," Palumbo says, "but making sure you that you can handle even the worst occurrences is the key to playing the game for the long haul."

After reading the aforementioned secrets, I tracked down Mike and asked him some additional questions.

Conversation with Mike Palumbo

MW: Mike, thanks for your time. Can you tell us why trading embodies a substantial amount of stress, and what can you say about handling tough situations?

MP: Dealing with stress, you have to have experience, and you have to realize that there are way more things in play than meets the eye. You have to have a certain mind-set where you are not able to get your butt kicked . . . and when you do, you have to deal with it. In my case, even if the bottom falls out, I can say, "No matter what happens I have four great kids and great friends and I'm going to be okay."

MW: What about on a more rudimentary trading level, for the guy who's just starting out? Can you put it into terms of a losing trade?

MP: For the individual investor, the hardest thing is to know when to cut a loss. The best traders think they are never going to lose. However, even the best traders make huge mistakes. You have to realize when you are wrong at the earliest possible juncture and then have the guts to get out of the wrong position as quickly as possible, and move on.

MW: If there were a few traits that you think make up a great trader, what would they be? Strength, intellect, intuition, and so on.

MP: The most important traits of great traders are basic IQ-type intelligence, ability to think unemotionally, highly competitive and also very humble. It is this humility that very few—even good—traders have. And humility is what allows you to admit to yourself when you are wrong and think clearly during times when you are losing and highly stressed.

MW: What would you say is the biggest problem traders have becoming successful?

MP: Remember that word I just talked about a few questions earlier? It's the one quality so few even good traders have: humility. Never think you know it all, and also be willing to learn from others and from mistakes.

MW: For the beginning trader who doesn't have the experiences you have, what would you say to him, when a position goes against him? In other words, what advice would you give him to calm himself and address the situation at hand on a more detailed level?

MP: The investor must analyze why the position has gone against him and then decide what to do next. To be able to make the right decision when figuring out what to do next, the trader must be unemotional about it. For the beginner that will be difficult to do. Then, once you have analyzed what went wrong and why, you must formulate a game plan for what to do next. That could be to completely get out of the position and possibly lock in losses, but if your analysis says that the position is likely to lose further, then that is what must happen.

MW: If you were advising a trader just starting out from the very beginning, what would you tell him or her to focus on? What's important, and what's not?

MP: This rule works for anything that you want to learn about in life. You must try to seek out [those who are] the best at what you want to do, and learn everything you can from them. I was lucky enough to get great training throughout my career, especially at Kellogg, as an analyst at Duff & Phelps, and then at Susquehanna, which is a big reason for my success.

MW: If you could do it all over again, what would you do differently?

MP: Absolutely nothing. I made my share of mistakes, but every one of them taught me something that I used later in my trading career—and sometimes later in other business situations.

Conclusion

Mike points out several times that humbleness is one of the most important keys to greatness. And coming from a guy as successful as Mike, we should probably take note of what he's saying. He said, "And humility is what allows you to admit to yourself when you are wrong and think clearly during times when you are losing and highly stressed." With this in mind, no matter what's happening around us, no matter how successful we become, it's so vitally important to remember to stay humble. By doing so, we will be able to remain in our purpose-center, living completely in the moment with a strong sense of esteem.

On a side note, I would like to also point out that when Mike was asked about what to do about a losing position, he replied that the trader must analyze the situation and make an unemotional decision. While this may be more of my point of view than Mike's, I would like to argue that the only way we can make an unemotional decision is to directly deal with the emotion of the losing position. As we covered in Chapter 1, we must simply accept the feelings that go with the loss in order to let them go and make an unemotional, unbiased decision at the next turn. At some level this is an unconscious action with great traders, who deal with a loss by immediately letting it go to make a calm decision to rectify the trade, or trade profitably in the next instance. When we are able to let go of our emotions, we remain humble and make the right decision. What's more, coming from a guy as successful as Mike, we see that some of his greatness is rooted in humbleness. In essence, taking notes from Mike's successful career, when we start to tackle the world and see the windfalls of trading profits, it is even more important to remain humble, so as to not let our egos overrun our ability to make great trading decisions. If we fall into the trap of becoming full of ourselves, we risk making sloppy assessments that will eventually cause great losses.

* * *

Humbleness is greatness, which is why a guy like Mike is at the top. No matter what happens, he remains humble. And, we're about to hear the importance of humbleness reiterated by Kevin Cuddie; another incredibly successful trader. Kevin has a track record of five consecutive years without one losing month, something unheard of in today's volatile markets.

BALANCE OF SELF: AN INTERVIEW WITH KEVIN CUDDIE

I began trading with Kevin Cuddie in 2002, and I have rarely ever seen someone who can return money more consistently than this guy. What's more, over the years, when I was on the desk with Kevin and thought I had digested all of the market's cues, Kevin would often insert some little bit of "commonsense" knowledge that blew all of my logic out of the water. Kevin approaches the market from many different angles, but from what I've seen, he has one outstanding asset that makes him the incredible trader he is. No matter what happens, he stays humble, partially (I think) through his stringent risk-management skills . . . all of which has helped him be such a profitable trader. What's more, his humbleness keeps him in the moment, and in a place of common sense, something that is an incredible asset to those stressed by any given day's market noise, news, and movement.

Also, Kevin is the only trader I know who *never* lets a little loss turn into a large one. At every turn, when a position goes against him, he immediately cuts the trade and begins looking for something new. What's more, over the years, I've never seen Kevin gloat over a trade. Ever. He remains humble no matter what happens... even when he's making a killing. I never knew whether Kevin was having a blowout day or a bad one. Well, let me correct that... once in a while he'd offer to buy lunch; he would say "I've got it today." I would instantly know he must have just made a ton of money... but he'd never admit to it.

Because of Kevin's outstanding track record, amazingly humble sense of self, and incredible trading knowledge, Kevin was a shoe-in for this book. His trading insights are so profoundly well thought out, I think at some level they can help any of us become better people and traders.

* * *

MW: Kevin, thanks for taking time out of your busy schedule to share some of your insights. First, can you open up a little about some of the pressure you face on a regular basis as a trader?

KC: I try to eliminate all possible pressure points before that develop. I try to contain any issues and plan for any circumstances before they can happen. What remains is the pressure to adapt to the ever-changing markets. Tomorrow the relationships, trends, catalysts, volatility, and volumes will all change to some combination we have never seen before—but which are very similar to many days we have seen before. My job as a trader is to adapt quickly to new patterns.

MW: What do you do to overcome the pressure within yourself as a trader?

KC: Preparation and circuit breakers are my best defenses against pressure. When I am trading for myself, I trade my best when I am down. I get real intense and focused. To me, when things are going wrong I put pressure on myself to get focused and adapt... focused on the market and what is happening. I adapt and change quickly to what I think will work in the current environment, and there is nothing like focus to get back to where you need to be in the market. That being said, we are all human. There is a cut-off point—a circuit breaker. At a point set in stone, I get up and walk away for a while. I will not trade for the rest of the day.

At some point in my career, trading became more of a game. The things that used to stress me out became almost laughable because they became so predictable. The market definitely repeats itself. But it does so in a way that is just different enough to throw most people off. It became more of a game when I noticed this. The more I researched, the more I would see these reoccurring patterns. That's when the pressure became largely containable.

MW: What are some of the techniques you use to calm yourself down and find balance?

KC: Because frequent change and adaptation is so important, I think visualization is really important. If a certain trade has been working for a long time, it can be tough to change when it stops working. Going back to the well is human nature, so it helps to visualize executing a new trading plan before you do it.

Balance is key. Trading profits are all for nothing if you have not given equal or greater priority to friends, family, and faith. Like everything in life, the more we put into these areas, the better they become. When the rest of my life is balanced, trading becomes less stressful, because it's not all consuming . . . it's not the defining center of my life. So when things go bad trading, I can stay focused and get back on track quicker because I can lean on the strength of the other areas of my life.

MW: In your opinion, what's the difference between remaining calm and being aggressive? What I mean is, are you trying to remain calm and stay centered, or are you aggressively thinking about making money?

KC: I guess it's about picking your spots. I try to stay calm most of the time. I think about 80 percent of the time the market calls for being calm and patient. This could mean sitting on your hands or passively entering or exiting a position. The other 20 percent of the time I am real aggressive. Many traders fail in this area. You need to be able to turn it on and off real quick.

I have seen all sorts of personality tests used to define what will make a successful trader. I think it comes down to a person who can be conservative for long periods of time, and then superaggressive. It's a person who can also admit when they don't know or when they are wrong. It's a person who has a small enough ego where they can not only get out of a trade, but reverse and go the other way if there is good reason to do it.

MW: In your experience, what's the balance between humbleness and trading for a living?

KC: Man, great question. At all times you have to be able to admit when you don't know what's going on or why. In that case, get out of the way until you can find out what is happening. The biggest sign of intelligence I have found is when a person says, "I don't know."

On the flip side, when you know what and why something is developing, trust your instinct. Your instincts should be built on preparation and experience, so don't hesitate. Waiting for confirmation kills traders. If you like it, take it; don't wait for me or someone else to take it from you!

MW: What advice would you give an investor or trader who's been humbled by the market and is trying to regain his or her footing?

KC: Don't be afraid to change how you trade. Get small and try lots of new styles and trades. Take as much time reviewing your trades as you do researching the markets. Talk to as many traders as you can who are making great money and ask what they are doing. Try to surround yourself with successful people and eliminate negative influences. Adapt. You must change or you will not regain your footing.

MW: What advice would you give the investor or trader who is doing very well? What I'm trying to ask is what happens to the guy who's lost his sense of humbleness?

KC: Ego kills. I can't tell you how many times I have seen a trader have a record day only to follow it with the worst day they have ever had. Keep your intensity level up, keep up the research. Don't let your guard down, or forget your discipline. And stay humble; it's one of the most important traits of every great trader.

MW: When incredibly difficult and stressful moments arise, what would you recommend that an investor do to calm him- or herself, to see the situation clearly?

KC: One: If you are taking too much pain, get out. Don't hesitate, don't wait for a bounce, don't try to justify that the position is oversold. *Get out.* Chances are you broke your rules getting into this mess, now just end it. Almost always, these situations don't get any better.

Two: If you don't understand what is happening and are uncomfortable with your position, get out.

Three: Remember that if you are properly prepared, these situations will not seem stressful, and you will have a plan that reacts to what develops. Stick to the plan.

MW: When you first began, did you have your entire career planned out, or did things just fall into place?

KC: I had no plan when I started. I just wanted to get into trading and make a living. It was much harder than I thought it would be to start, and took much longer to get set up properly than I would have anticipated. But I was lucky enough to get some great training early on from the B/Ds I worked at as well as some traders whom I sat next to when I started trading for myself.

MW: Looking back over what you have learned, if you were a beginning trader/investor today, what would you focus on?

KC: Get professional help. It's so competitive now, I have not heard of anyone who has started on their own in their basement who makes any money. The only traders who I know make it are those who sit down in the same room with other professionals and trade side by side with them. Once you know how to make money, you can do it anywhere, but early on you need to get plugged in with other successful guys.

MW: Can you please give some words of wisdom for traders just entering the business, and for those who have been around for a while?

KC: New traders: Get help from other full-time traders. Don't revolve your education around seminars, online subscriptions, or radio shows. Those may add ideas, but are unlikely to get you to where you need to be. Try to sit on a trading floor with successful traders—there may not be any better or quicker education. Plan on a long, hard road. The success rate is real low for beginners, so you should know going in you are likely to lose all the money you put up as risk capital. You should not plan on making any money for a year and a half . . . and maybe much longer or even never. Anyone telling you anything different is probably trying to sell you something.

Your personal life must be set up for these facts, or you are much more likely to fail. Trading part time will also diminish your chances. Working late hours at another job will likely hurt your chances. Remember that commissions add up fast—fight for the best deal possible. Stay level headed. Like any business, the first guy in and the last guy to leave is likely the guy who will make the most money.

MW: Any last words?

KC: For those who have been around for a while: buy low, sell high; if that doesn't work, buy high, sell higher. Of course, I'm kidding.

SUMMARY

This chapter has described the importance of humbleness in life and in trading. It has shown that both Kevin Cuddie and Mike Palumbo regard humbleness as a necessary trait of trading success. I've met a few very un-humble (read: megalomaniacal) traders in my time, but eventually, they all seem to fall. It's sad to see when it happens, but if ego gets ahead of common sense, we are eventually destined for some hard times. Ego causes us to shoot from the hip, while humbleness creates a calm sense of self that allows us to live in the moment, diligently making well thought out trades. From the perspective of Buddhism, this is also known as mindfulness, which you read about in Chapter 2.

* * *

The point is that when we are mindful of our surroundings and ourselves, when we flow with the market, chances are our ego is not the one driving. In this state, we are humble in our purpose-center, living in the moment. And by finding or staying humble, we are also able to take a good look at our own psychological makeup, which could be a lifeline to understanding why we are making the trading decisions that we are, when we are. If you are about to make a big trade, ask yourself, "Am I humble right now?" If you can answer no, perhaps hold off on the trade; chances are your ego is making the call.

But there's more to the story. Humbleness without forgiveness is really just exhaustion, and when we recoup, we will not remain humble. Thus, the only way for us to remain calm throughout our trading days is to understand that forgiveness is an equally important aspect of self that must be actuated to truly *stay* humble. Forgiveness is not something you will hear much about on Wall Street because for many, it's only about winning. But you will lose from time to time if you trade for a living; it's the only thing I can one hundred percent guarantee. To transcend our losses and bad decisions, we must be able to forgive ourselves in life and in trading. And that's why Chapter 5 is so darn important. Forgiveness can quickly be pushed aside as something that you really don't need to read about in the worlds of finances and trading. But I would like to argue otherwise, and certainly hope that you take the time to really dig deep into the next chapter.

CHAPTER 5

Be Courageous, Be Forgiving

W e've all made mistakes, but it's how we deal with them that defines our future. In confronting the emotions and decisions we've been party to in our past, we must remember one of the most critical points of moving forward in life is learning to forgive ourselves. You might be asking yourself if this discussion is really necessary in a trading book; I will passionately debate that it absolutely is. I have met many damaged traders who continually beat themselves up about poor decisions, missed money, or something trivial that happened five minutes (or five years) ago— so much so that they sabotage the trade at hand. And in life, many of us do the exact same thing on a day-to-day basis.

Even more important, I've met traders who can't forgive themselves for letting a winner turn into a loser, and thus always take money off the table at the first sign of profitability. And when this happens, they get stuck in "smallgainicitis," which is the state of never having any big winners. And then when they have a large loser once in a while, they wonder why their account is always red. Thus, this chapter isn't just for traders who are trying to overcome a long string of bad trades, but, rather, it is also for those who win, but never seem to win big. And, of course, this chapter is also for anyone who simply has a few regrets for decisions they've made in the past. I think that at moments in this chapter more than any while reading this book, some readers will ask: "What does any of this have to do with the financial markets?" which is certainly a valid question. But remember that trading is psychology, and most who have careers in the markets never stop to consider what you are about to read. While you may not directly read about financials or trading in this chapter, what you are about to read attempts to address a part of the underlying sense of self, and psychology, that we must acknowledge to be the best traders we can be.

See, part of the fundamental problem in healing from our bad trading decisions is that even when we forgive ourselves, we sometimes do it in a way that keeps us from completely healing. In the future, we can quickly fall back into old habits if we have not completely let go of the initial problem. And forgiving ourselves takes an immense amount of courage. Forgiveness and courage are amazingly well tied together, as we must first be courageous enough to accept forgiveness deep within our heart, mind, and soul. Without this courage, we will never fully complete the healing process. And with the courage to forgive ourselves, we will find an amazing sense of continued humbleness. Through courage and forgiveness, our humbleness will help us further develop a strong sense of self-esteem, while staying purpose-centered. And reflecting on the basics of self we touched on in Chapter 1, when we have the courage to forgive ourselves for our mistakes, we are also overcoming the false dogma of self that keeps us from living in the moment.

What's more, with the courage to forgive ourselves, we can also find an amazing sense of gratitude, which, as you will read about in Chapter 11, can help us live more happy lives, with greater expectations for the future. Forgiveness, humbleness, and gratitude all go hand-in-hand, but we can never achieve any of these three states if we don't have the courage to take the first step.

Forgiveness is a substantial part of the equation in becoming the best traders and people we can be. Forgiveness is something many people (and specifically traders) struggle with, although I'm not entirely sure why. Perhaps it's because in the code of capitalism we live in, we've somehow been subconsciously conditioned to think emotional self-punishment is a healthy way of recognizing that we've erred. But the problem is that when we harbor ill feelings for ourselves, or for those around us, we're the only ones who are hurt in the long run. Eventually, our lack of forgiveness turns into resentment, something that will cripple our personal and trading lives if not dealt with. And in this, we're about to see how vitally important forgiveness is for prosperity.

THE VACUUM LAW OF PROSPERITY

This principle was brought forward by Catherine Ponder, in the book *The Dynamic Laws of Prosperity*.[1] In the book, Ponder states that there is a natural vacuum in all things. If you remove something from a space, another thing must fill it. As the saying goes, "Nature abhors a vacuum." This argument dates back to the Greek philosophers, who had trouble conceiving that a vacuum in nature really existed. Specifically, Aristotle argued that a vacuum in nature is not possible, as all space is filled with matter.[2] His argument was that to have a vacuum, you must first have empty space, which from his point of view, was impossible. In quantum mechanics, we see Aristotle's view slightly validated, as vacuum energy can never truly be at zero. Even in the most perfect vacuum atoms still exist.[3]

Thus, there's misunderstanding of the word *vacuum* with that of disproportionate pressure. Though the definition of a vacuum differs slightly from person to person, it is commonly thought as an area or volume of space that is emptier than standard atmospheric pressure.[4] An area of less matter is subject to the pressure of the area where there is more. And this leads us to *The Vacuum Law of Prosperity*, where Ponder states, "if you want greater good, greater prosperity in your life, start forming a vacuum to receive it!"[5]

In other words, if you want to see your life (or trading) improve, you must rid yourself of the negative emotions that occupy your mind in order to make room for positive thoughts of greatness. And in forgiveness, we see this necessity as readily apparent. How can we ever truly make room in our hearts and minds for positive thoughts, or to learn new paradigms of trading, if we harbor grudges, feelings of anger, or resentment? According to the Vacuum Law of Prosperity, when we forgive ourselves and those whom we feel have wronged us, we open the door to fill our minds and hearts with greatness. When we remove something within ourselves, we create an area of less pressure, so to speak, that is filled with an area of more.

In trading, I often see someone upset with him- or herself for a bad trade, or blaming someone or something else for the loss in their account. The only way to overcome this fill of negative emotion is to recognize it, and completely let go through unconditional forgiveness. When we completely let go of these negative feelings, we open the door for other, greater successes. In essence, we have formed a vacuum in our life (or in trading) by removing the negative.

I know this concept seems a little flaky, but, really, it is an amazing theory that I firmly stand by. And, as Ponder wrote, "Forgiveness is the only answer." She asserts, "I have discovered from talking with hundreds of people about their problems and from corresponding with hundreds more that, inevitably, when a stubborn problem does not yield, it is because there is a need for forgiveness."[6] You might be asking yourself, how does this concept apply to trading? If you can't seem to find your swing in the market, perhaps it is because a sense of resentment is keeping you from seeing the situation clearly. I can give you a personal example: A while ago, I was writing for a financial newsletter, picking stocks for subscribers. But it seemed like everything I chose fell apart. And let me tell you, it's one thing to take a loss in your own account, but it's even more stressful to pick a stock and then have hundreds of people write you and tell you something similar to "you'd do a better job pumping gas." I knew I could find winners, but felt helpless because it seemed like every stock I chose to write about fell through the floor. No matter how I switched up my research, I just couldn't make the right decisions.

Finally, I looked deeply at myself and realized that at some level I was not forgiving myself for the first few bad trades, and thus was picking stocks defensively . . . mostly out of fear. I really wasn't trading my game. But after I completely forgave myself and wrote out, "I forgive myself unconditionally, and I'm going to move forward without hanging onto the past. I'm going to do the best job I possibly can, and if they show me the door, at least I can get a job pumping gas." Almost immediately by forgiving myself, and by adding a little humor to my losses, I found a few great plays that worked right away. I firmly believe that by forgiving myself unconditionally, I had formed a vacuum to open myself up to believe in my research . . . and myself.

I would like to point out that there's a difference between forgiveness and not accepting responsibility. True forgiveness of self, to create a vacuum of prosperity, comes from accepting responsibility for our actions and then letting them go. Shucking off the situation without truly forgiving ourselves keeps our subconscious full of bad emotions. The only way to truly clear our minds is to forgive and forget.

Trading is stressful business, and to be the best we can be, we can't harbor ill feelings when we make mistakes. If we are to truly move forward in our trading decisions, we must let go of the last moment, even if it was something that caused us to lose money. To paraphrase Mike Palumbo in Chapter 4, we have to be able to move beyond a losing trade by analyzing what went wrong from an unemotional, unbiased state—something we cannot do unless we first forgive ourselves for the losing trade.

Sometimes I wonder if we're so all intent on measuring up to some mysterious perception of success that we feel like we have to kick ourselves around little, even after the fact, just because it seems like the right thing to do.

But there's another way to live and trade. If we recognize the problem and then courageously forgive ourselves, we are free to make the most of the next moment a hand. We can remember the circumstances that led to the initial breakdown, but beating ourselves up about it is not healthy.

With this in mind, I've interviewed one authority that I think knows more about forgiveness than anyone else I've ever met, Dr. Michael A. L. Eckelkamp. I'm happy to publish his thoughts here:

INTERVIEW WITH
DR. MICHAEL A. L. ECKELKAMP

As a brief introduction, Rev. Dr. Michael Eckelkamp has served as a parish pastor for 17 years and currently serves on the Healthy Ministries Task for of the Rocky Mountain District. He completed his Masters of Divinity and Masters of Sacred Theology at Concordia Seminary and his doctorate at Westminster Theological Seminary. In addition, Pastor Michael served short-term missionary efforts to India and Kyrgystan . . . and I would like to add is an all-around nice guy. Except when playing croquet, that is.

Dr. Eckelkamp's outlook on forgiveness is something we all need . . . and after hearing him speak often, I quickly thought of him when considering this chapter on forgiveness. Regarding religion, I would like to ask all readers to keep an open mind while reading this section of the book. I am not trying to press religion on readers; I am trying to help us all find a little forgiveness in ourselves, something that is vital to the subject matter of this book.

MW: Dr. Eckelkamp, thank you for your time. Can you please tell us a little about yourself and your approach to forgiveness?

ME: I have served as a pastor for 17 years. It is a joy for me to see the transformation that occurs in people's lives as they discover the ability to receive forgiveness. On a daily basis, I am blessed to see the transforming power of forgiveness set people free.

MW: As you know, this chapter of the book is on forgiveness of self. Can you please share some of your thoughts on forgiveness?

ME: Forgiveness is a legal term. It rises above mere emotion. While it certainly impacts the way we feel, forgiveness is a conscious decision one makes. I take God at his word. If God has chosen to forgive me—I then live as a person who is forgiven. If God is no longer keeping a record of my wrongs, then it is my job to learn from them, but then move on. God's love is bigger than my mistake.

MW: In your history, have you seen people say that they've forgiven themselves for a few bad decisions, but then later sabotage themselves, or regress to previous behaviors, because they did not truly forgive themselves?

ME: This self-sabotage occurs because cheap grace has been extended. The decision to forgive was based on avoiding pain or ignoring the hurt. Healing begins when one takes full responsibility for their behavior and thoughts by saying, "Yes, I did wrong, *and* God has chosen to forgive me." It was God's choice, not mine! If I am declared not guilty, then the only logical decision is to live in forgiveness. The genuine challenge is to take ownership first of the wrong and then to take ownership of the gift of forgiveness. A person gives you a present. It is right for you to say, "Thank you!" Then you treat that present well out of respect for the person who gave it to you.

In a much greater way, God has given to us the greatest present of all: His forgiveness! Our response is to say, "Thank you!" with our thoughts and our lives. We live as God has declared us to be: *forgiven*!

MW: Given your experience, what is the best way for someone to forgive him- or herself for a poor decision, and then to truly let it go?

ME: I encourage the person to write down the bad decision that they have made on a piece of paper. Then the person takes the paper and holds it up with both hands extended upwards. I encourage them to hold onto the paper for as long as they can. In a matter of minutes the pain of holding on is too great to continue to hold onto the paper. We eventually see that we are in charge of our pain, and all we have to do is just put it down. If you can't forgive, turn it over to a force that can, but the pain will never finally go away until you accept your own forgiveness as well. Just put it down and walk away.

MW: Can you give us any other thoughts you have on forgiveness?

ME: Personally, I discover that when I am hurting because of mistakes I made, that when I honestly examine my life, I honestly need to take inventory of my life.

MW: Finally, are there any last words you would like to provide?

ME: Stop thinking about forgiveness as a right and start seeing it as a gift. Gifts are best used and shared! The genesis of forgiving oneself is to open their ears. The sound of God's extending grace is what begins the inner transformation of the heart. The hearing of God's love is the starting point for forgiving oneself.

Conclusion

Dr. Eckelkamp points out that in terms of life, real forgiveness never completely comes to fruition unless we turn from where we have erred and do not consciously repeat the same mistake. Cheap grace is doing something over and over and over. In terms of trading, if we continually break our money-management rules, we will find that we are slowly eroding our sense of self-worth, as we find ourselves on the losing side of ourselves... time and time again. When we have a bad trade, or a money management slipup, it's very important that we accept responsibility for the mistake, but then also make the commitment to let it go. We need to forgive ourselves for the moment and walk away from the negative thoughts surrounding the trade. Then, we need to consciously avoid the same behavior in the future.

It's much easier said than done, but I can assure you that if you are faced with a scenario where you have a chance to err a second time and you walk away, you will not only reassure yourself that you learned from the initial experience, but will further solidify to yourself that you have forgiven yourself for having lost money the first time. Forgiveness coupled with proactive behavior that fails to repeat the past leads to a solid sense of self-esteem and trading confidence. But we have to remember that it takes courage to take a step into the unknown. And in the next section, Vic Frierson is going to tell us his story about finding courage.

THE NEED FOR COURAGE: VIC FRIERSON

The interview you're about to read is for anyone struggling through trading in particular and life in general. When times get tough, moments often come about when we question everything. And Vic Frierson, Executive Director of Park Heights Community Health, is no stranger to what I'm talking about. His amazing rags to riches story is so powerful that it has to be shared here. Overcoming difficult times is something that takes courage and, even more important, the courage to change. You're about to read about one guy who had the deck loaded against him from the start, hit rock bottom, and then found the courage to create an amazing life.

The Courage to Change

Growing up in Kentucky during the 1970s was a difficult proposition for most African Americans, who often found themselves fending off tides of racism. But for those who were penniless as well, life was even tougher. And it's here that we meet Vic Frierson, a tall, athletic young man, who in 1972 was in the heart of his high school years. But while most were enjoying the irresponsibility of youth, Vic was fighting for his family's well-being, caught in the throes of poverty.

Standing at 6'4" and 250 pounds, Vic dreamed of becoming a professional football player, or a professional singer, both of which he found he had great talent for. Vic's friends also noticed his talents; and his stature as a very popular guy at school reflected the admiration his classmates had for him.

But what his high school friends didn't know was that he, his mother, three bothers, and one sister were so poor that often there wasn't food on the table at dinner. To help, Vic would hustle over to the local corner store after school or practice, where he would take out trash, stock shelves, and sweep the floors, just to take bologna ends home to his family.

At the time, his mother was mentally disabled and could not help the family whatsoever. Vic and his siblings were completely on their own. And Vic was desperately trying to hide his family's poverty from the people in his community.

Then, on a hot day in the middle of summer, Vic came home around noon to check on his baby brother (who was just over one year old), his mother, and the litter of six puppies their dog had just given birth to. When he walked in the door, he stopped dead in his tracks. He couldn't believe his eyes. His mother was standing over the puppies in the living room, smashing each with a large piece of firewood. She was killing each puppy, one by one, and Vic had no idea what to do.

Thinking, "That could have been my baby brother," Vic had to make the most courageous decision of his entire life. He phoned the police, who took his mother away to a mental institution. Several months later, with his mother slowly recovering, the family moved to the projects.

While Vic was telling me this story, at this point he looked up and beamed, "You might think the projects are a bad place, but compared to the conditions we had been living in, the projects were like moving into the Ritz Carlton. You never know how good or bad things truly are until you have some type of anchor to reference them to. Taking the smallest step up to the projects made us realize that somewhere in all of this, we were living in a very, very bad situation."

Fast forward several years after high school. Vic found himself struggling as his dreams of becoming a professional athlete were fading away. His life had turned into a $300 a day cocaine habit, which he was certain would kill him.

Desperately seeking answers, Vic looked back into his childhood, when he remembered the courage he'd mustered to make the telephone call to the police, many years earlier. And digging as deep as he could, he courageously made the commitment to himself to never touch another drug again.

Now Vic is the executive director of Park Heights Community Health and has been drug-free for over 20 years. Vic's story of overcoming incredible personal and social odds to find success has many pieces of hope for traders, or any of those who are struggling to make sense of tough times. Here's what Vic had to say.

* * *

MW: Vic, thanks for your story. Given what you know about hardship, and what you've overcome, what advice would you give someone having problems in their trading career, or in life?

VF: Listen to your angels and recognize that they are there. By this I mean, listen to the people who are around you, who are trying to help. We get so caught up in ourselves, we never stop to take a moment and look around. Listen to what the people around you have to say; you have to listen to them, and you have to accept what they are offering: help, advice, money . . . whatever. You have to believe in God's teachings that say, "When you take one step, I'll take two." You *have* to take action. Taking no action is the *worst* decision you can possibly make. And really, what it's called is: *courage*. You have to be willing to take that one step. Then, if you want to call it blind faith, do, but it's your own *courage* that will be the first step in *anything* incredible that you attempt.

MW: So would you say part of overcoming adversity is letting go of your pride and accepting help?

VF: Yes, but also letting go of your fears while stepping up to the challenge at hand, no matter what it is. Most people are so afraid of change that they are reluctant to take the first step. People settle. It's easy for people to do what they've always done. Accepting a different paradigm is hard.

MW: What about traders slugging it out with the market each day?

VF: I don't think it's any different if you're a million-dollar trader or homeless person. The same rules apply. If we are to step outside ourselves and overcome our fear of what we don't understand, what's to stop us from doing something so incredible that we can change lives? What's to stop that person from changing everything he or she knows? Instead, we have a tendency to put the blame on something or someone else. What we do is instead of stepping up to our fears and our responsibility, we blame someone or something else for the problem at hand. By doing so, we don't recognize our own responsibility to help facilitate change.

MW: What advice would you give the regular guy who is facing a tough year trading?

VF: Life is absolutely nothing without taking risks. It's like the risk of loving someone. People want assurances; they want to know that they won't be hurt. However, taking risks is an implicit part of any loving relationship. The same thing applies in every aspect of our lives. You're taking the same risk that that Fredrick Douglass took . . . it's all part of loving something, it's all part of trying to effect change.

MW: You said that traders and homeless people have similarities. What did you mean by this?

VF: In the realm of taking risks and effecting change, the paradigm is identical; both have to be willing to take the first step. Homeless people may not have as much to lose in a material sense, but emotionally they face the same struggle. At some level, we all find ourselves completely broken at some point, when we're at a humble bottom, we are open to the most change. We're all identical; it's only a matter of whether we can bring ourselves out of ourselves and find an ounce of courage within our sorrow that we can truly change the things happening around us. All that matters is that when everything is caving in, it's important to remember that *courage* is the very first step of reversing everything.

Conclusion

I was very inspired by Vic's story, and as I began to think about it, I realized that he is right about courage and change and all of our equality whether we are a million dollar a year trader or homeless. In fact, some homeless people might even live with better morals. But the point is that no matter where we are in life, when we're struggling, we're struggling, and the only thing that will effect change in our lives is our ability to be courageous enough to take the first step toward change. As traders, this may simply be approaching another trader and asking for help. Vic's story helps remind us that as people, we're all doing the best we can . . . and most people are always willing to help those who are trying to make positive changes. And if we're trying to make some big changes in our lives, we must be courageous enough to take the first step and also remember to ask for help.

> *Courage is the first of human qualities, because it is the quality which guarantees all others.*
> —Winston Churchill

SUMMARY

In this chapter, we have taken a deeper look at forgiveness and courage, which are certainly not items that most traders think about during the day. However, the point here is that by having the courage to ask for help, or to forgive ourselves for a bad trade, we open the door to humbleness and to a better understanding of the way we approach ego and esteem. All of the aforementioned are really parts of a dynamic circle of self that all contribute to one another. We must recognize all the small parts to see the whole. And to see the whole of our trading careers move forward, courage and forgiveness of self are vitally important.

It's easy to shrug off these concepts, but I want to take a moment to tell you one thing: I've been around several trading floors in my career and have met hundreds of traders throughout the years. Right now, at this very moment, there are only a small handful of those guys (and gals) still trading for a living. I've really taken the time over the years to dissect why so many traders have failed and I've come up with four reasons:

1. Those who are almost certain to fail in trading do not have the will, desire, or ability to truly be honest with themselves.
2. Most traders who have been unsuccessful do not have the courage to ask for help.

3. Traders who cannot stay humble eventually go down in flames.
4. Traders who cannot forgive themselves eventually take massive losses, while never being able to let a winning trade run.

* * *

After the previous discussion on the need for courage and why it's so important to forgive ourselves in trading and life, it's also important to look into the main cause of why we might not be able to do so. And the key emotion that keeps most of us from effecting change in our trading and personal lives is *fear*. In Chapter 6 you're going to read about how fear plays a vital part in our lives, what fear is, and how we deal with it. In addition, we'll cover what types of fear are good and what types are not. And then we'll unlock some incredible tools that will help us defeat useless fears at every turn.

ADDENDUM

An Additional Note from Dr. Eckelkamp on Forgiveness

Real forgiveness doesn't mean that we don't feel hurt. It doesn't mean that we won't think about it every once in a while. It doesn't mean that we won't have a setback on wanting revenge on a person and wanting them to hurt the way we were hurt. It doesn't mean that we have to be their best buddy. It doesn't mean that we will allow them to do it again. It doesn't mean that the pain will go away overnight after we forgive.

What it does mean is drawing from a source outside of ourselves. We cannot share what we do not first receive. Forgiveness flows from God. Because God tells me, "Michael, you are forgiven." I am then able to say to the person who wronged me: "I forgive you." Forgiveness is a legal declaration that I give up the right to get even. I refuse to hire myself as judge, jury, and executioner.

One of the words used for forgiveness used by Jesus is also used to mean to "unlock a chain." It is in our nature to hold ourselves and others captive. This personal jail sentence confines us to a prison of isolation and self-degradation. God makes a conscious decision to open the door of the prison. He has the right to issue the death penalty, but instead chooses to take our guilt, our shame, and our sentence upon Himself. Instead of an electric chair, God chose a cross. The law is fulfilled as the sentence is served. The punishment for your mistake has been issued and rendered.

Why continue to sit in the jail cell? Why continue to beat yourself up over the wrong? Instead, walk away from the prison a free person.

Forgiveness is also a mind-set. We are called to "write-over" our old and useless ways of thinking. Thinking differently leads to living differently. For example, when you delete a worthless document on a computer you make the effort of putting it in the computer's wastebasket. But it isn't gone from your computer.

You must make the additional effort to empty your computer's wastebasket. But even then it isn't deleted from your computer's memory. It's still there. All your computer did was replace the first letter with its own code symbol to say it may be written over if the space is needed. It is hidden from you. But it can be recovered even then by simply replacing the first letter.

Only after time will your computer write over that file. Then it will be completely gone. Forgiving others and forgiving self is much the same. We make a real effort, a definite decision, to live in the forgiveness God has given to us. Our memory is written over. Our mind filled with forgiveness writes over the hurt and desire for revenge.

CHAPTER 6

An Investigation of Fear

Fear is only as deep as the mind allows.
—Japanese proverb

Fear in itself is an interesting subject of research, as it transcends many levels of our psyche. At some level, fear is good, and at some level, it is very destructive. For some, a profoundly engrained sense of fear is something that has deep roots and should only be confronted with the help of a psychiatric professional. Keep this caveat in mind as you read this chapter.

Fear in itself is a very unpleasant feeling. When we feel fear, something in the situation that we are in is presenting danger. When we feel fearful, we are feeling a painful emotion, and we are feeling uneasy. And when we feel fear, we are alarmed. But to understand fear itself, before we even begin to touch on fear in relation to the financial markets, it's necessary to understand what fear is at a very core level, and then try to understand how and why we feel it when we do. In this chapter, we're going to dig into what fear is at a rudimentary level and the different types and manifestations of fear, and then see how fear applies to our lives and the markets. Fear is very serious business, something that should not be brushed off. However, in an effort to keep the tone from being too academic, I've tried to insert a little humor in this chapter.

FEAR DEFINED

You might think it's overkill, but do read all of the following definitions of fear. *Merriam-Webster's OnlineDictionary* (http://www.m-w.com/
help/citing.htm) defines fear as:[1]

1. archaic: *FRIGHTEN*
2. archaic: *to feel fear in (oneself)*
3. *to have a reverential awe of* <fear *God*>
4. *to be afraid of: expect with alarm* <fear *the worst*>
   intransitive verb: to be afraid or apprehensive <feared *for their
   lives*>

And in its definitions of fear, fearing, and fears, Answers.com holds:[2]

1. *a. A feeling of agitation and anxiety caused by the presence or
   imminence of danger.*
   b. A state or condition marked by this feeling: living in fear.
2. *A feeling of disquiet or apprehension:* a fear of looking foolish.
3. *Extreme reverence or awe, as toward a supreme power.*
4. *A reason for dread or apprehension:* Being alone is my greatest
   fear.

When we "feel" fear, we perceive some sort of elevated level of danger.
Our physiology is alarming us that something is not right. "Fear triggers
the familiar 'fight or flight' response, characterized by increased heart rate,
breathing, and muscle tension, which allows the individual to escape from
danger or defend itself against a predator."[3]

To get to the rudimentary understanding of fear, we need to understand
that some aspect of ourselves is being trailed by a predator.

ACKNOWLEDGING THE PREDATOR

For many, understanding fear by acknowledging the predator is very uncomfortable. Thinking of ourselves as prey is hardly a touchy-feely approach
to handling our emotions. But in the case of fear, it is what it is. And for
us to confront the emotion, at some level we're going to have to get strong
to do it.

Though this may sound easy, it's vital to know that there are different types of fears: internal and external. And if we are ever going to be the best traders we can be, we must be able to distinguish between the two.

When you're standing in the middle of the street and a cab is flying towards you, it's pretty easy to recognize that you may be feeling fearful. The fear is external. But there are times when you may not be able to recognize that fear is even present at all, simply because it is masked by our delusional understanding of trading, or from within ourselves.

Many traders begin to feel immense amounts of stress when putting on large positions or when their trades are either making or losing a ton of money. At these times, one may start to get very stressed out, thinking that the entire situation is simply part of the game. There's a threefold problem here. First, at these times, traders may not even be able to recognize that they are mistaking stress for what is really fear, and second, even if they do not mistake that fear has ensued, they may not be able to distinguish whether it is internal or external. Third, even if they are able to distinguish what the predator is, and where it's coming from, they may have no idea how to deal with it.

Let me break it down. In physical life, if a lion were chasing us in the jungle, we would probably instantly recognize that we were feeling fear. After all, most of us intuitively know that when a lion is on our tail, a painful experience potentially resulting in death could be right around the corner . . . and we're probably going to deal with it by running like greased lightening. But here's where fear gets tricky. Sometimes the predator isn't obvious, and we have no idea that we're even feeling fear in the first place. And even more troubling, sometimes the predator is so well hidden that we can't even see that the predator is actually fear itself. If you don't know it's there, how are you going to know to run?

If you stand at the edge of a cliff, you probably feel some sense of fear. It's only natural, because if you slip, the predator is death. The external predator is easy to identify . . . it's the cliff. But if you see a bag of M&M's (I will expand further on this in a moment), and you suddenly feel very fearful, there's probably something else going on inside you. After all, most people don't usually find themselves frightened when seeing a bag of candy. The fear is internal. And even if you acknowledge that a predator is present, if you focus solely on the bag of M&M's, you may never find the true predator, because the predator is either something entirely different than the bag of M&M's or simply fear itself. In trading, there are two points here. First, many traders can't recognize that fear has ensued because it is so well hidden (like seeing a bag of M&M's and feeling fearful), and second, sometimes there is no predator at all except our own dissolution playing havoc on us.

Thus, the first step in recognizing fear is acknowledging that a predator does exist. We must be able to recognize the signs of fear and to know that we are feeling fear when it surfaces, even when it isn't obvious. It sounds easy, but it's not always so.

When you're trading for a living, external and internal fear (and the inability to recognize and distinguish the two) can become our greatest enemies. Fear can cause us to make horrible trading decisions based solely on irrational emotions of the moment. Those who trade with fear, and cannot recognize it, eventually go broke.

The primary step in overcoming our sugarcoated denial is to be honest with ourselves. When we find ourselves with sweaty palms, on a common-sense level, we can assume something stressful is happening. As a result, we need to ask ourselves, "Why am I feeling the way I am? Is the stress that I'm feeling actually fear in disguise? And if it is really fear, what is the predator, and is it external or internal?"

Before we get too much further, I want to take a moment to state that for some people, fear is beyond their control. For these few, fear is actually a chemical issue within their physiology, and no matter how I cover it here, it simply won't help without medical attention. Take a moment to read the following:

In *The Neurobiology of Fear*, Laurel Duphiney Edmundson asserts,

Based on the presence or absence of a stimulus, the brain appropriately regulates the strength and duration of this coping mechanism. When this regulatory system malfunctions, however, it can lead to excessive fearfulness in certain individuals. For some reason, these people have trouble suppressing the body's response to stress. While a lot of progress has been made in understanding the mechanisms that initially trigger fear responses, the precise method of turning them off remains elusive. Researchers continue to use animal models to gain further understanding into the regulation of the neurobiological reaction to fear. [3]

What you've just read was written in 2000. In 2005, however, cutting-edge research at Harvard University showed that fear is formed in the amygdala brain structure and is linked with the protein stathmin.[4] When mice were genetically modified so that they could not produce stathmin, they "showed deficits in neural transmission and exhibited decreased memory in fear conditioning and the failure to recognize danger in innately aversive environments."[5]

The bottom line is that some people have physiological issues not subject to mental conditioning that may be causing fear-based behavior. The point is that if you make an honest attempt at overcoming fear by yourself and nothing seems to work, it's time to see a doctor, because something physical may be going on. But honesty is the key. And it's here that we take the next step: we will distinguish when fear is being made by our own worst enemy (us) and learn how we can both recognize and control it.

GOOD COP

At some level, fear is a natural emotion that ensures our survival; it is good because it is something that can save our lives. Good fear can be natural or it can be learned. In the state of *natural* fear, we are truly in danger. When we feel this fear, adrenaline and cortisol[6] are released in the brain in an effort to make us more alert, to ready ourselves for, evaluate, or escape from, the threat at hand.[7]

Thus we see that having fear is actually something that can help us navigate dangerous situations, such as when you're about jump from a moving train onto the back of a horse. (It's a good example because I'm sure we've all had to do this at one time or another.) At the level where fear is a natural reaction to danger, our ability to perceive fear is thought to depend on our individual genetic makeup. In research, "The ability to detect and anticipate dangerous situations seems to be crucial for survival, and individual learning might not be entirely quick enough to ensure survival chances. Moreover, even potentially dangerous stimuli might be rare and thus impossible to learn—leading an individual into danger when the stimulus is encountered for the first time."[8]

Somewhere within us, we all have a natural ability to sense when something might harm us. Some might be able to better handle or feel less fear than others, but at some level and to some degree, we all feel natural fear when something very dangerous is confronting us.

The second type of good fear can be both instinctual and *learned* fear.[9] This state occurs when subconscious or conscious memories cause our physiology to reflexively trigger the fear emotion.[10] For example, when a child first puts his hand on a hot burner, chances are that up until that point, he has no idea that it will hurt him. However, the painful occurrence of having his hand burned will provide a learned sense of fear that will keep him from putting his hand on the burner a second time. (Hopefully, anyway.) When learned fear is a valid sense of fear that keeps us from physical or mental harm, it is good fear. This is also known as adaptive fear and is helpful in our survival.

Good fear is a benefit when it helps us, but is destructive when it causes us to make the wrong decision or to not be able to make a decision at all, for that matter. An example of this would be "watchful immobilization," which is a level of fear where we reflexively shut down to evaluate or protect ourselves from the danger around us.[11] In terms of trading, this could happen in a situation we've never encountered, and though there is nothing negative in the situation, we have no idea what the outcome will be. Without having anything to directly associate with the situation, our fear level begins to rise, and the neurobiology of our brain causes us to freeze. With this in mind, when something happens that makes us feel fear at all, even if it's good fear, it creates a situation where maladaptive bad fear can manifest itself.

BAD COP

Maladaptive fear, or bad fear, occurs when we find ourselves in an elevated sense of alarm, doubt, anxiety, terror, or panic due to misplaced conditioned fear. When we are experiencing bad fear, we are reacting to something from a conscious or unconscious memory that doesn't necessarily have any correlation to the situation at hand. And if we leave maladaptive fear unchecked, chances are we will only restrict our ability to prosper as people, friends, lovers, and traders. A little fear is good; unnecessary self-made fear (maladaptive learned fear) is bad, potentially leading to anxiety. Remember the earlier statement, "if you see a bag of M&M's, and you suddenly feel very fearful, there's probably something else going on inside you"? This is an example of maladaptive, bad fear. Somewhere along the way, something negative happened that is stuck in our subconscious and somehow a bag of M&M's was in the picture too.

It's as simple as Pavlov's dog. In 1927, Pavlov published his paper on conditioned reflexes, which basically proved that a neutral occurrence (bell ringing) paired with an unconditional stimulus (food) causes a conditioned response (salivation).[12]

In terms of maladaptive fear, a neutral occurrence (something that isn't good or bad) is paired with an unconditional stimulus (something that provokes an emotion or physical reaction) or an adverse stimulus (something bad) that causes a conditioned response like salivation or fear. Putting this concept into the trader's perspective, when a neutral stimulus (buying a stock) is paired with an adverse stimulus that is painful (losing a ton of money), the two form a relationship, and the unfortunate outcome can often be a conditioned reflex of fear. However, taking this one step further, when a neutral stimulus is combined with an unconditional stimulus *and* an adverse stimulus, the conditioned response can be even worse, because we may not truly know what the true cause of the adverse stimulus is. Our reaction to the adverse stimulus in relation to the neutral and unconditional stimuli will end up clouding our judgment in the future. In our minds, we have linked the neutral and unconditional stimuli to the painful outcome, and from that moment forward, we will associate the two. And it's in such circumstances that we see why maladaptive fear, or bad fear, can become so destructive. If we do not question the fear we are feeling and cannot recognize that it may not be genuinely protective fear, we will slide down the hill of fearful thinking until it takes over our ability to make rational decisions. What's more, when fear manifests itself as a way of life, it evolves into anxiety (see Chapter 7).

DECIPHERING THE DIFFERENCE BETWEEN GOOD AND BAD FEAR

In the initial stages of understanding how to combat fear, we must first diagnose what type of fear we are feeling. If we are feeling good fear, there's probably a genuine reason we should be worried about the situation. However, if we are feeling bad fear, we might be manufacturing the fear ourselves, and the situation may not actually be as dangerous as we think.

Signs of Good Fear

Good fear arises when the situation at hand has some sort of clearly identifiable, tangent form of danger that is presenting us with a sense of alarm. And in the case of trading, when we are in a situation where things are falling apart quickly, or clearly appear that they are about to fall apart, the fear that we are feeling is most likely valid in the sense of good fear. Our minds and bodies are trying to make us aware that something dangerous is at foot.

Signs of Bad Fear

If the situation does not have any clearly identifiable signs of imminent danger, then we may be feeling bad fear. In this case, this sense of fear may not be coming from the actual situation itself, but, rather, from a memory or feeling of a situation that we've experienced in the past. What's really happening here is that while the situation itself isn't presenting any clear danger; we are creating the sense of fear within ourselves based on the feelings from another painful event that have somehow attached themselves to the current scenario. If you see a bag of M&M's and you find yourself filled with fear, the fear itself is probably not derived from the candy. Instead, the fear is a learned reaction, where some sort of stimulus that prompted genuine fear has somehow become linked to a neutral stimulus that really poses no true threat. Regardless, in your subconscious, the bag of M&M's means danger. In trading, such learned bad fear may come from associating a loss with a completely unrelated event.

Here's a picture of how this can happen: Say that you have just bought a technology stock the day of a Federal Open Market Committee (FOMC) meeting where a quarter-point drop in the federal funds rate is expected. You perceive that the market will rally on news that the Feds are loosening the money supply and fully expect tech to move higher with a broader market rally. That afternoon at 2:15 p.m. EST, the Fed announces that it is lowering rates a quarter point, and the market reacts favorably. You're ready to rake in the cash, as the tech stock you've bought should run with the rest of the market. But it doesn't go up at all, and around 3:00 p.m. it begins to fall rapidly. You look for news, but there isn't any, and so the sell-off in your stock seems completely irrational. And then the stock starts dropping even faster, and you start to feel terror, just before complete panic sets in. By the time you get out, you've lost a huge chunk of money. You don't know why that happened, but you suspect that the sell-off in your tech-sector stock had something to do with the announcement on interest rates. From that day forward, whenever an FOMC decision looms, you will stay as far away from the market, and tech stocks, as you possibly can. You experienced pain from the trade, and from now on, the correlation between an FOMC announcement, and the unpredictable volatility in tech, will tie the two together as something to fear.

But what you don't know is that on the day of the FOMC announcement, a massive pension fund decided to change its strategy slightly and move the bulk of its assets into transportation. And its main holding is the same tech stock you bought just before the FOMC announcement. To make matters worse, the head trader at the pension fund is a very brash guy, so instead of slowly trading out of the large position in the tech stock, he instructed his desk to "dump it."

In reality, the FOMC announcement had nothing to do with the tech stock you bought getting crushed. Subconsciously, though, the FOMC announcement and the tech stock sell-off are correlated because they happened at the same period in time. The neutral stimulus (buying the stock) is paired with an unconditional stimulus (the FOMC announcement). In the future, when you think about buying a tech stock on an FOMC announcement day, you will feel fearful because you remember the previous experience. The conditioned response to the thought of buying a tech stock when the FOMC announces is fear. But the fear is misplaced. In reality, the FOMC announcement had nothing to do with the tech stock tanking.

In identifying the signs of bad fear, we simply have to ask ourselves if, when one thing provokes fear within us, could there possibly be a separate event that triggered fear? Does the item causing fear stand alone, or is it secondary to something else? We must look at all causes of the fear and make sure that what we are feeling isn't just a conditioned response to something that really has nothing to do with the true situation at hand. If the fear that we're feeling cannot be identified as stand-alone (like a cab that's about to hit us in the street), it is more than likely some sort of conditioned reflex.

EVENT TIMING AND THE CONDITIONED REFLEX

Another conclusion that Pavlov made in his study was that if you ring a bell after a dog has eaten, he will not salivate. The unconditional stimulus (the food) must come after the neutral stimulus (ringing the bell); otherwise the conditional response (salivation) will not occur.

In the case of the tech stock and the FOMC, the unconditional stimulus (FOMC) would have to come after the neutral stimulus (buying the stock) for the conditioned response (fear of losing money) to happen. If you'd waited for the FOMC announcement to occur before buying the tech stock, chances are that you would not associate the two when the tech stock dumped.

When you feel fear, you can ask yourself about the order of events that occurred to help pinpoint the true cause of fear. When we can clearly identify the true cause of the fear, the predator, we have taken the first step to overcoming the fear itself.

OVERCOMING GOOD FEAR

Normally, when good fear comes about, like our feelings of flight when the building we're standing in is burning down, we probably don't want to analyze the situation too much. Standing around roasting marshmallows while the roof's ablaze is not where we want to consider our options. But if we are feeling good fear when the market is moving against us, and we're sure there isn't a neutral stimulus that is associated with the situation, we might want to evaluate the good fear for a moment. When your stock is buckling, are you fearful of losing money? The predator is loss. And the predator is valid, because loss hurts and could hinder our trading decisions in the future, if we begin to be bereaved of our financial solvency.

When we recognize and acknowledge the predator, we can look at it directly in the eyes, while asking ourselves, "How dangerous is this situation?" If we assess the total risk of the losing trade, we can begin to make a rational decision to get ourselves out without panic or terror. Basically, this is learning to remain calm in the eye of the storm. When we're losing money, we know the predator is loss, but the greater predator is losing even more money and then having to deal with our personal loss of self-worth, self-confidence, and efficacy, and questioning our purpose-center, or the wife at home, who's not a big fan of a negative paycheck. And if we're not careful, we can log the situation in our memory, thus setting ourselves up for unhealthy fear-based trading decisions in the future.

Thus, to stand up to good fear and make sure we are confident in ourselves, we have to consciously acknowledge the predator and then become the predator ourselves. When something is trailing us and we figure out how to turn the tides of the situation, we not only defeat the fear itself, but also promote a healthy sense of self-efficacy and esteem as well. It's important to note that to stand up to the fear, we must acknowledge the fear in order to move beyond it. As you know from Chapter 1, we must accept the emotion as something we can't directly control, though we can stand up to it by acknowledging it. When we accept fear and then lean into the discomfort, we are taking on the predator, without trying to control the predator.

Defeating good fear that is surfacing at a time when we are not in physical peril requires us to step back from the situation and look at things from an unbiased standpoint. When we do, we have the opportunity to make the conscious decision to approach the fear-based situation with a rational mind, which, in a sense, defeats good fear. Keep in mind that there's a difference between analyzing the situation and being stuck in watchful immobilization. We want to proactively think about how to get out, not completely shut down.

When we logically defeat good fear from a Zen-like stance of calmness, we are taking control of our lives. We don't want to completely tear down or take away our ability to react as our physiology demands in sincerely fearful situations. However, we do want to make sure that we are conscious of our bodies and what they are doing when they are in the process of effecting chemical changes within us. Lastly, from our stance of purpose-centered mindfulness, the most important aspect of defeating good fear is to acknowledge and accept that we are feeling fear in the first place.

DEFEATING BAD FEAR

Defeating bad fear is a much more difficult task because it requires us to not only look at the situation, but also look at ourselves. When a bad fear situation surfaces, we must stop and recognize that we are feeling fearful. It's one thing to look at the bag of M&M's and say, "Those things scare the heck out of me," but it's another to see them and run out of the room screaming at the top of our lungs. When we acknowledge that fear is present, we are approaching the situation from a calm stance of inquiry. When we bolt from the room because the bag of M&M's is too much for us to handle, we're reacting to the neutral stimulus, while completely disregarding our ability to think rationally.

The *first step* to defeating bad fear is to recognize and acknowledge that we are feeling fearful. Once we do this, we want to then determine what the predator stalking us is. If we are afraid for our lives, it's death. But when you are standing face to face with the bag of M&M's, if you're attempting to think rationally even though you're in a state of fear and panic, at some level most of us will recognize that the M&M's are harmless.

The *second step* is to analyze the true danger of the predator and determine whether our fear is valid, or is a conditioned response. On a logical basis, if it is not truly as dangerous as we feel it is, it is probably a neutral stimulus that we have a conditioned response toward that really stems from a completely separate unconditional or adverse stimulus.

The *third step* to defeating bad fear is to dig into ourselves and try to find out what the adverse or unconditional stimulus really is. (I want to add that if you think dredging the adverse stimulus from your memory might be too disturbing, consult your psychiatrist first.) When we figure out what the true adverse stimulus is, we can begin to understand that the neutral stimulus was simply in the wrong place at the wrong time, when the true adverse stimulus surfaced somewhere in our past.

The *fourth step* to defeating bad fear is to evaluate the timeline of the prior neutral stimulus and adverse or unconditional stimulus. Pavlov's studies generally teach us that for a neutral stimulus to correlate to an adverse or unconditional stimulus in generating fear, it usually appeared prior to the adverse or unconditional stimulus.

Here's an example of what I mean: One day in your past you were walking down the street, minding your own business, eating some M&M's. While waiting to cross the street, you looked down at the bag to read the ingredient list, when suddenly someone conks you on the head with a golf club and swipes your wallet. The next time you're at the store and you reach for the bag of M&M's, you find yourself with sweaty palms and for some reason decide to pass them up. Here we clearly see that the neutral stimulus (M&M's) is now correlated with the adverse stimulus (a golf club whacking your cranium), creating a conditioned response of fear for M&M's.

But let's replay the situation out from a different angle. Say you are walking down the street, minding your own business, whistling the theme song to *Rocky*, when suddenly someone bonks you on the noggin with a golf club. When you wake up on the pavement, you have an M&M's wrapper stuck to your face. As you peel it off, you take a good look at it. By Pavlov's study, the next time you are at the grocery store, when you reach for the M&M's you might think of the wrapper stuck to your face that day when you woke up after being bonked on the head, but, in theory, you should not directly associate the candy with the attack. The M&M's might remind you of being bonked on the head, but (in theory) won't trigger symptoms of fear. (Note: I think at some level, if we've been through actual bodily harm or our life was truly in danger, this part of Pavlov's theory falls apart, but because trading generally doesn't usually involve physical peril, we'll conclude Pavlov's theory holds true.) What's important here is that we can generally assume that the true cause of the conditioned response (the unconditional stimulus or the adverse stimulus) generally had to occur at the same time as or before the neutral stimulus, not after.

The *fifth step* in defeating bad fear is to recognize that the neutral event is not correctly correlated with the conditioned response. We have to admit to ourselves that M&M's do not always mean a golf club clunking our head. Recovery at this point can take significant time, depending on the level of fear you feel when you look at the M&M's. But the only way to truly get over it is to admit that you're afraid of being bonked over the head again, while accepting that it's okay to feel what you're feeling. What's more, it would be necessary to then accept that M&M's make you feel fearful and let yourself feel what you are feeling. Then, by accepting the emotions, you are validating the fear, while also properly addressing to your subconscious that the M&M's are not the real cause of fear. At that point, it would be a good idea to try to buy some more M&M's, but it might be a good idea to go to the store with your therapist.

In the case of the FOMC announcement, we must recognize the maladaptive fear and accept that what we are feeling is valid. With complete acceptance, it might be a good idea to take a position in another tech stock the next time the Fed announces—with tight stop-loss plan—just to let ourselves know that we are in control of the situation. Even if the stock moves against us, if we close the loser before taking a big loss, we will reaffirm to ourselves that we are in control of our trading destiny and defeat the conditioned response of bad fear at the roots. Most likely, when the trade is closed, we will say, "What was I thinking?" Importantly though, we can never have this epiphany unless we first identify the true fear stimulus in the first place and then admit that it is valid. At that point we can face it head on. As Franklin Delano Roosevelt said, "The only thing we have to fear, is fear itself."[13]

FEAR AND MORITA THERAPY

In Chapter 1 we discussed Morita therapy and overcoming our emotions by simply accepting them. By doing so, we are able to live in the moment. But fear is a little more complicated, as you've probably already surmised. If you remember the discussion about getting back on a bike after we've fallen off, I mentioned that it's not enough to just get back on the bike to overcome our fear, but we must also admit that we are feeling fear to truly overcome the situation. And in this chapter you've read much about facing the predator. It's important to distinguish that facing the predator (fear) does not mean to just get back on the bike, but, rather, to first accept the emotion and then figure out what type of fear it is that we are feeling. In the case of the M&M's and the FOMC announcement, we will eventually want to "get back on the bike," but not before first accepting our feelings of fear as a valid emotion.

Morita therapy tells us to just accept our feelings, and while I completely agree with this advice, at some level, fear also needs an additional degree of analysis to understand the root of it. Thus, unlike most of our emotions, fear can sometimes require some introspection rather than simply accepting it. Thus, once we take the time to figure out the true causes of our fear, the next important step in healing is to simply admit to ourselves that what we are feeling is valid.

FEAR IS THE ONLY PARADIGM OF THE MARKET

When you are standing in the middle of the street and a cab is screaming towards you, the fear predator is bodily harm or death. And it's coming from both mental and physical levels. Physically your body is pumping adrenaline, and mentally you're trying to figure out how to evade the situation, all of which is happening in the blink of an eye.

In terms of trading, though, when the market is moving up quickly, the fear predators that stalk you are greed, desire, and regret, not bodily harm. And so we have to understand that while the fear predators in trading have some similarities to physical fear, they are really not the same. We can control our trading fears if we understand the fear itself, while also understanding the fear paradigm of the entire market.

Markets move on fear, and fear only, because greed is fear. Markets move on the fear predators that make us take action. And when we want to make money, the fear predator that is prompting us to invest is greed . . . it is the self-interest of people that prompts market action.[14] Greed is a manifestation of fear.

Greed is defined as "a desire to obtain more, a desire to obtain more money, wealth, material possessions or any other entity than one needs."[15] We have to ask, why would any of us want more than we need? The answer is because when we feel we have abundant wealth, we feel strong, protected, safe, successful, and happy—all of which factors protect us from having to be fearful. You most likely won't have to fear paying the mortgage ever again if you have a million dollars, and the only way to get a million dollars is to acquire abundant wealth. And abundance is greed. We are greedy because we don't want to have to fear, and abundance through greed is perceived by many to overthrow fear.

Markets move up because someone is buying more stock somewhere. And he or she is only doing so because they see the opportunity of increasing their wealth by buying stock in an upward-moving market. The desire to acquire greater monetary wealth (abundance) is greed, which, as we just covered, is a manifestation of fear. Thus, we can infer that the greater the market speed, the greater the fear level. When markets and stocks are moving up rapidly, the investing public is fearful of missing the opportunity of abundance and is buying at a faster rate. (As a side note, the Market Volatility Index (CBOE: VIX) is a measurement of fear that trades inversely to the major indexes. When the VIX is low, markets move up, because it is said people are complacent about the market and are buying stocks. I would like to argue, though, that they are buying stock because they are equally fearful of not making money.)

As we understand that greed is actually a manifestation of fear, we see that fear is actually the only paradigm of the market. And once we understand fear as the greater whole—or, from a Jungian prospective, the "collective unconscious"[16]—we will see that in understanding fear, we tap into the market. However, there is a fine line between understanding the collective fear, or lack of fear, and understanding the fear in ourselves. We must understand how to immunize ourselves from market-based maladaptive fear in order to recognize the greater fear of the broader market and the collective unconscious of the market. To give you an idea of how this plays out, let's look at Jungian psychology in relation to the Dow Jones Industrial Average, an FOMC announcement, and the collective fear of the market. Then we will see how utilizing Morita therapy with our purpose-center can help us have a better understanding of the fear-based emotions of the market.

The Collective Unconscious and the Market

Carl Jung worked in analytical psychology and brought to light the separation of personal unconscious and the collective unconscious. As a definition, "the collective unconscious can be adequately explained as arising in each individual from shared instinct, common experience, and shared culture. The natural process of generalization in the human mind combines these common traits and experiences into a mostly identical substratum of the unconscious."[17] Basically, we can assume that all investors share the collective unconscious desires to make money and avoid losses. What's more, as people, we have a cognitive map that helps us find direction through life and the markets.[18] Our personal understanding of the market can often be similar to one another's understanding simply because when something works for one, it is passed to another. When we understand that the collective unconscious and the cognitive map of individuals are often related in terms of market movements, we are able to see beyond our personal unconsciousness and perceive the greater collective unconscious at work. In short, when we take the time to understand the fear at work in the market (fear of losing or missing the opportunity to make money), we have a greater chance of perceiving more accurately the events that could potentially transpire as the herd moves. More important, we can proactively plan our behavioral reaction to the events that are about to happen. To put this into actual market actions, we will look at an FOMC announcement and a chart of the Dow Jones Industrial Average. (As a side note, you can probably see that we are stumbling on the concepts of intuition here, which are discussed in detail in Chapter 10.)

In Figure 6.1, you can see that the index hit a high in May of 2006, before falling over 900 points. As investors, we must try to understand not just the fundamentals behind why the index lost ground, but also what the collective unconscious was thinking at that time. It is important to note that, for the sake of simplicity, this example leaves out many other events that were transpiring in the market at the time, including political tensions, economic data, and rising energy prices.

After examining Figure 6.1, take a moment to read the following FOMC announcement from May 10, 2006.

* * *

Release Date: May 10, 2006
For immediate release

The Federal Open Market Committee decided today to raise its target for the federal funds rate by 25 basis points to 5 percent.

Economic growth has been quite strong so far this year. The Committee sees growth as likely to moderate to a more sustainable pace, partly reflecting a gradual cooling of the housing market and the lagged effects of increases in interest rates and energy prices.

As yet, the run-up in the prices of energy and other commodities appears to have had only a modest effect on core inflation, ongoing productivity gains have helped to hold the growth of unit labor costs in check, and inflation expectations remain contained. Still, possible increases in resource utilization, in combination with the elevated

FIGURE 6.1 Federal Open Market Committee press release. (Chart courtesy of StockCharts.com, http://stockcharts.com.)

prices of energy and other commodities, have the potential to add to inflation pressures.

The Committee judges that some further policy firming may yet be needed to address inflation risks but emphasizes that the extent and timing of any such firming will depend importantly on the evolution of the economic outlook as implied by incoming information. In any event, the Committee will respond to changes in economic prospects as needed to support the attainment of its objectives.

Voting for the FOMC monetary policy action were: Ben S. Bernanke, Chairman; Timothy F. Geithner, Vice Chairman; Susan S.

Bies; Jack Guynn; Donald L. Kohn; Randall S. Kroszner; Jeffrey M. Lacker; Mark W. Olson; Sandra Pianalto; Kevin M. Warsh; and Janet L. Yellen.

In a related action, the Board of Governors unanimously approved a 25-basis-point increase in the discount rate to 6 percent. In taking this action, the Board approved the requests submitted by the Boards of Directors of the Federal Reserve Banks of Boston, New York, Philadelphia, Cleveland, Richmond, Atlanta, Chicago, St. Louis, Minneapolis, Dallas, and San Francisco.

* * *

There are three statements to take note of in this report. First, the press release states, "The Committee sees growth as likely to moderate to a more sustainable pace, partly reflecting a gradual cooling of the housing market and the lagged effects of increases in interest rates and energy prices." Here we see that the FOMC is really saying to beware of housing markets dropping with rising interest rates and that higher oil prices could negatively affect the economy, while higher energy prices cause growth to slow.

Second, the statement, "Still, possible increases in resource utilization, in combination with the elevated prices of energy and other commodities, have the potential to add to inflation pressures" translates to, "watch out, more interest rate hikes to come."

Third, "The Committee judges that some further policy firming may yet be needed to address inflation risks but emphasizes that the extent and timing of any such firming will depend importantly on the evolution of the economic outlook as implied by incoming information" really means, "We'd like to reiterate, more hikes to come."

From this FOMC announcement alone, the collective unconscious perceives tightening money supply based on inflation risks and higher energy prices. Moreover, continued rate hikes are indicating a slowing housing market. At the end of the day, from this press release, the collective unconscious is full of fear.

Looking at fear from a rational stance, we know that the neutral stimulus is the trading action of the Dow Jones Industrial Average, while the adverse stimulus is the worrisome tone of the FOMC release, creating the response of fear, or sell-off. In short, we can perceive that the indication of more interest rates hikes in the pipeline will not give investors a reason to buy. As a result, the Dow Jones Industrial Average declined from May to June. Now that we see the macro level of fear, we can look at the fear within our personal unconscious to see how we can make more accurate trading decisions.

PERSONAL UNCONSCIOUSNESS

If we were to stop for a moment when news like the FOMC report hits the market and recognize that the collective unconsciousness is full of fear, we could then shape our decisions to profit from the emotions of the market at hand. To do so, we must first check our fear level and exposure. Once we identify what our fears are in the situation at hand, we have recognized the market dogma that will move markets in the near term. And, taking one step further, if we then put this in the back of our mind and live in the now—in accordance to Morita therapy—we will sell the positions we have and possibly open up short positions.

When this FOMC announcement surfaced, I purchased puts options on the Diamonds, a Dow Jones Industrial Average tracking stock (AMEX: DIA). In doing so, I put my fears that the market would fall to rest, knowing that I had hedged my portfolio. I had protected myself from the fearful collective unconsciousness of the market by accepting the fear as a possible indication of near-term movement. But it's important to note that I took the action I did from a stance of fear. I was afraid the market was going to sell off, which was the catalyst for seeking a protective position. I admitted that I was fearful of a sell-off, which cleared my mind to make a rational trading decision. At the end of the day, I decided to open the put position because I decided that the market was fearful of the FOMC announcement, not just me. I removed myself from the equation after admitting that I was fearful of a downswing. And after I did, the collective fear of the market still resonated and a sell-off ensued.

By admitting my own fear and analyzing the fear of the broader market, the puts I opened not only gave me a sense of relief, because I knew I was protected from my fear, but I also didn't have to worry about a downswing and thus was able to go about my normal day-to-day trading. By recognizing the collective unconscious of fear in the market, I breached the monetary dogma at hand and made the correct decision. In essence, when I recognized the fear in the market, I was able to make an intuitive decision while trading in my purpose-center.

SUMMARY

As described in this chapter, it is vitally important for us to understand what fear is and to identify good and bad fear within ourselves. Only then can we see how fear plays into the broader collective unconscious of the market and our personal trading consciousness. When we take these steps, we see the big picture and are able to make sharp intuitive decisions in regard to larger market movements and our own purpose-center.

What's more, by understanding what fear is at the very roots, we are able to recognize when we are operating under maladaptive learned fear. This simple recognition can stop us from associating two completely unrelated events and, thus, make us more profitable traders for being able to see ourselves and the situation clearly.

Also, when we are able to take a step back after recognizing that valid good fear exists, we are able to rationally make non-fear-based decisions while staying calm in the middle of a market storm.

With all of this in mind, there will be circumstances when we will find ourselves completely sideswiped by events we could not predict and, of course, by a string of bad trades. We need to recognize that single and compounded tragic events can be overcome by looking into ourselves, while also seeing that if we do not stop to understand our emotions, we may subject ourselves to continued anxiety, which is devastating in and of itself.

* * *

Putting what we have just learned into action, and going one step further, in Chapter 7, you're going to read about an investor who overcame a massive life tragedy and who thus has some great points for anyone struggling in life, or in trading. Bob Williams is a successful trader today because he has taken the time to investigate fear and anxiety, two things that riddle most traders. In addition, you will read an interview with Sue Myers, PhD, APRN, BC, who will discuss the inner workings of anxiety and how we can overcome that most destructive condition.

CHAPTER 7

Overcoming Adversity and Anxiety

T ragedy can strike at any time in life and in the markets, and when it does, we can often find ourselves completely upended. The fallout from adverse circumstances out of our control can devastate us. When one of these events happens, the fallout is beyond fear, and we can be left with immobilizing anxiety that can forever hinder our chances at success. And anxiety is all too prevalent in the trader's psyche, as at some point unforeseen losses always occur. To overcome the aftermath of such, we must recognize both the devastation that has occurred and the resulting learned fear. If we do not, we will fall victim to the horrible issue of never being able to think clearly when the pressure is on. Anxiety can cripple any of us in our day-to-day lives and in our trading decisions. Thus, in this chapter, you're going to read about how Bob Williams faced a near-death experience, hit an emotional rock bottom soon after, and then recovered. Moreover, Bob will give us some insights into what he learned from this experience and how it correlates to the worlds of trading and investing. Finally, Sue Myers, PhD, APRN, BC, will explain anxiety from a medical perspective and describe the tools we need to overcome this alarming product of fear.

TURNING THE TIDE ON DEATH— BOB WILLIAMS

I consider myself blessed to have met Bob Williams, an amazing guy who survived a tragedy that made national headlines. What Bob went through, most of us probably can't even fathom as a reality. But the understanding of self and anxiety that Bob has to share from his experience is truly informational and inspiring. What's more, Bob is a trader, and one of the best I've ever met at that. And it's no wonder that he's as good as he is, considering that because of his devastating experience, he's had to look way deep inside and question all of himself . . . something most traders never, ever do. Of importance, an additional item that you will read about in Bob's story is how we can lose trust in the world and ourselves after a devastating experience takes place. And in the world of trading, this is very poignant, as after one takes a huge hit, trust in one's own decisions can quickly fade. Bob's story is truly a gift and should not be glanced over. As traders, we have much to learn from Bob.

In March of 2004, Bob and his fiancée, Julie, boarded the *Lady D*, a pontoon water-taxi at Fort McHenry, Maryland, bound for Baltimore's Inner Harbor. Shortly after the boat set out, a sudden storm came from nowhere . . . with 50 mph winds and waves that began to violently rock the boat from side to side. In a few brief moments, the *Lady D* capsized with 23 passengers and 2 crew members aboard.

In the blink of an eye, Bob and his fiancée found themselves—with the other passengers—trapped 12 feet beneath the water's surface, in the cabin of the overturned boat. After being violently slammed to the opposite side of the cabin, and as the near freezing water quickly flooded the cabin, Bob and his fiancée had just enough time to gasp for one breath of air before being completely submerged in the ice-cold coffee-colored blackness of the harbor. Miraculously, even though sheer panic had broken out with the passengers scrambling over one another (underwater) they were able to open a window and swim out of the cabin.

On the surface, the freezing storm waters made climbing to safety almost impossible, but both somehow made it. In all, about five minutes had passed from the time the water-taxi flipped to the time Bob and Julie were safely atop the boat's floating wreckage. It didn't take the couple long to realize that all were not accounted for, and people were likely still trapped beneath the boat. With hypothermia already setting in, there was nothing they or the other survivors could do except wait for a rescue team to arrive.

When the navy arrived roughly 20 minutes later, the rescue boat was used to lift one side of the water-taxi out of the water, while several divers leapt in to look for potential survivors in the underwater cabin. Almost as quickly as the military divers swam underneath the overturned boat, they returned . . . empty-handed. The military divers were only able to stay in the water for just over two minutes because the water was simply too cold, even for the trained professionals. Over the next few minutes, Bob and Julie helplessly watched as lifeless bodies were pulled from the water and brought aboard the wreckage.

Of the 25 people who boarded the water-taxi that day, 5 died.

While listening to Bob's story, I was completely in awe of his calm and positive outlook, despite having been through a tragic experience that would emotionally cripple most of us for life. And even though I like to think of myself as a tough guy, hearing Bob's compassion for the others who also lived the experience, and his amazing outlook on life, I couldn't help but feel tears welling in my eyes.

* * *

MW: Bob, thank you for telling us your story. I'm so sorry you had to go through such a horrific experience. As you know, this chapter is about overcoming adversity, something that you know a ton about. And in getting a better feel for what you went through, can you explain what happened to you emotionally after the accident?

BW: I felt extremely fortunate and grateful to be alive, but those feelings were quickly replaced by tremendous sorrow for the people who lost their lives and the families that were torn apart that day. I slowly retreated inward and didn't even realize I was doing it. The gratefulness I felt days after the accident was being replaced by a sense of confusion and apprehension as I tried to make sense of the events.

MW: Bob, when we were speaking before the interview, you mentioned that there was also a bereavement of trust, which was one of the major "self-losses" that occurred with the entire situation. Can you elaborate a little more on this?

BW: What did I lose that day? I lost the basic trust in myself and in the world. When you wake up each morning and don't have that basic trust, it can really be a struggle.

What I needed to do was realize that I hadn't really lost anything—it was still there; I just needed to realize it was there. I felt like in order to feel better or whole again that I needed to get back to the shoreline, but really I was already there, I just had to realize it.

You mentioned Pema Chodron's book[1] [mentioned previously in Chapter 3, which Bob and I spoke about before the interview], and tying it back, we are all born with basic goodness. We can't let our thinking or perceptions change that, because that's where you get into trouble.

My mind was altering how I saw the world. I was filtering everything through my experience on the boat, and the way I saw things became skewed. It took some time to tap back into the basic goodness in people and in the world. It's so important to remember that this "goodness" is always there—it's one of the few things that you can count on every day.

MW: How did you come through full circle?

BW: One would think that after you go through a near-death experience, you'd be grateful for life, but many times the exact opposite occurs, and you feel cut off or isolated. This feeling of separateness or isolation is dangerous because it's where fear manifests itself. I decided to explore Zen Buddhism and meditation as a way to accept and relax with my experience.

MW: So in other words, you were feeling separated and isolated from the world. You mentioned in our earlier conversation that these bad emotions can eventually fade, but it takes work. Can you expand?

BW: Yep, exactly. It's called "mindfulness training"; learning to bring a moment-by-moment awareness to life's experiences.

MW: How do you live in the moment and not think about the past?

BW: . . . or the future. What you try to do is only experience what your eyes are showing you. That's true reality. Letting go of the "thinking mind" is a very difficult concept to grasp and one that I still struggle with daily. It's particularly helpful when you're caught up in a moment and feeling bad about things—just relax and return to the present.

MW: With everything in mind, can you give us some additional insights about what we can expect after going through a difficult time?

BW: We all have a tendency to want security and want ground under our feet, whether it's in our jobs or in our personal lives. I'm learning that if you can relax with the whole concept of groundlessness—and be okay with the fact that there's no security in tomorrow—you'll build the strength within yourself to overcome any situation.

MW: Bob, when we were talking about the whole story, you told me about the intuition you felt when things seemed like they were getting dangerous before the boat flipped. You and your fiancée are alive today because you trusted your intuition and told Julie how to escape the cabin by opening a window underwater, should the boat capsize. You perceived the outcome before it ever happened; you somehow had a glimpse into the future. This is so amazing; I'm having trouble putting it into words. Can you shed some insight on your feeling regarding intuition?

BW: It all boils down to genuine trust in oneself. The more we have, the easier it is to trust our intuition and let our own internal compass be the guide.

MW: How would you put this in terms of trading?

BW: Trading will bring forth just about every negative emotion out there. At least it has with me. It's so easy to second-guess yourself or beat yourself up if a trade doesn't break your way. You just can't be emotionally vested in every single trade and expect to hold up very long. Remember why you made the trade in the first place, you had a vision—don't let your discursive mind spook you out of the position.

MW: I think what you're saying is don't get spooked by your fears, right? Can you elaborate a little more on this and fear in the market?

BW: When you start having thoughts like whether you're the last person to buy into a rally or the last person to sell off in a panic, and facing the indecision that comes along with that mind-set—forget it, you've had it, you're scared to death. I don't think you can earn any type of significant return with the fearful mind in charge. You've got to step aside, out of the market, and get you're bearings back.

MW: Would you say that any of the emotions you went through that day have come up again in trading. I guess what I mean is, are there any similarities to the emotions or fear that you experienced that day to what the average guys go through in daily life and trading?

BW: Certainly it's not a life-and-death struggle out there in the financial markets but it's incredibly demanding. Fear is going to be a part of the equation, whether you like it or not. But fear is only a bad thing when it is not based on anything real. Fear can be good...very good; it warned me of the storm and the winds that day and ultimately led me to come up with a plan that saved Julie and me. In terms of trading, I've had fears that a sell-off was imminent—the fear had a base in real market news and events and ultimately led to that wonderful feeling of selling right at the very top of a move.

MW: What have you specifically taken away from this experience that helps you handle the pressure and fear that comes with trading?

BW: Be comfortable with uncertainty in trading and in life. The catch-22 is that you really don't have a choice; markets can be the epitome of uncertainty. You've got to make good decisions and follow a discipline to be effective. You can only make these good decisions with a clear and relaxed state of mind.

MW: Are there any specific things you do to handle fear and anxiety when you are trading?

BW: Being informed I think is key—I mean really being in tune with the market. If you truly understand each position and the news and events affecting that position, then you can make wise decisions and minimize the effect of fear.

MW: With everything that we've covered, can you give us some additional insights into what makes us great people able to handle adversity and change?

BW: Really look inward and make loving peace with yourself. If you don't have a core belief in yourself, it's going to be a challenge whether you're trading or teeing it up on the weekend with some friends. I'm not referring to any level of arrogance or ego; I'm talking about on a real, genuine level, to really love and trust in who you are.

MW: Any last words, Bob?

BW: Remember that "tough times don't last, tough people do." There's also a favorite story of mine I'd like to share. It's about a group of people, maybe 20 or so, who set out to climb a mountain. After the first day's ascent, the group stops and looks down over the edge of the cliff... and 4 or 5 people decide it's too much... they bail.

The group continues up the mountain the next morning, and again, after another exhausting climb, they stop and look over the edge, and a few more feel overwhelmed and retreat down the mountainside.

This happens one more time until there are only a handful of brave souls that navigate their way to the peak. The view from the top is simply magnificent and each rejoices in conquering the mountain. They achieved their goal.

The moral: The folks who bravely managed their way to the top are no better than the people who bailed out. They simply haven't hit their wall in life yet, but they will; we all will. As for the people who did not make it to the top, if the effort was genuine, then the experience will make them greater people, and perhaps next time, they will make it all the way.

With this in mind, you *don't* know what's around each corner, and it's okay if you're going through a period of emotional or physical strife—it's unavoidable. There's an amazing sense of freedom when we're able to simply let go and understand that we're not always in control.

* * *

Bob Williams's interview shows us that fear and anxiety in life situations have direct correlations with trading, and when we understand the connection, we can improve our trading careers. When we understand that fear and anxiety are natural states of being, we can transcend them through acceptance. What's more, by clearing our minds and accepting our emotions, Bob points out that we have a greater chance of seeing the situation openly. The key, then, is to work hard to uncover the information that will keep us ahead of the game. I've heard this information called "market intelligence," which means we have a good idea of what is driving stocks. When our market intelligence is low and we don't really have a good idea of why things are happening, we stand a greater chance of making an irrational decision driven by our emotions. And, as we've seen over and over in this book, trading assessments from a stance of non-emotion gives us the greatest shot at success in the markets.

The next section of this chapter looks a little deeper into anxiety with an explanation and interview with Sue Myers, PhD, APRN, BC. Anxiety and trading can often go hand in hand; thus, it's vitally important for us to have a deep understanding of what anxiety is and how we can combat it, if we are to live our lives to the fullest, while trading with passion and purpose.

THE BASICS OF ANXIETY

Anxiety itself is a manifestation of fear, apprehension, and worry. But anxiety is a dangerous emotion, as it can often cause us to have negative physical reactions such as hyperventilation, heart problems, and hypertension. For many traders, these physical problems become a regular part of life, as the markets constantly evoke stress and fear. Without a deep understanding of anxiety, we stand the chance of cutting short our trading careers, and lives in general. But there are solutions to anxiety, and if we tackle the subject head on, we will find our lives liberated from the negative emotions derived from this problematic issue.

Anxiety itself is a complicated animal because it has cognitive, somatic, emotional, and behavioral components. Before we get too far, it is important to look into each of these aspects. Specifically:

The cognitive component entails expectation of a diffuse and uncertain danger. Somatically the body prepares the organism to deal with threat (known as an emergency reaction); blood pressure and heart rate are increased, sweating is increased, blood flow to the major muscle groups is increased, and immune and digestive system functions are inhibited. Externally, somatic signs of anxiety may include pale skin, sweating, trembling, and pupillary dilation. Emotionally, anxiety causes a sense of dread or panic and physically causes nausea and chills. Behaviorally, both voluntary and involuntary behaviors may arise directed at escaping or avoiding the source of anxiety. These behaviors are frequent and often maladaptive, being most extreme in anxiety disorders. However, anxiety is not always pathological or maladaptive: it is a common emotion along with fear, anger, sadness, and happiness, and it has a very important function in relation to survival.[2]

With this brief explanation in mind, Sue Myers, PhD, APRN, BC, has been gracious enough to explain anxiety, the manifestations of it, and how we can diffuse it at every turn. This incredible woman has much to teach us about anxiety, what we need to know about the dangerous condition, and how we can overcome our own minds to live an anxiety-free life.

* * *

MW: Can you please give us a more detailed explanation of anxiety and how it affects us, both mentally and physically?

SM: In many ways, anxiety is good for us! When there is a normal response to anxiety, the brain adapts to the stressful situation at hand and we become more alert, more responsive, and often more creative! However, anxiety becomes harmful when the mechanism that causes the tense state becomes impaired. Our bodies can begin to work against us, causing a full-blown anxiety disorder. Understanding how someone develops an anxiety disorder has been the subject of intense scrutiny and research over the past two decades.

Anxiety affects us both emotionally and physically. The emotional reaction to anxiety is made up of feelings of worry, nervousness, and restlessness, or feeling keyed up or on edge. Physical reactions include an array of signs and symptoms such as a pounding heart, palpitations, rapid pulse, chest pain, hyperventilation, sighing respirations, nausea, and abdominal distress, to mention a few. There is little or no conscious control over these uncomfortable physical experiences.

Understanding some basic concepts of the central nervous system can help to better understand anxiety. The central nervous system has two broad divisions: (1) the somatic (voluntary) and (2) the autonomic nervous system (involuntary). The autonomic system helps to keep our minds and bodies in balance by two opposing subsystems: the sympathetic or excitatory portion and the parasympathetic system or inhibitory portion. When someone feels anxious or fearful, sympathetic nerve fibers are activated that produce an automatic involuntary response. Norepinephrine, a powerful chemical mediator, is released to multiple organs of the body. The purpose of norepinephrine is to prepare the body for "fight or flight." As a result, the surge of norepinephrine causes (1) the pupils to dilate (hyperalertness); (2) the heart rate and force of each heart contraction to increase (rapid, pounding pulse); (3) the respiratory rate to increase in depth and rate (hyperventilation); (4) blood to be shunted away from nonessential organs (cold, clammy hands); (5) blood to be shunted to the brain and muscles (mentally, physically alert); and (6) the gastrointestinal tract to slow down or stop (cramping, nausea).

MW: Does the physical reaction of anxiety cause the emotional reaction, or is it the other way around?

SM: The exact relationship between physical and psychological manifestations of anxiety is not clear. A psychological perspective, such as Freud's, theorizes that psychological symptoms are primary and lead to the development of physical symptoms. More recent theories, based on extensive research, include a more physiologically based explanation. In short, parts of the brain's limbic system (including the hypothalamus, hippocampus, amygdala, and cingulate gyrus) are interconnected and are involved in the fight or flight response. The limbic system also communicates with higher cognitive centers of the prefrontal cortex and lower temporal lobe areas. This is a slower communication that occurs after the initial rapid fear response. During that slower communication time, the individual makes a more reasoned decision about subsequent action or inaction. For example, imagine that an individual who has a conditioned fear of snakes decides to take a stroll in a local zoo and accidentally comes to the snake cages. There is an immediate physical anxiety response caused by release of norepinephrine. The slower track impulses that are sent from the limbic system to the prefrontal cortex may help the person reason that the snakes are in a cage and will not cause harm—or the individual may reason that there is safety in fleeing. Regardless of the action taken, in this theory the physical response is the initiator of the anxiety manifestation and the psychological or emotional response follows.

MW: How do people develop an anxiety disorder?

SM: It is believed that the development of an anxiety disorder centers on a conditioned fear response that originates in the amygdala and is communicated within the entire limbic system. Repeated experiences that the individual perceives as fearful (even if under normal circumstances they are not fearful) will cause an anxiety response because the autonomic system has learned to overrespond to certain stimuli. For instance, individuals with an anxiety disorder may respond with fear to certain smells, sights, or locations even if they are unrelated to the actual fear itself.

As an example, a Gulf War veteran was visiting a war memorial several years after she became a civilian. On entering the archway of the memorial, she broke out in a sweat, became dizzy and nauseated, and felt like she was suffocating. A diagnostic workup later concluded the veteran had posttraumatic stress disorder (PTSD), a debilitating anxiety that, in this case, was activated by sight of the war memorial.

In addition to the conditioned fear response theory about the cause of anxiety disorders, the neurotransmitters serotonin, norepinephrine, and gamma-aminobutyric acid (GABA) have also been implicated. These findings set the path for discovering medicines that alter the neurotransmitters and successfully alleviate moderate to severe anxiety.

A genetic basis of anxiety has also been identified, in which a familial pattern is often elicited during a careful taking of the family history. For example, in the condition known as general anxiety disorder (GAD), studies have demonstrated a strong family tendency, in which 25 percent of those diagnosed with GAD have a first degree relative who has similar symptoms (of being a chronic worrier, being chronically "stressed out"). These biologic/familial factors interact with situational stressors and trauma to contribute to anxiety disorders.

MW: Can you explain maladaptive anxiety and how this situation can hurt our ability to make clear decisions?

SM: Since nearly everyone experiences mild to moderate anxiety at some point (test taking, traffic backups, punctuality demands, dating, meeting new people, and so on), it is important to differentiate adaptive from maladaptive or pathologic anxiety. Maladaptive anxiety can become debilitating and even crippling without treatment. The good news is that today much more is known about the diagnosis and successful treatment of anxiety than in past years. With skilled diagnosis, treatment, and consistent follow-up, patients can be relieved of troublesome or incapacitating anxiety. Unfortunately, currently only about 30 percent of patients with anxiety disorders receive treatment, while it is estimated that 4 to 8 percent of the U.S. population has a moderate to severe anxiety disorder that would benefit from diagnosis and treatment.

Let's look at an example of adaptive anxiety. Tim O. is a 25-year-old stock investor who was about to give a presentation by videoconference to the board of directors of a West Coast firm in which he had a major contract. As Tim waited while IT staff set up the conferencing cables, he began to experience a rapid and pounding heartbeat and felt a tightness across his chest. He became more anxious as he realized the 15 board members were now visible on the screen and poised to hear his report. With no hope of escaping the board members, he refocused himself to the task at hand, and drew on his prepared report and self-confidence to begin his presentation. Tim soon forgot about his anxiety symptoms and went on to give a successful report. In this case, Tim's pre-presentation anxiety, though causing a degree of discomfort, was short lived and ultimately served to assist Tim in overcoming his apprehension.

Maladaptive anxiety, in contrast, presents quite a different picture. Joan B. is a 27-year-old computer programmer who was required to travel across a one-half mile bridge span every day to reach her place of work. Several months earlier she had begun to worry the bridge would collapse when she was at the bridge's highest point. While driving on the bridge she visualized herself being in a car crash and careening off the bridge into the water below. She pictured herself submerged in her car, trying in vain to open a window to get out. Two weeks ago she became so anxious about driving over the bridge she called in sick for work. Her apprehension escalated and she became nauseous, had heart palpitations, and began breathing so fast she became dizzy at the thought of getting in her car to drive to work. Joan's husband did not understand her predicament, but encouraged her to seek help, saying she has had "spells" before. This latest bout of anxiety was worse than it had ever been. Joan declined to seek treatment, saying that her boss would think she was crazy and she could not afford to lose her job. She has not been able to go to work for two weeks and is reluctant to leave her home at all.

Joan has classic signs of an excessive fear or phobia. According to Joan's husband, she has a tendency toward being anxious, but has never sought treatment. Again, returning to important recent research, there is evidence that certain patients will carry memories that can immediately trigger negative thoughts (such as a fear of heights, a fear of drowning) and in susceptible patients (i.e., perhaps those who have an active norepinephrine release system), a phobic or other serious anxiety response is more likely to occur.

Let's compare the two individuals, Tim O. and Joan B. On the one hand, Tim's anxiety response clearly helped him to focus his energy on the videoconference presentation. Joan, on the other hand, had developed a crippling anxiety disorder, later diagnosed as agoraphobia, requiring treatment and close follow-up.

MW: In your previous two responses, three words stood out to me: anxiety, fear, and stress. Do they all mean about the same thing?

SM: The quick answer is no and yes, in that order. The fact that these terms are used interchangeably at times does not help to differentiate between the meanings, but there are distinct differences. Fear is a term, just like anxiety, that spans a range of feelings. Fear can be trifling such as fear that has little consequence, for example, a fear of volcanoes. The other spectrum of fear can be such that the individual is frozen in place, such as a fear of people. This end of the spectrum includes phobias, terrors, and feelings such as paranoia, horror, or persecution. In these instances an individual may feel overwhelmed with a sense of impending danger or disaster.

Anxiety is a term that describes fear. For example, the woman who had a snake phobia (extreme fear) became anxious because of that conditioned fear when she encountered the snake cages at the zoo. Her fear was manifested by anxious feelings (rapid heart rate, pounding in chest, cold clammy hands) caused by the release of norepinephrine (fight or flight response). As with degrees of fear, there are also degrees of anxiety, from anxiety that alerts us and helps us perform better, to debilitating anxiety. In keeping with this rating scale, individuals who experience severe fear, such as with a phobia or feeling of dread, will manifest extreme anxiety. An example of extreme anxiety can be demonstrated physically by uncontrollable trembling and emotionally by uncontrollable worry, apprehension, or *fear*. As you can see, the meanings of anxiety and fear have converged, because severe anxiety can manifest itself by a display of extreme fear.

The third term you asked about, stress, is easier to clarify. Stress is the result of a physical or emotional situation that requires the individual either to adapt or suffer physical or mental strain or anxiety. For example, a soldier stationed in Baghdad is under constant stress, which very likely will engender anxious feelings about being killed or killing another in battle. The soldier's maturity, resilience, coping mechanisms, past experiences, family history, combat training, and neurotransmitter system will influence his ability to rise to the challenge of successfully handling stress. Because of the extreme nature of the stress of war, the soldier will experience some degree of anxiety, no matter how well he or she adapts. Taken one step further, providing emotional and psychological support to soldiers in battle and after battle can reduce those stressful feelings that promote anxiety disorders, such as PTSD.

MW: Are there other types of anxiety disorders that require treatment?

SM: Yes, there are several anxiety disorders that have a cluster of treatable symptoms. At the center of each disorder is a major finding of anxiety that is out of control, interrupting an individual's usual coping patterns and making normal everyday activities impossible.

A panic disorder is an attack in which symptoms suddenly appear and last anywhere from 5 to 30 minutes. There can be a predominance of physical or emotional symptoms. Physical symptoms include feelings of choking, chest pain, sweating, tingling, dizziness, or chills and hot flashes, for example. Mental or emotional symptoms can include fear of losing control, a feeling of being detached from reality or detached from one's self, or fear of dying. Clinicians who diagnose these symptoms are first bound to rule out physical causes of these symptoms. Once a diagnosis is made, there is effective treatment to alleviate these troubling signs and symptoms.

Phobias are an unreasonable and extreme fear about a specific event. A severe phobia, known as agoraphobia (literally, fear of the market) is a fear of leaving home. Agoraphobia often follows untreated panic attacks because the person may fear that leaving home will cause a panic attack. Other phobias can include an abnormal fear of crowds, snakes, spiders, and, as mentioned in the case study about Beth B., a fear of bridges.

Obsessive compulsive disease (OCD) manifests anxiety whenever a person is confronted with a recurring obsessive thought or compulsive action. Examples of compulsive actions are repetitive hand washing, counting, or checking something. Obsessive thoughts may include fear of the death of a loved one or fear of becoming infected with a fatal disease, for example. There tends to be an awareness by the individual about his or her compulsions or obsessions. If untreated, OCD can progress and become severely handicapping.

Post-traumatic stress disorder (PTSD) has received a great deal of research attention following such infamous events as the Vietnam War in the 1970s, the Gulf War in the 1990s, the terrorist attack on September 11, 2001, and, currently, the Iraq War. Wars represent severe stressors that occur outside the range of normal human emotion. Signs and symptoms vary in patients with PTSD and span from psychological numbness to a persistent reliving of the experience accompanied by recurrent anxiety and depression.

While other types of anxiety disorders often have a genetic component, PTSD occurs from overwhelming traumatic environmental stimuli.

However, it is not known why some individuals who are exposed to the same harmful stimuli do not develop symptoms of PTSD. Typically, the severity of physical and emotional manifestations of PTSD is proportionate to the severity of abnormal environmental stress. Sophisticated tools are able to measure the neurobiological effects in the brain of patients with PTSD, aiding in the understanding of a strong mind-body interconnectedness.

MW: These types of anxiety sound very serious. How can a person get help?

SM: Help is available, but an individual or family member must first recognize their symptoms as being abnormal and enter the health-care system by making an appointment with a primary care clinician. At other times, symptoms may be acute, such as during a panic attack, and an emergency room visit is required. For example, if a patient presents to the emergency room with chest pain, current standards of care for diagnosing a heart attack are carried out immediately. If the patient's diagnostic tests are negative, the clinician will investigate other causes of chest pain, which include, among other possible causes, panic attacks.

Following a provisional diagnosis of anxiety disorder, the primary care clinician or emergency room clinician will refer the patient to a psychiatrist or mental health clinic for a definitive diagnosis. Fortunately, over the past 20 years, research has come a long way in understanding the causes of anxiety and effective treatment.

MW: How does the clinician diagnose an anxiety disorder?

SM: Specific signs and symptoms of anxiety disorders have been published in the *Diagnostic and Statistical Manual of Mental Disorders*, 4th edition (DSM-IV) [American Psychiatric Association, 1994]. If the patient's clinical picture meets the criteria, a presumed diagnosis of anxiety disorder is made. However, the clinician must keep in mind that, though rare, there are other organic causes of anxiety. During the history-taking process, a nonpsychiatric diagnosis is considered if (1) there is a sudden onset of symptoms, with no previous history of anxiety; (2) the onset of anxiety symptoms begins after age 35; (3) there is a lack of personal or family history of an anxiety disorder; (4) there is a lack of a childhood history of significant anxiety; (5) there is an absence of life events that would generate or exacerbate anxiety; and (6) there is a poor response to antianxiety drugs. Other diagnoses to consider would include hyperthyroidism, cardiac arrhythmia, congestive heart failure, chronic obstructive pulmonary disease, neoplasm, adrenal insufficiency, nutritional deficiency such as vitamin B_{12}, mitral valve prolapse, and others.

Other important history that will help to make an accurate diagnosis are to evaluate if the patient uses caffeine, amphetamines, marijuana, cocaine, alcohol, or other sedative-hypnotic drugs. Also, determining if the patient is taking drugs that heighten anxiety is important, such as theophylline, corticosteroids, thyroid hormone, psychostimulants, and any herbs. Herbs such as ginseng may trigger or worsen anxiety and a herb known as Mahuang contains ephedrine.

MW: What kind of treatment is there for anxiety disorders?

SM: First, I would like to mention that not all individuals need treatment for anxiety. As we discussed earlier, normal anxiety arouses us and alerts us and actually assists us in meeting daily challenges. But for those people who have been diagnosed with an anxiety disorder, treatment can help bring a patient back to normal functioning. In fact, if severe anxiety disorders are left untreated, they will likely become worse and cause more problems, such as avoiding work and social or family responsibilities. In addition, severely anxious patients tend to develop comorbidities such as depression and have a greater tendency to abuse alcohol and other drugs.

Recent studies have demonstrated that a dual approach to treatment of anxiety disorders is more effective than medication alone or psychological treatments alone. Depending on the type of anxiety diagnosed, benzodiazepines are typically prescribed initially, for short-term use of up to one month. Benzodiazipines have been used over many years as a mainstay of treatment for anxiety disorders. However, any medication must be prescribed with caution. Several recent studies have identified a loss of cognitive functioning in patients who have taken benzodiazipines over a long period of time.

Other drugs that have demonstrated relief of anxiety symptoms include the serotonin reuptake inhibitors (SSRIs) such as Paxil or Prozac, which act on releasing more of the neurotransmitter, serotonin.

Patients who have significant performance anxiety or fear may be benefit from short-term use of a beta-blocker such as propanolol, which will block the effects of norepinephrine and decrease the physical symptoms of anxiety.

No matter which drug is prescribed, the patient and clinician should strive to be in a partnership, so that the patient understands completely what the drug will do and how it should be taken, side effects to monitor, and how long the drug should be taken for. For most patients, an interactive collaborative approach with the clinician is the most effective way to get relief from this treatable but troubling illness.

A nonpharmacologic treatment that has been recommended to treat anxiety disorders is cognitive behavioral therapy (CBT). The main focus of CBT is to help patients understand their anxiety behaviors and then apply strategies that will develop acceptance of realistic thoughts and discard thoughts that are unrealistic and anxiety provoking. Outcomes for this type of therapy are favorable, in part because patients are actively involved in their own recovery. For most favorable outcomes, it is important to have continuity with a primary therapist who will periodically evaluate and re-assess the patient's progress.

Self-help or support groups are effective in providing additional help to learn insight into one's own anxiety problems plus learning about coping strategies others have used. In addition, talking to a trusted friend or family member may also provide additional benefit.

MW: Can you please illustrate some nonmedical ways to combat mild anxiety, before it develops? A sort of proactive anxiety toolbox to ward off anxiety is what we're looking for!

SM: Combating anxiety is a great idea. Having a proactive toolbox to prevent anxiety is an even better one! Even though we know that some stress and subsequent anxiety helps to keep us challenged and alert, there are times when too much stress creeps in and can threaten our equilibrium. For those individuals who do not have an anxiety disorder that needs medical attention, some of the strategies that follow can be helpful in keeping anxiety at bay:

- Maintain a "first things first" approach. Know what a healthy lifestyle is and work at it every day.
- Know and understand your family history with respect to anxiety and mood disorders.
- Maintain a life-long habit of daily exercise.
- Learn ways to relax, including yoga, deep breathing, or conscious muscle relaxation.
- Seek trust and comfort in relationships with others.
- Talk about anxiety with a friend or spouse.
- Become involved in an activity that can be controlled (e.g., working in a garden).
- Take advantage of down time or weekends to regroup, refuel, and relax.
- Get enough sleep.
- Avoid abuse of alcohol and drugs.
- Avoid caffeine and caffeine-containing products.
- Learn about anxiety and how it can be adaptive and maladaptive.

These points are pretty obvious! Yet heeding these suggestions can leave us saying, "I know I should do these things, but I don't have the time... besides, I like to relax with my friends and have a few beers... besides, caffeine keeps me going... besides, who has time for exercise?" and so on. Research has convincingly established a higher rate of anxiety when substance and drug abuse exist. Research has also demonstrated a lowering of coping ability when there is lack of sleep, excessive caffeine, lack of exercise, and lack of recreation.

MW: Can you please give us any additional thoughts on anxiety and, of course, the relationship between anxiety and the stressful life that we all face on a daily basis?

SM: Today, many of us are fortunate enough to live a life filled with previously unheard of conveniences such as instant access to worldwide information, cell phones everywhere, machines that save hours of housework and cooking time, and amazing opportunities for recreation. Yet we are more vulnerable than ever to developing an anxiety problem. Pathologic anxiety does not occur overnight and tends to follow a natural course. Recognizing normal and abnormal anxiety symptoms and knowing how these symptoms can help or hurt us is a first step to breaking the cycle of or treating a full-blown anxiety disorder.

THE BULKHEAD OF ANXIETY

Dr. Myers pointed out that anxiety left unchecked could become a cumbersome condition that can harm our lives. And for many who trade for a living, anxiety is very dangerous threat. In Dr. Myers's example of the woman who develops anxiety about the bridge that she must cross on the way to work collapsing, we see some similarities to trading. Left unchecked, constant feelings of worry that our financial portfolios will fall through the floor will become an extreme hindrance when we need to make good trading decisions. As Dr. Myers pointed out, some anxiety is good, as it raises our level of alertness, which can help us make the right trading decision at times. However, when our anxiety begins to impede our decisions and lives, it's time to get help. Anxiety is serious business and is something that we must look at on a very serious level when trading for a living; after all, with every decision to buy or sell, loss can be just around the corner.

SUMMARY

In this chapter we've learned about anxiety as a potentially crippling issue that left unchecked can cause serious health and mental problems in our lives.

Combining what we've learned from Dr. Myers and Morita therapy (which was actually created specifically to combat anxiety), we must accept our feelings and not try to control them. When we accept the anxiety that we are feeling, we are able to also recognize, during or after the fact, that it was anxiety that we were indeed feeling. And, as Dr. Morita professed, when we accept the things that we cannot control, we have a great chance of bringing ourselves back into the moment and letting go of our anxiety. For the trader who has trouble overcoming anxiety through the principles of Morita therapy, professional help is needed.

* * *

When battling both fear and anxiety, we must also look at the larger part of the equation, especially in the world of trading. And sometimes many of our problems may come from the way we are approaching the markets and problems at hand. At times, when we try to reason through everything, we can become so overly logical that we may actually be drawing the wrong conclusions all together, thus creating anxiety for ourselves. And it is in this area that we begin to look at cause and effect as an essential part of our psyche.

In Chapter 8, you're going to read about cause and effect from a trading standpoint while also hearing from the famous Joe Ritchie, founder of Chicago Research and Trading, which in its heyday of the late 1980s and early 1990s traded more option volume than any other firm in the world. Ritchie sold CRT in 1993 for $225 million, a mind-boggling amount of money for any trader. With Ritchie's superstar success, his thoughts are an excellent contribution to our discussion of cause and effect.

CHAPTER 8

Cause and Effect

A ll facets of our lives (including our finances) are affected by our emotions and how we understand ourselves. Understanding this fact, we can begin to look into the principles of cause and effect to gain additional insight into our psychological approach to the market. Throughout this chapter you will read about cause and effect and how we can sometimes unknowingly create false logical thinking by not having an in-depth understanding of the true cause variables of every situation. In addition, you will read an interview with supertrader Joe Ritchie, who sold the options trading powerhouse, Chicago Research and Trading (CRT) for over $200 million in the late 1990s. You should walk away from this chapter with an understanding of how cause and effect creates experience, which is one of the most important building blocks of intuition, and something we desperately need in life and in trading.

Cause and effect is a relationship that touches all of our lives, yet many of us hardly ever stop to really take a look at what's going on. Almost everything that happens in our trading and personal lives can be traced back to a certain starting point, where we made a decision that specifically created or contributed to an outcome. Sometimes, when the outcome is negative, one of the toughest things for us to do is actually face that we've erred. It's human nature to avoid pain, but if we walk through life trying to protect ourselves from the truth of ourselves, we stand the chance of never truly gaining ground. With this in mind, when we have a great understanding of cause and effect and we work hard to comprehend the relationship, we can effect great changes in our trading and in our lives.

THE FOUNDATION OF CAUSE AND EFFECT

The first step in dissecting cause and effect is to understand that there is a fallacy in the typical perception of the relationship between the cause (variable A) and the effect (variable B.) The Nizkor Project gives a great explanation of this mode of thought.[1] Usually we assume that A always causes B, especially if the two have a direct relationship that's easy to see and understand. However, to be successful in the markets, we need to understand a new paradigm of thought where A is not the pure cause of B, even if the two are related.

Here's why: In the technocentric 21st century, we are constantly inundated from all directions with information that can change the outcome of almost any situation. And for many, the constant influx of information can create a state where even when we think we are reading things clearly, we are not. For example, a trader might say, "My trading has been very poor [the effect] lately because the market always changes direction right after I get in." However, the real problem isn't the issue of the "market always changing," the real problem may be that he or she simply isn't sticking to their stops. Here's where it gets interesting though. It's true that A (not sticking to the stop) creates B (losing money); however, the actual cause of B was not completely A. Rather, B is not B at all, but is X in a larger equation. Thus, the "market always changing" and the stop-loss problem are multiple-cause variables creating loss. We then arrive at the conclusion that there are multiple variables of A instead of an A by itself.

In coming to this conclusion, we give rise to a new paradigm of cause and effect, with multiple variables that make up the equation. The new equation would be more like $X = A, B, C$, etc.[2] This thinking asserts that to have a true understanding of X, we must investigate all of the underlying cause principles or variables that make up A, B, C, etc., thus creating a sum of the whole.

If we adhere to the logic that $A = B$, then we run into a "false dilemma."[3] With this concept we can assume that:

1. Either $1 + 1 = 4$ or $1 + 1 = 12$.
2. It is not the case that $1 + 1 = 4$.
3. Therefore $1 + 1 = 12$.

Instinctively, you know that assumption 3 is not true, but if we follow a model of pure logic we may not see that 3 is flawed, even if somewhere deep in our perceptions we know it is. I often see such flawed thinking in the markets, as traders struggle to figure out why the floor is caving in. We have to be careful not to overanalyze our trades by using too much logic that eventually leads us to seeing things in false logic. When we add too much logic to the equation, we can end up at the wrong conclusion. Hard logic without common sense prevents us from noticing what's real and keeps us from seeing the situation clearly.

What we have to understand, then, is that following simple cause and effect logic with only two variables can result in a breakdown in our logic if (1) we fail to recognize that there is more than one cause variable in every situation and (2) we overanalyze the situation with a static cause and effect formula without using common sense.

It's simple to say, but I see it day in and day out, especially with new traders who are trying to figure out a system to beat the market. What's more, it's common knowledge that the people who are most usually wrong about market direction are economists. And while I'm not trying to lash out at economists themselves, my point is that because they are almost overeducated, their attempt to reason out every aspect of the market eventually keeps them from seeing the reality of the situation around them. Fact is, the market moves on emotions, something that can't simply be summed up by applying a formula. Things change, and we must know that emotions are an inherent part of the cause variables that create effect in the market.

CAUSE AND EFFECT IN TRADING DECISIONS

Markets move up and down because of the emotions of the people who are trading. But the emotions of traders are also fueled by their own personal baggage, the day's news, individual financial well-being, and various other components that change the way the individuals feel at any one moment during the day. And when we are trying to understand the day's trading action, we certainly can't ask each market participant what he or she is feeling. Thus, on some level we must look at macrocause variables to create an intuitive understanding that the microcause variables drive trading action. The bottom line is that market direction is derived from the emotions of each individual within the market.

Markets move up and down because of the decisions traders make to buy or sell, but the application of this understanding in regard to each of our individual accounts is a completely separate thing. Imagine the following:

One day you hang the stock page of a newspaper on the wall. Then you take a small, sharp dart and throw it at that stock page. When that dart pins down one particular stock, 20 traders immediately decide to buy it. The entry point for each person is the same, so each trader's

profitability will solely depend on his or her individual perception
of when to exit. Most likely, the investor with the greatest aptitude
for risk management will show the healthiest profit and loss from the
position.

In other words, any dingbat can buy a stock, but it takes someone with
trading talent to know when to sell it. And selling a stock has much to do
with keeping our emotions in check and understanding all of the variables
(including ourselves) that will result in the greatest outcome (X). Thus, in
our trading decisions we must add ourselves into the cause variables as
something pertinent to consider in the emotion of the market. After all, we
are part of the market, and as much as we strive to remove our emotions, it's
probably almost impossible for us to completely do so. At some level, trust
becomes a cause variable for our own trading success, because we have
to believe in our capacity to make incredible decisions. Call it the "cause
variable of self-efficacy," if you will.

If we expect to be good traders, we have to trust ourselves to know
when to sell more so than knowing when to buy. More important, we have
to understand all of the variables of cause that create the final outcome,
including what prompts us to sell when we do. Exiting a trade is as much of
a cause variable to the total gain, or loss, of a position, as buying the stock in
the first place. Our decision to sell a position and our emotions contributing
to that decision are all cause variables to the equation.

As traders, information and actions are the causes, all of which make
up the effect. Again, markets only move up or down because investors and
traders feel emotionally compelled to buy or sell stocks. It's simple to say,
but only great traders can actually feel the true emotion of the market before
something happens.

Sometimes, we can blame the elusive "them" as one of the cause variables for our losing position. When we speak about the market in terms of
"they took the stock down" or "they moved it up," we simply have yet to
open our own minds to our own personal abilities and realize the multiple
variables influencing our decisions. What we have to consider is that "they,"
or outside influences, never push the buy or sell button for our individual
account. We are the sole directors of our financial portfolios, and without
having a solid sense of emotional balance within, we can become blamers or
become hypnotized by a host of influences that leave us unclear, unsure, or
ambivalent about our options. In essence, our lack of understanding of the
true variables that create the structure of our trading know-how can defeat
our ability to trade with instinct and intuition based on the knowledge we
have worked so hard to learn.

For example, when the market is declining, if we are short-term traders,
our centered self will recognize that it's time to sell our longs and open short

positions. We recognize that not only were our positions losing money, but that a greater macroreversal occurred, and it is time to change our mind-set. This recognition is the key. By being able to change our overall mind-set, we have altered one more variable in the equation of outcome. But in doing so, we have created a variable within itself. We then see that a revision of the previous cause and effect formula of $X = A, B, C$, etc. would now look like $X = A(a, b, c), B(a, b, c), C(a, b, c)$.

ALTERING THE CAUSE VARIABLES

Changing our cause variable mind-set may seem easy, but it can prove challenging for all traders. I think when we hear that a trader has "turned the corner," what we are really hearing is that he has finally achieved the ability to intuitively infer all of the cause variables to make winning trades. And more than likely, he has probably finally come to grips with the reality that he is solely responsible for the outcome of his trades. Somewhere inside, when a trader begins to really understand the market, he or she has really finally gained the ability to see multiple layers of cause variables, while also understanding that cause variables are also constantly moving and shifting with the market. Such traders do not buckle when market conditions get tough. If they did, it would be a sign that they weren't honestly looking at all of the cause variables of the present situation. For example, if the market is going against us and we look the other way, the effect is a losing trade, but the cause is our own bad decision, which, in essence, was really derived from a lack of understanding of the situation. The initial decision that got us into the trade was sparked by our translation of the information at hand, but looking the other way when the trade moved against us was the result of not having the proper tools to change the outcome or seeing that the cause variables had changed.

In the book *The End of Karma*, Dharma Singh Khalsa, MD, asserts that everything in this entire universe is bound to the principle of cause and effect.[4] And he's right; we reap the seeds that we sow. It's not enough for me to say that the stock I owned went down "unexpectedly" because of a negative earnings report, and that's why I lost money. I might be able to say the *effect* was that I lost money, but the *cause* was *not* the negative earnings report; it was only *one* of the variables of the true cause. And in this case, the misunderstood variable was that my money had exposure to a potentially negative earnings report ... due to the decision *I* made to buy the stock (or at least hold it) prior to earnings. In this case the real responsibility may have been with my own lack of diligent research or understanding of the company's potential earnings outcome prior to the announcement. In life, and investing, we do get lucky from time to time, but more often than not we get exactly what we deserve. Thus, we have to understand all of the emotional causes of "why" we make our decisions *before* we make our decisions if we ever hope to prosper in the market.

To explain a little further, I ask you to consider about what your money management plan is in 60 seconds or less and write down that answer here:

* * *

* * *

If you had to think about your plan for more than 60 seconds, it might mean that you don't have a core money management plan in place. It's hard to understand the effect when we haven't taken the time to understand the causes. If we haven't given enough consideration to the variables contributing to the outcome, we are standing on dangerous ground, especially when our money is on the line. And this is how so many of us live our lives . . . on dangerous ground.

I challenge you—for one single day—to visualize the exact outcome of every situation you encounter, as soon as you encounter it. Every time you speak to someone, imagine how the conversation will end. Every time you make a trade, know exactly how much money you will make or how much you are willing to lose. Imagine exactly how you will park your car before you even get in to drive away. At every turn, just for one day, imagine the outcome—the effect—of everything you do, before you do it. In doing so, you will begin to see how important it is to consider the causes that play a part in the outcome. I think what you will notice is that none of us can predict the outcome of every situation, but if we try to consider all of the cause variables that could possibly contribute, we have a much better chance of perceiving the effect correctly. Thus, we also have to understand that perceiving the effect, or outcome, also has to shift from a simple two-part equation to a new paradigm with many variables, including our intuitive and perceptive ability to change our thinking on the fly.

One example of a cause variable that has significant impact on the effect, would be our money management plan. But, even with covering our cause variables with things like a foolproof money management plan, not everything will always work out as we initially hoped. Things change continually in the market, and these constantly shifting waves of instability demand that we move with the market, like water in a river basin. We must flow with the current, moving over and around all obstacles in our way. Bottom line, to be the best traders we can be, we must take a look at the cause variables that shape the outcomes of our decisions. And to constantly create our desired effect, we must be in harmony with change, which leads us to our interview with Joe Ritchie. Over the year, I've been able to get to know Joe's story a bit, by not only interviewing him for this book, but also for one of my columns in *TraderMonthly* magazine. At first I was very intimidated to talk with Joe, because he is truly one of the most successful traders in the history of the world. But what I found is that he's one heck of a nice guy, and everything I'd heard about his market genius is true. What I noticed is that Joe seems to have an incredible ability to see the outcome, or the big picture, while also still examining all the cause variables, without overanalyzing them at the same time. Maintaining such balance is very hard to do, and over the next few pages, you will gain some insights on how Joe keeps a level head in the market.

INTERVIEW WITH JOE RITCHIE

As a little background, Joe Ritchie was the founder of the infamous firm Chicago Research and Trading (CRT), which in the 1980s was the world's largest options trading operation. Joe eventually sold CRT to NationsBanc in 1993 for $225 million. In addition, you may have already read some of Joe's thoughts, as he was a contributor to the book *The New Market Wizards* by Jack Schwager.[5]

In his "next life," Joe would go on to found the JV Dialog (which spawned scores of companies in the former Soviet Union, employing over 5,000 people nationwide), assist Rwanda's President Paul Kagame in the economic redevelopment of the impoverished nation, back a plan to challenge the Taliban, serve as mission control for Steve Fossett's last two (and successful) around-the-world solo balloon attempts, and set eight verified speed records in Ritchie's own Avanti P180 turboprop plane.

Now he's back in the thick of Wall Street as the head of Fox River in Chicago, an equity trading firm specializing in automated execution. Though Fox River has only been around for six years, the firm is already becoming a major player in New York and Chicago. Given all of Joe's success, he's the type of trader that we definitely want to listen to.

* * *

MW: Joe, thanks for taking time out of your busy schedule to give us some of your thoughts. In Jack Schwager's book, *The New Market Wizards*, you said that instinctive traders tend to succeed more than analytical traders. Have you changed that opinion whatsoever?

JR: Instinct is high trump. The word "instinctive" is important, but the word "balance" could be used in the same sense as well. G. K. Chesterton wrote a famous chapter [in his book, *Orthodoxy*[6] (Ignatius Press, 1995)] called "The Maniac." The Maniac is a man not bereft of his wits, but bereft of everything except his wits. The Maniac thinks that everyone is out to get him . . . and if you point out that no one cares, he would say that's exactly what they want you to think. If you use pure logical reasoning, your decisions are insane. There's a reason why some of the most unsuccessful people in our business are PhDs—because they would like to squeeze the world into a certain mold, and when it doesn't work, and they try to force it, they get killed.

Instinct captures it all. It's a fact that the people who are the most hopeless—in the trading world—are the ones who are extremely highly educated in economics. It's an attempt to reason out everything. There's nothing wrong with a lot of facts, but you need to put them under your belt and forget about them. When you aren't thinking about the things you've learned, the things you've learned are still in there! Simply put, if Michael Jordan tries to reason his way through a drive to the basket, it just isn't going to work!

MW: What advice would you give an investor or trader who has taken some hard licks in the market and is trying to regain his or her footing?

JR: First, Stop. Clear your head. Second, size down your trading units until you regain your rhythm. Third, resolve to wait for the right trade rather than force it.

MW: What advice would you give the investor or trader who is doing very well? What I'm trying to ask is what would you tell a trader who has turned the corner and is beginning to see an ego consummate with his or her bottom line.

JR: *Gradually* size up.

And don't get cocky. If you're starting to think you're hot stuff just because you're making a lot of dough, then you'd better hope you lose it all and get your soul back in the bargain.

MW: When difficult and stressful moments arise, what would you recommend that an investor do to calm him- or herself, to see the situation clearly?

JR: Cut your position by half. It's amazing how that clears the mind.

MW: When you first began, did you have your entire career planned out, or did things just fall into place?

JR: I had nothing planned out. Some things fell into place, some didn't. All were healthy, especially the latter.

MW: Looking back over what you have learned, if you were a beginning trader/investor today, what would you focus on?

JR: Finding the "gaps," that is, the places where something is getting overlooked. In pit trading, there's a saying that "the glory's in the front month, the money's in the back months." Find niches that aren't overtraded.

MW: Can you please give some words of wisdom for traders just entering the business and for those who have been around for a while?

JR: Newcomers: Well, nah, don't get me started. But good luck.

Old-timers: I hope you're grateful. In most times and places we'd be the village bums.

MW: Thanks, Joe, your insights are very much appreciated!

ADDING ON TO JOE'S WORDS

Taking another look at understanding the effect of making money in the markets, instinct captures many of the variables of cause. I'm going to add my opinion to Joe's words here, but if Michael Jordan were to take time to break down each situation as an $A = B$ relationship, many of his drives would be thwarted by the movement on the court. What we see is that at some level, we must know our cause variables, but the logic becomes instinct, not a hard-and-fast plan. Instead, when Michael Jordon drives, he already has his cause-related variables toolbox in place, so he's instinctively able to work out the equation while he's in motion.

Obviously, trading is a little different than playing basketball. When you are in the middle of a trade and an economic report or earnings numbers surface that affects your position, you may have to stop and do some actual fundamental valuation-related math—but the principle is the same. The trader's tools are the financial and personal items he or she has worked hard to understand prior to the game. And in understanding these multiple cause variables of trading and self, he or she has a greater chance of making the desired outcome become a reality by acting quickly and calmly when the heat is on.

With this in mind, solidifying the cause variables of intuition means having a personal understanding of:

- The larger picture of trading, finances, and market emotions
- Economics and the application of economic numbers
- The trading platform you are using
- Fundamental analysis
- Technical analysis
- Your personal money management plan, including your stop-loss strategy and your desired profit points
- Your trading style and plan
- Your risk plan
- Your psychological profile and how you perceive the market

By understanding these factors, we can then begin to put together a loose cause and effect formula, with multiple cause variables in every trading situation... that will help us persevere when times get tough. If you remember back to Chapter 1, we discussed taking an inventory of what we know by writing down all of the things we know in the market. And in doing so, you will certainly want to cover all of the items we just listed. We are taking a look at the cause variables that make up our trading knowledge, which is exactly where we may find that we are missing some important knowledge that is holding us back from trading at our highest level. What we cannot do, though, is simply write down what we know and assume that we have all the tools we need (known as cause variables) to trade profitably in every situation. We have to understand that the effect (in terms of the market, and perhaps life) is a moving target, and our intuitive ability to make changes (based on previously considered variables) is what will help us to be the best we can be. To be the best we can be, and to trade with passion and purpose, a deep understanding and feeling of the cause variables that we hold as our fundamental market knowledge will make us sharper traders at every level.

With this in mind, and once again touching on Joe's words of wisdom, one of the most important variables of trading success is good instincts. Balanced traders are instinctual traders. Their ultimate view of reality is formed by the unconscious reasoning where logic actually gives way to intuition. Sometimes even when it doesn't look right on paper, you can intuitively feel the correct outcome. Remember in the beginning of this chapter where we demonstrated that simple $A = B$ logic can create a false dilemma? This is certainly the case in trading. At times, when we apply simple (or too much) logic to the market, our conclusions are wrong because we are not letting all of the cause variables filter through the most important facet of profitable decision making: us. It is this instinct and intuition that ultimately perceives the larger reality... or trade.

Again, this is why we need to take inventory and write out the variables that make up what we know as self. Preparing this list (or *personal balance sheet*, for lack of a better term) is something that requires intense honesty, which is probably why not many people do it. What's more, after you've done this, you will intuitively know when to back away from a situation that you do not have the right tools for. And knowing when not to trade is just as important as knowing when to trade. As the old adage goes, "An ounce of prevention is worth a pound of cure." And when we know our cause variable weaknesses just as well as we know our strengths, we find ourselves suddenly empowered by knowing when to step away from the plate, if need be.

With all of this in mind, perhaps one equation we can then use to determine effect is:

Intuition + Plan + Knowledge + Experience + Knowing our limits = Winning trades

This equation leads us into the next section where we will examine one of the most valuable commodities of all: experience. I don't care how smart you are, what college you went to, what Nobel Prize you won—the markets have a funny way of handing derrieres to people who have not been around for a while. It's experience that seasons traders for the long haul and fills their bank accounts with oodles of money.

EXPERIENCE AS THE MOST IMPORTANT CAUSE VARIABLE

Often overlooked, experience is one of the most important cause variables of profitable trading. No one in this world can instantly create the effect they desire in the trading world without experience. In fact, it may just be *the* most important variable in the cause and effect equation of success. With this in mind, don't ever get frustrated if you've just walked away from a horrible day and are trying to figure out what went wrong. Using the "winning trades" equation, you may have thought everything was worked out prior to the trading day when things went wrong. But the one variable that isn't included in that equation is having seen the situation that you just did. It's important to remember that this one variable (which can eventually consume all variables) is the greatest equalizer of them all. If you've been there once, chances are when you get there again, you will know exactly what to do, and you might just be able to do it intuitively. Thus, when we add experience to the cause variable equation, we know that we have strengthened our instinctual and intuitive abilities to handle "the next time" slightly better.

SUMMARY

In conclusion, we have to challenge the conventional cause and effect relationships as we know them and understand that the markets never present a simple $A = B$ formula. Let me rephrase that. You may see an $A = B$ formula once or twice, but eventually, as the markets and the emotional buying and selling of traders shifts, the equation will too. And if we haven't taken inventory of our market knowledge (the cause variables), we stand a chance of not being able to intuitively change when the market does.

Finally, when our trading fails, it is because we (unfortunately) were not able to see that the equation of the market (or stock) had altered. However, even the rough days are actually a gift, as they add one more cause variable (experience) to the equation of profitability. And with each day that passes, the experience variable becomes even more of an intrinsic asset that will only help in the future. As the old saying goes, "Never forget where you came from," but I would like to add, "and never forget where you are now." You know what you know, and unless you take inventory to figure out what it is that you may still need to learn, there will be many rough days in the market ahead.

What we have just covered in this chapter leads into the discussion of emotional intelligence, or, as I like to think of it, trading maturity, in Chapter 9.

CHAPTER 9

Emotional Intelligence: The Intuition Wild Card

I n the world of trading, a quarter and all the smarts in the world won't get you on the bus. Trading successfully requires more than just book smarts, it requires *emotional intelligence*, which "describes an ability, capacity, or skill to perceive, assess, and manage the emotions of one's self, of others, and of groups."[1]

In that definition we see why emotional intelligence is so important to the trader. If we do not have the "ability, capacity, or skill to perceive, assess, and manage the emotions of one's self, of others, and of groups," we will never make it in the fiancial markets. In fact, I think this definition of emotional intelligence just about sums up most of the best qualities in successful traders I've met over the years. The guys who make it know how to read themselves and those around them.

Perhaps you know the game Liar's Poker? In this game, the participants all use the serial numbers on each others dollars (not showing one another, of course), in an effort to end up with the largest sum of similar numbers. If there were two people playing, you and another, the guy next to you might say "one two," and then even though you don't have any twos on your dollars, you could say something like "three twos," upping the bet that there are three twos between the serial numbers of both dollars. Obviously in this case, you are betting that all three twos are on his dollar. In essence, you are bluffing in an attempt to get him to raise the bet. However, he can call "bull" when it's his turn, and if there aren't three twos between the dollars, you would lose, because you bluffed. In this game, those who always win are the people who can read whether their opponent is bluffing or are just really good at bluffing themselves. It is the ultimate test of emotional intelligence.

To win you have to have the "ability, capacity, or skill to perceive, assess, and manage the emotions of one's self, of others, and of groups." Trading is exactly the same. It's a constant game of bluffing and emotions. Those who make it are just exceptionally good at reading the emotions of the collective whole.

As individual traders, we are putting our money on the line every day, and our livelihood is driven primarily from our ability to do so profitably. Unlike someone who gets a regular 40-hour workweek paycheck, our emotions, otherwise known as "fear, pain, and desire," are what primarily determine whether we eat or go hungry. We must have a great understanding of our ability to interact with the greater whole that's happening around us. This is known as our "Emotional Intelligence Quotient or EQ."[2] Without EQ, as traders we potentially risk not being able to dynamically read the emotions that surround us at every moment during the trading day.

With this awareness in mind, we will dive into the concept of emotional intelligence in an effort to determine how we can more adequately understand the markets we are trading in and ourselves as well. In this chapter, we will go over the roots of emotional intelligence, with an admonition about making sure to "keep it real." We will progress to applying emotional intelligence in day-to-day life and in trading, in an effort to really dig into how we may better understand the greater moves of the market on an emotional level. Finally, we will wrap up the chapter with a brief discussion of the connection between emotional intelligence and intuition.

THE ROOTS

Emotional intelligence studies date back to the 1920s, when E. L Thorndike first began using the term "social intelligence" in regard to our ability to interact with others.[3] However, it wasn't until much later in the century when the term was primarily coined by Wayne Leon Payne in 1985 in his dissertation, "A Study of Emotion, Developing Emotional Intelligence." In the abstract of the paper, Payne states, "Since emotional intelligence involves relating creatively to fear, pain and desire, these states are explored in detail and guidance is offered on how to relate to them in emotionally intelligent ways."[4]

It's also important to note that the term "social intelligence" was further used by David Wechsler in 1943, though the evolution of the term did not take further form until Howard Gardner began to write about "multiple intelligence" in 1975, in the book *The Shattered Mind*.[5] When Payne put the term "emotional intelligence" in the title of his dissertation in 1985, the term was solidified as an important area of study. Later, the term emotional intelligence was popularized by Daniel Goldman, the author of *Emotional Intelligence*, but was also brought to the public in 1990 by John D. Mayer and Peter Salovey.[6] The latter two figures put together several papers on the subject, taking the concept one step further.[7] Their efforts created a multi-million-dollar industry aimed at training those in business to better understand their emotions. Many corporations and major universities are now using emotional intelligence as a way to help executives and employees move beyond their emotions . . . to manage employees effectively, while making efficient business decisions. Really, what has happened over the past three decades has been an expedited curve in the evolution of emotional intelligence thought. This is good news for those in the financial markets, as the subject is certainly pertinent to each of our lives.

The meaning of the term *emotional intelligence* is still in flux, and our understanding of the emotions behind the decisions we make is evolving with the times and technology. Computers make decisions without emotion, and, sadly, in many cases it appears a lack of emotion is the goal for many business leaders. Nevertheless, we can learn many things from this area of thought and apply the good to our trading lives while hopefully retaining our appreciation for the aspects of self that make us incredible individual people.

If life and business are emotional, from the perspective of this book, trading is even more so. If you've ever traded on a floor, you know what I'm talking about. Trading at our highest level requires a substantial amount of emotional intelligence to understand and see all situations clearly. The issue that I'm getting at is that when we trade purely from our own stance of egocentricity, we fail to see the things happening around us. What is egocentricity? From the perspective of a psychiatrist (to lead to a very important point that has much to do with trading), "Egocentric thinking means that a child will take everything personally. . . . The impact of not having one's parents' time creates the feeling of being worthless. The child is worth less than his parents' time, attention or direction. The young child's egocentricity always interprets events egotistically. 'If Mom and Dad are not present, it's because of me. There must be something wrong with me or they would want to be with me.'"[8]

Here's the deal: Children don't have much emotional intelligence—everything revolves around them. It's not a bad thing; it's just the way we're wired. But as adults we can have some of those childish behaviors, because somewhere in our mid-teens, we seemed to falter slightly in our emotional development. What I'm getting at is that there has probably been a time when you said to yourself, "If I buy the stock, it will go down." And I'll admit right here, I've been guilty of this in the past. What I had to recognize was that I was thinking from a sense of childishness, because the market has absolutely nothing to do with whether I'm buying or selling a few thousand shares. And, to be perfectly honest, I've heard the old, "If I buy it, the stock won't go up" routine from almost every trader I've ever met. Facts are facts. When we're trading for money, our emotions are on the line. And when we get punched in the nose by a bad trade, it's hard not to regress a little. But the problem is that if we do, we are falling way off the mark to operate as highly evolved emotionally intelligent people. What's more, we are only cutting ourselves off from our own ability to think with knowledge, logic, experience, and intuition. And when the world is revolving around our portfolio, chances are our overall emotional intelligence will have regressed to a point that we sure as heck won't have a chance at recognizing the emotions of the market, outside of ourselves.

Thus, recognizing when moments of egocentricity surface, we stop ourselves from sulking in the dreadful feelings that the market is a bully. Of course, there are many similarities to life here, as when we make all of our life decisions based on "me," life usually becomes somewhat of a soap opera. Thus, in trading and in life, we must find a happy median between feeling emotion and making sure to stop ourselves when we are thinking in an egocentric fashion. We don't want to become emotionless trading robots, but if we catch ourselves thinking that the markets revolve around us, we're more than likely regressing to some sort of a childish behavior.

Again, it's crucial to note that there's a fine line between letting ourselves feel emotions and regressing. We must recognize that to be emotionally intelligent people, feelings of worry, doubt, or anger about a certain market environment are absolutely going to surface. But when they do, we need to realize that these emotions are just part of trading, because of the stakes at risk. At this point we must be very honest with ourselves (when we are feeling a little blue), in order to stop ourselves from slipping further into childish behaviors. The point here is that we want to recognize that there will be negative emotions created by our trading decisions that are valid, but we must make sure we handle them as adults. And trust me, if you hang around trading floors long enough, I can assure you that this theme will come up again and again.

EMOTIONAL INTELLIGENCE WITH EMOTIONAL IDENTIFICATION AND ACCEPTANCE

As a society, we often think that an individual's intelligence quotient (IQ) is one of the main determining factors of success. However, study after study has proven that IQ without the ability to relate to others, and life on the whole, can often impair our ability to make progress. Of course, there is always the one in a million success story of someone with no social capacity who changes the world ... but for most of us, dealing with others is a very important part of life. Take the Somerville study, a 40-year study following the lives of 450 boys from Somerville, Massachusetts, for example.[9] Without going into too much detail, the study concluded that actual IQ had almost nothing to do with success. The most successful of the group were those who, as children, were able to control their emotions (like anger and frustration) and at the same time, get along well with those around them. What we are beginning to see is that the adult careers of those who did not have the ability (as children) to cope with the social aspects of life were hindered from the start.[10]

At some level though, as soon as we become aware of the aforementioned ideas behind emotional intelligence, it doesn't matter where we've been, the road to change is just around the corner. And I would like to assert that even if you have no emotional intelligence issues, if you trade for a living, you should read about these concepts.

One of the most vital points in understanding emotional intelligence is to have a solid sense of emotional identification. In trading, even if you're a well-balanced guy or gal in the majority of your life, when the floor starts to buckle, emotions are going to ensue. And for some, overwhelming emotions are just a normal aspect of life. If this is the case, these traders stand the chance of not being able to identify when something within them has shifted. In short, the lack of emotional awareness will hinder them from ever being able to even see that emotions are running the show, not intellect. It's as simple as this: We have to be able to recognize how we feel *when* we feel it, if we ever hope to keep our emotions from forcing us to make horrible decisions at the most stressful and critical moments during the trading day.

I firmly believe that if you deeply and honestly understand emotional awareness, you are head and shoulders ahead of the market. Why? Because if you can honestly recognize when potentially negative or overwhelmingly happy (leading to sloppy mistakes) emotions surface inside of you when you are losing, winning, or simply about to even pull the trigger on a trade, you have already beat half of the market. By knowing what you are feeling, you will have a better understanding of why you are doing what you are.

But here's the really important part: If you have a solid sense of emotional awareness, you will have the ability to stay clear of emotional infection. Here's what it means: "Emotional infection, in which B's experience of the signs of an emotion or mood in A cause B to 'catch' that emotion or mood, but without knowing, in the case of an emotion, what it is directed to. In a herd of animals, one animal is alarmed at something. The others, seeing, hearing or perhaps smelling the signs of its alarm, themselves become alarmed. In the same way panic or hysteria sweeps through a crowd. People go to parties in order to become infected by the jovial atmosphere."[11,12,13]

Sound familiar in the market? If you've ever watched Jim Cramer's *Mad Money*, you know it's hard not to follow his calls ... the guy's full of emotion.

But for the serious trader, we have to make our own decisions based on our own emotions. Thus, emotional awareness is not only important to recognize what we are feeling within our own trades, but even more so to make sure that we don't follow the herd off a cliff.

Here's an example: John has a tough day, and he's feeling very frustrated with something one of his co-workers said earlier that morning. When he was at the water cooler, he was talking to Jack about some reports that are due, when Jack said, "Yea, we can get the reports done on time, but that's assuming you don't goof up the numbers again." John, who doesn't handle conflict well, laughed a little and replied, "Don't worry," partly because he didn't know what else to say and partly because he was caught off guard by the comment. Later that day, he finds himself grinding his teeth, and he's really pretty upset about the comment from Jack, who messes things up quite often too. He broods, and broods, and broods. He finishes the numbers, sends them to Jack, and then goes home. Later, when his wife asks him why he didn't put the trash out yet, he comes completely unglued, replying with, "Because, I'm tired of doing every damn thing around here." And they launch into a horrendous fight, where they both end up feeling bad.

The next day, John is still feeling frustrated and upset, and is still mulling over the comment by Jack. In his first interaction with Jack, who has the report in his hand, Jack says, "You did great, *this time.*" John whips back with, "Yea, glad you didn't screw it up either." The two begin a hushed argument about who messes up more, and in the end, both end up exhausted. The one change in John though, is that though he is frustrated, he is no longer angry, because he finally told Jack that he screws up too.

The point here is that when John finally confronted Jack, he was released from his anger because he was able to acknowledge it. True, he might still be a little frustrated with John, but at least he's not angry about the comment at the water cooler the day before. And he'll probably realize that he owes his wife an apology.

Instead of having gone through all of the brooding and frustration that John did and then having some sort of blowup, if he had just admitted to himself that he was angry about the comment in the first place and accepted that it was okay to be angry, he would have probably let it go, or walked right into Jack's office and calmly talked about the subject. But because John did not know how to let himself acknowledge the emotion (i.e., had no concept of emotional awareness) and allowed himself to fall victim to emotional infection, he was forced to brood about it until the festering discomfort bubbled into his evening with his wife.

If you acknowledge and accept your emotions when they appear, in theory, you will be rewarded by being able to let go of the emotion. So often we never admit to ourselves that it is okay to feel what we are feeling. If you are as mad as heck, just admit to yourself that you're really angry. It's hard to stay mad when we tell ourselves, "I'm mad, and it's okay to be mad." When we acknowledge our uncomfortable emotions, that's usually when they start to dissipate. Some think it's too touchy-feely to acknowledge and accept our emotions, but, really, it's just good business.

APPLICATION TO TRADING

We often think of trading as a world of its own, but really it's not. In every decision you make to buy or sell, there's some sort of interaction with others and the information of the world, if even only on a subconscious level. While we like to think that much of our decisions are based on the facts received, we are actually reacting to our emotions based on the information at hand. We are trading based on our belief that a certain outcome will occur. But, in doing so, we can often find ourselves wrong or, in the case of something that is working for us, right but at a loss for what to do next.

I've seen many traders let winning positions turn into devastating losers simply because they don't know what to do when a position moves in their favor. Book the profits or keep the position open? Fear or greed? Even more intriguing, I've seen traders hang onto positions that go against them, only to close them when the position gets back to breakeven . . . and then gripe when they realize that they could have not only "flatted" the position, but also actually closed the trade significantly positive if they had hung on. No matter what *could* have happened, the basic fact is that we made a trading decision based on the emotion that we were overcome with at the moment we effected a trade. Shoulda, woulda, coulda . . . the real question is why did or didn't ya?

To have a solid understanding of the decisions we make in trading, it never hurts to give ourselves some training time to identify what's happening within us when it's happening. With this in mind, one of the best ways to accomplish this is to keep an "emotional trading journal."

To help with trade analysis, I've seen traders record every buy and sell they make, with a brief comment detailing what was happening in the market when they made the trade. I would like to take this technique one step further. For one week, keep a journal of your entry and exit points with an explanation of what was happening in the market when you stepped in or out. Then add another entry noting what you were feeling when you made the trade. Were you emotionally aware, or were you emotionally infected? What's more, clearly label the moments when you felt egocentric. For example, two entries in the journal might be:

Trading Journal

10:41 AM—Bought Immersion (Nasdaq: IMMR) at $6.73.

Reasoning: Nasdaq and Technology Index are showing some signs of possible strength. The stock pulled back within 10% of the volume weighted average price (VWAP) in a strong uptrend.

Emotional Awareness: I felt optimistic about the trade because it seemed the market would rally all day. I felt calm when I entered the position, as I let the stock pull back, before just "jumping in." I feel that I can make at least 25 cents on the trade before considering taking profits. My stop is 5 cents under the VWAP, or with a significant downturn in Nasdaq futures.

Emotional Infection: No. The market was trending laterally, and there was buzz circling that the major indexes were going to sell off. I was not taking on the attitude of the herd.

Emotional Trigger: Optimism, aka greed.

Egocentricity: No. I recognized what I was doing and stepped back to look at the greater market.

11:17 AM—Sold Immersion at $6.60.

Reasoning: The market doesn't seem to begin going anywhere, and there have been almost no prints on the ask (buys on the tape). The stock isn't dropping a ton, but I'm negative, and I don't want a big loss.

Emotional Awareness: I'm afraid the market is going to turn over, and momentum will bring the stock way below my stop before I can trade out. I'm worried that the bids will fall apart and I will have to trade under the bid to ensure I get filled. I am worried and fearful of taking a hit.

Emotional Trigger: Fear.

Egocentricity: Yes. I'm tired of the feeling that everything I touch goes to pot.

If we read closely here, we see that many of the old market ideas hold true, namely, that of fear and greed. We generally buy because we think we're going to make money and sell because we're afraid of losing it. But many of us believe we're emotionally beyond this type of thinking, and we feel we make rational decisions all the time. Looking closely at the preceding entries, though, we can see that in this hypothetical situation, it would be really

hard to not look at it and say, "You know what? I've got some work to do."
I really believe that if many of us really—honestly—kept a trading journal,
quite a few of the entries would be similar to the sample entries just pro-
vided. But the question is, how honest can you really be with yourself? Don't
forget, self-honesty is one of most important aspects of being emotionally
intelligent.

EMOTION VERSUS INTUITION

At the moment we are about to buy a stock, if we take a brief second to
ask ourselves why we're doing what we're doing, on an emotional level,
we might have the chance to reroute our decision from one based on emotion to one based on intellect-based intuition. In the sample trading journal
entry, when the entry was made to buy, suppose the trader had said to
himself:

> *I accept that I am feeling optimistic, much of which is due to the
> elation of the upward momentum of the market today. In accepting
> this optimism, I am going to briefly reconsider what I am thinking,
> in an effort to not let my optimism of the moment get me in over
> my head. Am I chasing the stock, or would it be better to wait for a
> continued pullback?*

Reviewing the above comment, he would have been immediately aware of
the emotion prompting his decision. And acknowledging the emotion and
then inquiring if a non-emotional approach would be better could have most
likely saved him a ton of stress.

Here's where we can get a little muddled, though. As Joe Ritchie pointed
out, intuition is high trump. To be able to trade intuitively is one of the best
assets of successful traders. What I would like to argue, though, is that there
is a great difference between trading intuitively and trading emotionally. The
intuitive trader is one who trades based on the internal understanding that
an event has a high probability of occurring. And the intuitive trader is
one who is extremely emotionally intelligent. The emotional trader takes
action because he is so overwhelmed by the moment that he simply reacts to the situation. Intuitive traders move proactively; emotional traders
move reactively. And those with a great understanding of emotional intelligence through emotional awareness, infection, and egocentricity are more
apt to make proactive decisions based on an understanding of self and
the market.

SUMMARY

No matter how you slice it, the bottom line of emotional intelligence is to take responsibility for the emotions inside of yourself. If you do, you will be far ahead of the investing public, who often have no idea why they do the things they do. Many get a hot tip or hear a talking head on television say "the stock is going up," and they buy. But the problem here is that when the stock tanks, who do you think the first one blaming the market will be? You guessed it, the guy who was duped by his own emotions in the first place.

If you aren't aware of emotional intelligence . . . if you are constitutionally unable to be honest with yourself . . . if you cannot become aware of your emotions . . . if you allow yourself to become emotionally infected by the crowd . . . and if you operate from an egocentric stance of trading . . . there's a good chance you may suffer some huge losses.

However, those who take the time to quietly work on their EQ stand a much greater chance of evolving into boldly intuitive traders, adeptly prepared to handle the roughest market circumstances.

* * *

So far in the book we've covered a ton of ground attempting to understand why we do the things we do. Some of the points included our purpose-center, Morita theory, dogma, esteem, ego, humbleness, forgiveness, fear, anxiety, cause and effect, emotional intelligence, emotional awareness, and egocentricity. We also know that intuition (see Chapter 10 for a more in-depth discussion of intuition) and gratitude (Chapter 11) are vitally important parts of trading and life.

I want to take a moment and mention that these items are the fundamental building blocks of self that are vital to layer your financial knowledge on. After all, it's so important to know why we're buying or selling when we are, beyond just seeing an attractive chart or fundamentals. And all that we've covered are really the greater part of a larger evolution in our plight to trade with passion and purpose each and every day.

What's more, when we incorporate all of these characteristics into our lives, we can achieve a well-rounded purpose-centered self that will allow us to remain calm in the fiercest life and trading storms. And even more exciting, when we are able to mindlessly put all of the concepts covered so far into play, we are well on our way to trading at a high level of intuition . . . a quality of the best on Wall Street. In Chapter 10, we will take a deep look at what intuition is and how we can further develop this valuable skill.

CHAPTER 10

Developing
Intuition

I ntuition is the most important characteristic that we can possibly develop in trading. For some, intuition comes naturally, and for others, it's
learned. And even if you feel you already have plenty of intuition, there's
always room for additional knowledge and evolution. This chapter covers
what intuition is, how it is formed, and how we can develop our intuition
as traders.

LEVELS OF INTUITION

To begin, it is important to understand that intuition is the transcendent
application of knowledge, skills, and experience by what can be called "unconscious reasoning." When we operate on a level of unconscious reasoning,
we have truly evolved to a higher state of movement within the markets,
often being able to perceive events before they occur. Before we get too far
though, it is important to recognize that on a rudimentary level, there are
different levels of primary intuition:

- *Gut-feeling intuition:* a spontaneous impulse to take an immediate,
  unplanned action, which in retrospect proves to be the most beneficial
  action to take in order to positively influence an unknown future event
  or situation.

133

- *Knowledge-based (educational) intuition:* understanding without apparent effort; quick and ready insight *seemingly* independent of previous experiences or empirical knowledge.
- *Sensing:* Although sensing is the opposite of intuition, it is noted here so we can clarify it from the start, and avoid confusing it with actual intuition along the way. Sensing is one of the four axes of the Myers-Briggs Type Indicator, and it is the way we take in some sort of information that helps form our thoughts.[1] Sensing can help form intuitive thoughts, but is not the actual intuitive process itself.

Gut-Feeling Intuition

A gut feeling can be viewed as intuition as a type of common sense. Before we go further, let's take a moment to differentiate fear (covered in Chapter 6) from gut-feeling intuition. It's common sense that if you walk into a highway, you're going to get hit by a car. But this knowledge is different than learned fear, as even though you've been told not to walk into traffic on a highway, you probably never had to learn the lesson the hard way. We just know that being hit by a car that's traveling 55 mph will cause bodily harm. This understanding has some similar properties to fear, but, for the most part, the concept of walking onto a highway is something that we just feel is a bad idea. And the stand-alone feeling is indeed fear, driven by our physiological ability to institutively perceive danger. We are fearful of being hit by a car, and so we know instinctively not to walk on a highway.

In trading, this type of gut-level intuition can be similar to buying a stock when the market begins to drop. We know downward movement will cause a stock that we are holding to lose value, and so, intuitively, most of us know buying is a bad idea. (Of course there are exceptions to the rule, but, for the most part, buying in a rapidly declining market is a bad idea.) Our feeling that buying in a sell-off situation is based on fear. From our stomachs, we know that danger is present. At this level, we are sensing gut-level fear, which can be called the most primal level of intuition . . . as the danger is so clearly apparent that most have no trouble perceiving the outcome. For now, we will leave our discussion of gut-level intuition where it is, as it is first important to cover educational intuition. And we will also come back to our senses in relation to intuition as well. Once we cover the latter two, we will go over all three together in an attempt to gain a greater understanding of the trader's highest level of intuition: unconscious reasoning.

Knowledge-Based (Educational) Intuition

When we have knowledge-based intuition, we know and feel something because we have learned it, or can match the pattern of the situation to something else we have already experienced. In psychology, this learned intuition is known as the recognition-primed decision (RPD).[2] The RPD model was developed by Gary Klein who argued that as people, we can make quick decisions without having to compare every outcome that could happen. His study says we form a mental simulation of the event unfolding, and in doing so we are able to make a quick decision. Our intuition allows us to quickly match the situation to something we perceive as to apply best to the situation, by matching the pattern of the situation to something we know. For the rest of this chapter, we will call this *experience-based intuition*, which may more accurately describe it, as used here.

To accurately make the correct intuitive decision, the pattern must match something that will provide the best possible outcome. Thus, it's easy to see how inexperienced traders can lack experience-based intuition. However, there are some who have the ability to match other life experiences to the world of trading and, in essence, actually be very intuitive traders without much trading experience. Thus, we have two types of learned intuition traders:

1. Experience-based intuition: Achieved by years of directly correlated hard work.
2. Nonmarket intuition: Achieved through the application of other life situations to trading.

One type isn't more correct than the other; they are simply different. As an example of the first type of intuition, when a trader has seen many different examples of market action and has experienced various positions, he or she is able to match the previous experiences with the current events. And in doing so, he or she is able to make the best possible decision . . . to create the greatest outcome. However, such decision making can only be accurate if he or she has taken the time to properly examine all facets of self and past experiences to make the most of them in the future. And, it's important to note that if we've learned incorrectly from a past experience, the intuition we exercise in the future could lead to a loss.

As an example of nonmarket intuition, let me illustrate with a brief story. One day, two young professionals begin their first day of trading on the floor. With all that they've learned, both are excited to jump into the trading action. Both worked hard as clerks and believe that they've learned all that they can. The only difference between the two is their backgrounds. On the one hand, John majored in finance in college and, afterward, worked for his father's budding law practice. Jane, on the other hand, majored in statistics in college and, for a short while after college, worked at a casino calculating odds for various games. On their first day trading on the floor, both take a position in stock ABC, which quickly begins to tank. John holds on to the stock, while Jane exits. John takes a huge loss, while Jane takes a small one.

What I've just illustrated is an extremely simple example of nonmarket intuition playing a part in one's trading life. Jane, who knows probability, intuitively knew to exit when the tides turned against her. John, however, had to learn the trading lesson the hard way. Statistics and probability alone won't make us expert traders; however, being able to match other areas of our life to the markets will help us trade with intuition when we encounter a situation that we have never seen. Jane's experience calculating probability gave her a greater ability to match a life situation to the trade at hand, and she was able to take a small loss. John took a large loss, but if he goes back and reviews the situation, he will have the learned experience in the back of his mind and be able to act intuitively the next time around.

Senses and Intuition

Though we've already briefly covered sensing and intuition, it's important enough to note that our physical senses are strikingly different from intuition. Intuition is a product of senses, but senses are not a product of intuition. In short, "senses" refer to the means for receiving data via sight, smell, touch, taste, or hearing.[3] It's important to take notice of our senses if we are to have a greater understanding of our intuition. We know sensed data is something we feel, see, smell, taste, or hear. In contrast, our intuition is how we perceive the data that is coming to us, often with minimal exposure. But sometimes our intuition can get drowned out by our senses. Here's how: If you were looking at a computer screen all day, you might perceive the trading data without emotion. However, if you were in a trading pit, the smells, sounds, shoving of traders, and the sight of the emotions around could all affect your intuition. Even if you are able to properly match the situation at hand with another profitable experience, the mere fact that the guy next to you is screaming his head off to buy a stock might influence your decision to sell when you are long, even if you were just thinking about taking profits off the table a moment ago.

Here's the kicker: If you don't sell and the stock tanks, you might be mad at yourself for not using your intuition. You will feel duped by your senses, which allowed you to be influenced by the things happening outside of your body. With this in mind, the next time the guy standing at your side is screaming "buy!!!!" and you're about to sell, you might listen to your inner self . . . and actually discard the position. Your senses deceived you the first time, but your intuition will keep you in line the next. Thus, if you are a trader communicating with other people, via computer or in person, and you're about to do something that goes against your intuition, stop and ask yourself, "Am I being deceived by my senses?"

PLANNING FOR INTUITION

Intuition and planning aren't something that usually go hand-in-hand, but they can be. In the book *Divine Intuition* by Lynn A. Robinson, she asserts that sometimes when we are trying to make a decision, we never have the ability to truly—intuitively—recognize the answer to our question, simply because we don't know what the question is in the first place.[4] Let me paint a clearer picture of what I am talking about. If you are struggling with trading, and you are looking for some sort of answer on how to improve your bottom line, there are many facets of the entire trading universe (and yourself) that you probably need to look at. But when you just look at the larger, overwhelming macropicture, it's hard to see any clear answers. Thus, to help intuitively find the solution you are looking for, you must break down the question. To easily do so, write down two or three paragraphs about what the problem at hand is and what you are seeking... in as great detail as possible. Once you have written down all of this information, sum all of it up in one question. What you've done is taken the larger picture and narrowed it down to one point. You have asked one very specific question. And when you intuitively perceive an answer, you will be able to recognize it, because you will be looking for it. Simply put, your mere intention to understand how to improve your bottom line begins a process that opens up your receptivity to the answer.

Basically, we trying to ensure that when we're driving on the road of life, we know what street we need to turn on to get to where we want to go. If we don't know the name of the street we need to turn on, we'll never know where to make the correct turn, even when we're there.

Much of this planning is as simple as just writing down your life and trading goals every day or once a week. When we write down the things that we truly want, we open ourselves up to being able to see the roads we need to turn on when they appear in our lives. Without knowing what we want in the first place, how can we ever expect anything brilliant to ever happen? Moreover, how can we ever intuitively recognize when the world is handing us a true opportunity if we have no idea how to recognize the opportunity. When we intuitively know to do something, we know it from within... because at some level in our subconscious, we've already asked the question. This leads us into our discussion regarding developing intuition, where we will examine how to consciously further our abilities of perception. Simply being conscious of the things that are happening within us (including when we are feeling something intuitively) will give us that much greater of a shot at being incredible traders.

DEVELOPING INTUITION

In understanding how we develop intuition, I would like to reference an excerpt from the book, *What Is and What Will Be: Integrating Spirituality and Science,* by Paul P. Budnik Jr. In this exciting book the author is trying to merge "science with values and meaning by making the simplest possible assumption about the connection between physical structure and conscious experience."[5] In his book, Budnik hits on the concept that the implications of intuition move beyond philosophy, but instead "extend to the foundations of mathematics and physics suggesting that Einstein's intuition near the end of his life was correct."[6] (Budnik is alluding to Einstein's contributions to quantum mechanics based on "intuition.") Budnik further states, "Intuition can play with ideas at a looser level. Intuition can leave the conceptual framework of classical particles that quantum mechanics is trapped in."[7]

In another part of the book, he states,

> *How can we develop intuition, let it lead the way and yet hold it back from leaping into the abyss as Einstein did? Of course I do not think that Einstein was wrong but in his lifetime he was not able to accomplish what he intended. We can afford to support a few Einsteins without practical results, but for intuition to become more universal it must become more developed and differentiated. We must know when and how to use it and we must know with some, albeit imperfect, reliability when it leads us to far afield from what is practically possible.*[8]

What we see here is a complex statement of intuition. Additionally, I would like to assert that what we are really seeing is an elevated emotional awareness of fear that our intuition may be misleading us. As you know from earlier in the book, fear is something that is of both physical and mental nature. However, at some level, intuition attempts to transcend fear and is the amazing ability within all of us to overcome all aspects of self (or physics, in Einstein's case) to see a situation clearly. But, at some level, we all question or ignore our intuition during times of stress, and this is no more apparent than in trading. If you are standing at the helm of a losing trade, and in your deepest, quietest moment, you have an inexplicable notion that holding on to the potentially losing trade just *feels* comfortable, safe, and right (and you are sure it's not just your subconscious trying to avoid taking a loss), then it's probably a good idea to listen. As a trader at this certain crossroads, we can always effect hard rules to override our intuition, just in case we are wrong. This type of thing would be as simple as a stop-loss.

When faced with situations where our intuition is telling us one thing, and yet we still want to do another, or we are so driven by outside pressure that we can't even hear our intuition, stop! If we create a set of trading rules that keep our emotions in check, but at the same time let our intuition give guidance to the situation, we are basically creating a plan to overcome our weaknesses when things get hazy. Really, what I'm talking about is taking *all* of the things in this book and putting them into play—unconsciously. When we confidently establish a solid sense of ourselves and trust all of our knowledge, we expand our incredible sense of intuition. After all, intuition is said to be the ability to see, read, or learn something without the conscious act of reasoning. With this in mind, we are about to hear about intuition from a very successful woman who is at the helm of The Oxford Club, one of the most successful financial newsletters in the country. Over the years, she's trusted her intuition to help along the way.

INCREDIBLE INTUITION THROUGH THE EYES OF A PUBLISHER

Julia Guth is top dog at The Oxford Club in Baltimore, Maryland, a private investor network and financial publishing group with over 320,000 readers. Since 1990 she's been the executive director and watched it grow into a $30 million success. As with the markets, there've been good years and bad, but during this volatile time, the organization has constantly grown because of the incredible information provided to investors. And along the way, there were plenty of instances where her intuition led her in the right direction. With Julia's incredible track record, I'm happy to publish her thoughts here.

MW: Julia, can you tell us a little about yourself and your position at The Oxford Club?

JG: I'm in a great business that capitalizes on current global trends by coming up with new ways to play the market. Then, to get people interested, we have to be bold and innovative with the way we communicate these new plays. At the same time we keep things grounded by emphasizing certain disciplines and traditions to growing wealth over the long term.

Given my adventurous spirit, I never would have imagined being with one company for so long. I went to college in Boulder, worked in the music business, graduated with an MBA in international management from Thunderbird in Arizona, traveled around the United States and overseas, lived in

Brazil and in Spain. But I'm thrilled to have landed in this particular financial publishing business: There's never a dull moment. I wear many hats, and I love it that way: entrepreneur, corporate manager, personnel director, talent scout, business analyst, marketer, editor, leader, and learner.

MW: You've worked very hard to make it to the top. Can you fill us in on some of the difficulties you faced?

JG: I'm not going to pretend there were dire times, because there weren't. Just a couple of corrections, both in the markets and therefore in our business too—where I had to trim some fat from the business—but often times you are looking for an excuse to trim anyway. And, of course, there are always the irregular and sometimes long hours. I think the biggest challenge for me was coming to terms with the fact that I was a very young female, and certainly an atypical-looking financial executive, heading up a conservative, contrarian financial network of mostly men in their 50s to 70s.

MW: Did you use your intuition?

JG: I suppose you could call it that. Nobody told me I was the wrong figurehead, but I sensed that for The Oxford Club to grow, I better get together an A-team of financial experts that I could put on the front line who could be the face of the Club, the "intellect" of the Club, and I could be the "heart." The positioning has worked well for the organization over the years. In the industry, I have built a reputation for hiring good people, who have, in turn, hired even better people . . . and that makes us all look good! Finding great talent is my number one challenge always, but then there's finding those talents who will also be a good fit for our team. Then there's knowing how best to place them—and motivate them—within the organization. I often need to rely on intuition in the beginning when I don't know someone.

One thing I know how to do is make a quick decision. In our business we need to keep moving forward, test new ideas, analyze the results, and retest, while staying ahead of the trends. There is no time for bureaucratic committee meetings or hierarchical approval processes. But team members will come to me when they are at a crossroads and I need to give them direction, or help them make the next move. I have to rely on my ingrained experience and what I "sense" is the best decision.

MW: How would you define intuition?

JG: For me personally it means moving and thinking in an organic, nonforced manner. When we do things right—in sports, in business, in relationships, in trading—it feels right. It feels natural. But often, through excitement, impatience, or frustration, we try to force an outcome. We block our intuition so we can rationalize the forced move forward. This actually takes extra work and stress . . . and the results? Well, sometimes we get lucky and we're successful, but we're also exhausted and feel a bit out of control, and maybe uneasy that we pushed our luck. More often, we fail and we say,

"Why was I compelled to do that? I should have known better! Why didn't I listen to that inner voice?" That's "intuition" talking. Why did I ignore it? Is it fear, an insecurity, or an addiction that forces me to act this way?

MW: How important is intuition in trading and business?

JG: As in all relationships, including your colleagues and customers, life is so much easier when you seek quality over quantity. Intuition is critical when trying to figure out if you have chosen the right person for the right job. Intuition is critical when you are trying to solve a complex problem that has more than one right answer. Or in choosing the highest quality idea... the one that will evolve into a great product that will serve your customers for the long term. In my business, intuition guided us to specialize in our information, be personable and opinionated, independent of the brokerage houses, go up market, and stay out of the mainstream. We didn't know exactly why we were inspired by this positioning; it just felt right for our ideals and corporate culture. We were also one of the first financial publishers to push global investing (in the late 1980s, early 1990s). Intuitively we believed that's where investors would want to go . . . the next stage in their asset diversification. That by itself set us apart as a more adventurous organization. In the beginning independent financial newsletters like ours we were considered "outcasts" on Wall Street and among the mainstream media. Regardless, it felt good to us to be outcasts. In the end, as Wall Street's "unbiased" recommendations became discredited, investors flocked to publishers like ours for truly independent advice. Now we have to work hard to keep our ideas "alternative," on the cutting edge.

MW: Can you give an example of how your intuition ever misguided you, and what you learned from it?

JG: I've certainly had plenty of bad ideas and made some poor decisions, but I wouldn't say that I was misguided by intuition . . . I would say that I was misguided by lack of intuition.

Sometimes I couldn't rely on intuition because it simply wasn't there. I didn't have the experience or knowledge to even sense what the next move should be, so I would guess. I've since learned to build a consensus when trying to make a decision or take action where I have no inner sense of what would be right or wrong. I seek the advice of others I believe can think through the problem intellectually and intuitively.

MW: What is your perception of intuition in the financial market?

JG: Beyond the fundamentals, I use intuition in investing to ask myself: "Am I making a smart move or an emotional move?"

I use it to measure the quality of an investment or the person recommending a company (people). I also use it to measure the energy behind the market (momentum behind the trend). Then there's the good sense of putting some disciplines in place in case I make the wrong investment decision. I suppose that is using your intuition to know thyself as an investor...how much risk can you truly accept in any given position? Certainly my experience and intuition tell me to not be lazy and always have an exit strategy, and one of the easiest to employ is the trailing stops.

Intuition can serve as a yellow or red flag alerting us to those superficial, impatient, emotional, and undisciplined desires to act. We just need to pay attention.

TOP-DOWN PROCESSING

After all that we've read so far in the chapter, we will now take another step into our investigation of intuition though top-down processing and then apply what we've learned to trading. Finally, we will bring all of our knowledge together with Julia Guth's insights to wrap up the chapter.

In psychology, the mind's ability to process outside stimuli is called "top-down" processing, whereby we are using the information our senses are sending us, while simultaneously accessing the experiences that we have already logged in our minds. When our intuition misguides us, it is because we have a perception breakdown and are not processing all of the data correctly. One example of this type of breakdown is Weber's law, which holds that for us to perceive a shift in something, the shift must be proportionate to the stimulus that is causing change. In other words, if you put 10 apples on a scale and take one off, chances are you will notice. However, if you put 10,000 apples on a scale and take one off, there's a good chance that the disappearance of a single apple could go completely unnoticed. In the trader's world, pennies are often overlooked, but quarters and dollars are not.

What's more, when we see a huge shift in a major market index, or we see some head-turning economic news come forth, we stop what we are doing and take notice. But here's where market intuition comes into play. With Weber's law in mind, those who have the ability to sense small shifts have the intuitive ability to read the market better than those who need a major event to effect a trade. At the end of the day, those who can sense one apple leaving the scale of the market are more likely to make the right decision when they need to. And most likely, they will have already been thinking about making the decision anyway.

For example, if crude oil goes up 5 cents a barrel, investors who understand the economics of oil will know that 5 cents means a ton of money coming out of consumer's pockets. And when consumers are paying more at the pump, they're likely to spend less money on nonessential goods, like upscale clothing, perfume, and jewelry. Those who simply look at the uptick in the price of crude oil as an inflationary part of life, without looking into the true implications of the move, could be in for a loss. For these people, it won't be until crude oil rockets $5 a barrel that they stop and take notice. In this situation, we see that the most intuitive traders are those who are able to sense small changes in market, mentally match the situation to something relevant, and then make the correct decision to profit.

What all of this comes down to is that in order to effectively top down process the information that we are receiving, while also effectively utilizing Weber's law, we must remain consciously cognizant of the information we are receiving. And, even more importantly, we must have the ability to recognize that something in the air of things may be shifting, which we have not actually realized, but feel through a slight touch of intuition. I believe that if you've done your homework and have worked hard to be the best trader you can be, your intuition will nudge you when opportunity is right around the corner. This may be as subtle as a slight twinge of thought that an index is overbought or that a major rally is right around the corner. What's happening is on a deeply subconscious level; your intuition is feeling Weber's law and is perceiving a minute imbalance. If you find yourself with a seemingly insignificant thought in the back of your head, listen. Try to figure out where one apple has been removed from the 10,000 on the scale. Chances are, if you acknowledge this intuitive feeling and begin looking around (perhaps through research), you may find that a major shift is about to occur, but is currently too small for the broader market to perceive.

INTUITION IN TRADING

Obviously, intuition plays a substantial part in trading, as at every turn there's an opportunity at hand or an opportunity disappearing. Because of these simple two facts, intuition is the most important characteristic of becoming a successful trader. Without intuition, we will never have the dexterity or overall ability to sense when something is about to happen or not happen.

In the famous book, *Reminiscences of a Stock Operator*, the infamous Larry Livingston (Jessie Livermore) makes many of his trades on a gut feeling.[9] In one particular example, he's on vacation, taking a break from trading, when he decides to step into a brokerage office. Soon after, he notices that the Dow is up on heavy volume, and as a result he decides to short 1,000 shares of Union Pacific. Eventually, he accumulated 5,000 shares short, on the feeling that something just wasn't right despite upward momentum in the broader market. At the same time, he decided to depart from his vacation early and return to New York in order to keep a closer eye on the position. Soon after, San Francisco was hit with a devastating earthquake. Though the market didn't immediately sell off, he held onto his position for several days, "intuitively knowing" that when the market finally digested the entire situation, he would walk away with a windfall. Other traders were telling him to cover, but intuitively he knew to hold. And he profited handsomely because of it.

At some level, we may say that the windfall was simply pure luck, as no one can (especially in the early 1900s) accurately forecast an earthquake. And given that the trade was made on heavy buying volume in the Dow, the reasons for Livermore getting into the trade probably had more to do with him being a contrarian. But his intuition told him to hold . . . and he made a lot of money because he did. This is merely an example (and fiction too!), but what I'm trying to relate is that during the trading day, when your intuition is tugging to tell you something, take a moment to listen.

SUMMARY

Overall, intuition is not something that you either have or you don't. Intuition is something that all of us can develop and enhance. But to do so, we must take the time to analyze how we process information, and where we may have missed intuition in the past. In doing so, we will be able to match future situations to those that we have already experienced. Over the years, I've heard, "practice makes perfect" and "practice make progress," but I would like to add, "There is no perfection, but with intuitive perception and vigorous practice, we become progressively better."

The unconscious act of reasoning, in business and trading worlds, is something that incredible people like Julia Guth perceive as second nature. And given that she has been able to use her intuition as a warning light when something is amuck, we may want to do the same. At times, we will have to stop and reason things out, but our intuition is something that should never be overlooked. And while intuition is something that comes naturally to some people, our life experiences help grow our intuition by giving us the ability to match more situations whatever we are facing and accurately perceive how to create the greatest outcome.

With a solid understanding of intuition at the most basic levels, we know that with every day's trading action, we are gaining experience, which will only add to our perceptive capacity in the future. What it really boils down to is that though there is some sense of gut feeling in the market, true intuition comes from being around day in and day out . . . and taking some hard licks along the way. When we hear about the wisdom of older people around us, it's no wonder—these people have been around the block a few times and have seen many things. The more we see, the more we can match our past experiences with the situation at hand and act intuitively. With every gain and loss in the market, we are building intuition and, at the same time, are enabling ourselves to be better traders in the future. The longer we're around, the greater our chances of developing incredible unconscious reasoning.

* * *

Throughout Chapter 10, we have covered a ton of ground on intuition, something that you may recall supertrader Joe Ritchie speaking very highly of. At this point, you may notice a subtle shift in direction as Part I comes to an end. In Chapter 11, we will look into gratitude as an important facet of trading. For many, it's hard to ever imagine that gratitude will help us be more proficient traders day in and day out. However, what I hope to relay to you is this: Trading is very, very stressful, and by proficiently adding gratitude in our days, we will not only be able to handle all situations better, but will be able to more effectively apply everything we've covered in the book so far, while also simply just having a better attitude overall.

CHAPTER 11

Expressing Gratitude

*Derived from the Latin word "Gratia," or "grace",
gratitude generally means an attitude, a moral
virtue, a habit, a personality trait, or a coping response.*

—Robert A. Emmons, *Counting Blessings versus
Burdens: An Experimental Investigation of Gratitude and Subjective Well-Being in Daily Life*

What you're about to read is much different than anything else found
in publications related to the trading world. Trading is a tough
game, and most of the time we never think about considering things
such as gratitude as a viable part of our trading psychology repertoire, but
it's a concept that is as important as understanding why a stock moves
at all. Utilizing gratitude every day will help us achieve trading greatness,
and in knowing gratitude, we have the ability to understand ourselves on
a more fundamental level. If you prefer, call it the human PE ratio. Those
who are filled with gratitude have a greater capacity to remain humble when
times get tough, while dynamically perceiving that change is needed when
market conditions become difficult. And when you trade for a living, there
are definitely going to be tough times; I can assure you this one thing with
every ounce of my being.

With all of this in mind, throughout this chapter, gratitude is presented
as a tool. We will see that with constant practice of thankfulness, we become greater people and more optimistic traders. Case in point, the recent
study Dimensions and Perspectives of Gratitude by Robert A. Emmons and

Michael McCullough proved that through gratitude we become more optimistic people,[1] which is something that trading for a living commands.

As a brief excerpt from Emmons and McCullough's study, their synopsis states,

> *Although a variety of life experiences can elicit feelings of gratitude, prototypically gratitude stems from the perception of a personal positive outcome, not necessarily deserved or earned, that is due to the actions of another person.*[2]

In this statement, we see that the authors are pointing out that when we are grateful for one particular thing, we are thanking someone, or something, that made the event happen. However, as Emmons and McCullough will show, when we truly live in gratitude, we are thankful to everything that is, and everyone that we come into contact with. And living with this greater sense of gratitude (on a personal level), we benefit immensely from the thankfulness we extend into each day. There is a distinct difference between just being grateful for something we have received and living in gratitude for everything that is.

When asking ourselves, "What is gratitude?" perhaps a better thing to ask is, "What is it not?" We can assume that when we are feeling grateful, we are not mad, resentful, angry, upset, disenchanted, or feeling other negative emotions. There's a difference between saying thank you and feeling grateful. And when we are feeling grateful, we are not muttering lip service.

Basically, it's hard to be grateful for something *and* be mad. At some level, expressing gratitude, even when everything's going wrong, forces us to alter our perception of the situation and the outcome. Gratitude is linked with happiness, pride, and hope. In addition, gratitude can also present feelings of admiration, respect, trust, and regard . . . all positive emotions, at the end of the day. Really, gratitude is, as Emmons and McCullough put it, an "intrinsically rewarding state."[3]

When we look at life from a perspective of gratitude, we turn each day's negative experience into a positive one. In the world of trading, this positivity is something that we all certainly need. There's almost no other career on the face of the planet that embodies directly negative feelings, on an immediate basis, than what is experienced during the normal trading day. At every turn, there can be a loss, and, as we all know, losing money is not a positive experience. However, when we look beyond the trade and consider our fortune to be in the situation—*at all*—we can turn the tide of the negative emotions that surface.

Being constantly aware of our blessings makes the small things much less important. Even in the case of trading, through the constant awareness of our life prosperity and the chance to help those around us, we can realize that every losing trade is a wonderful chance to learn something new. Gratitude may seem a little silly, but it's not. Gratitude is the foundation of all greatness, and something that none of us will have continued success without.

Gratitude takes work. It's not an emotion that always comes naturally, and to continue to express it in our day-to-day actions, we must remember to make an effort to express it at every moment . . . even when it seems there is nothing to be grateful for.

GRATITUDE AS A PSYCHOLOGICAL STUDY

As previously noted, Robert Emmons (University of California) and Michael McCullough (University of Miami) conducted a study in which one group of people were subjected to conditions of hassles, neutral events, and situations and were instructed to keep weekly journals of these happenings. In another group, several people with neuromuscular disease were also subjected to conditions of gratitude, or conditions that did not necessarily favor such. In both groups, those who focused on conditions of gratitude found a "heightened well being" across the board.[4] The study shows that focusing on gratitude instead of other more negative (or even neutral) facets of life can help us to achieve greatness at every turn.

When defining exactly what gratitude consists of, Emmons and Mc-Cullough cite the 1985 study by B. Weiner illustrating a two-step cognitive process.[5,6] In the first step, the individual recognizes that the outcome is positive. In the second step, the individual realizes that the outcome is due to an external source playing a large role in the making the outcome a reality. One point that the researchers made was that gratitude is generally always connected with some sort of positive emotion. What's more, citing a separate study on gratitude from 1998, Emmons and McCullough agreed that gratitude is an activating emotion that allows us to focus on the things that are important to us at a higher level.[7,8]

At the beginning of an academic quarter, 192 participants were given packets organized into three different groups: gratitude condition, hassles condition, and events condition. In the gratitude condition, each week the students wrote five things that they were grateful for or thankful of. In the hassles condition, each week the students wrote five things that hassled or irritated them. These items included all facets of their lives including family, friends, work, school, finances, and outside affairs. A simple example, as stated in the dissertation, would be, "Hard to find parking."

In the events group, students listed five things that had affected them in the last week, though no emphasis was put on whether the occurrence was definitively positive or negative. They basically recorded the neutral events like, "talked to a doctor about medical school" or "learned CPR."

In addition to listing five examples of one of the above three groups, the students were also asked to rate their mood, physical symptoms, reactions to social support received, estimated time spent exercising, and two "global life appraisal" questions. Within this ratings section, 30 affect terms were selected: interested, distressed, excited, alert, irritable, sad, stressed, ashamed, happy, grateful, tired, upset, strong, nervous, guilty, joyful, determined, thankful, calm, attentive, forgiving, hostile, energetic, hopeful, enthusiastic, active, afraid, proud, appreciative, and angry.

The study also assessed physical symptoms of the students with questions that asked about "headaches, faintness/dizziness, stomach ache/pain, shortness of breath, chest pain, acne/skin irritation, runny/congested nose, stiff or sore muscles, stomach upset/nausea, irritable bowels, hot or cold spells, poor appetite, coughing/sore throat, or other." Lastly, the students were asked about their help-giving (receiving) situations. In other words, the students were asked how they coped with the most detrimental problem of the week. The possible responses included "accepted sympathy from someone," "talked to someone about how they were feeling," or "received concrete help or advice from someone." They were then asked to rate their feelings toward the person who had given them help. All of the data was then measured via descriptive statistics to provide the most accurate results.

First, the researchers noticed that for the participants, there was a direct correlation (.86–.92) between the words "grateful," "thankful," and "appreciative," meaning that the three terms are seemingly interchangeable. Second, when looking toward the week ahead, participants in the gratitude group rated their lives more favorably and looked toward the near future more optimistically than the hassles or neutral groups. What's more, the gratitude group participants were less likely to experience symptoms of physical illness and spent 1.5 more hours a week exercising than those in the hassle or neutral groups. Lastly, it was found that "grateful emotions in response to aid giving were significantly associated with higher ratings of joy and happiness."[9] Generally, when students were extended some sort of aid, well-being was more in evidence than not.

Overall, the study revealed that those who kept gratitude journals on a daily basis not only felt better on the whole, but performed better at work and in life, slept more, and felt less physical pain (see Table 11.1). The inevitable conclusion of the study is that those who incorporate gratitude as a part of their regular lives generally live more happy lives.

In short, when we are grateful for all of the things that come from outside of us, such as the support of our family and friends, we tend to focus more on the benefits we receive from others, instead of on the negative issues, both small and large. What's more, when we remove focus from the

TABLE 11.1 Comparisons of Groups by Measures of Well-Being

Dependent Variable	Condition			$F(2,189)$
	Grateful	Hassles	Events	
Life as a whole	5.05^a	4.67^b	4.66^b	4.08*
Upcoming week	5.48^a	5.11^b	5.10^b	2.81*
Physical symptoms	3.03^a	3.54^b	3.75^b	3.06*
Hours of exercise	4.35^a	3.01^b	3.74^a	3.76**

Notes: $N = 192$. Means that do not share a letter are significantly different;
$P < .05$; *$P < .05$; **$P < .01$
Source: Emmons and McCullough, *Dimensions and Perspectives of Gratitude.*

negative items and look more at the benefits we receive from those around us, we flourish as people because we feel loved and cared for. Emmons and McCullough assert, "Therefore, gratitude appears to build friendships and other social bonds."[10]

What we need to realize is that by concentrating on the positive aspects of our lives, beyond the hassles, we enable ourselves to live happier, more focused lives, with a more positive outlook for the near future. The implications to trading are somewhat staggering, as trading in itself is an extremely stressful business, which directs us to the question, "How do we use gratitude as a trading tool?" In the next section, I paint a clearer picture of how gratitude can help us in the markets, and additionally, how through gratitude we can pull together everything in this book to be the best we can possibly be.

GRATITUDE AND TRADING

When we lose money, it's difficult to find *anything* to be grateful for. But, if we find some sense of gratitude in the markets, even when things are going against us, we open ourselves up to finding new solutions. What's more, it's hard to be grateful without forgiving ourselves for the mistakes we have made. By expressing gratitude, we are also helping to clear our heads of the poor decisions that led to the loss in the first place. Gratitude is more than just a feeling of thankfulness; it kick-starts many of the other things we have talked about in this book to help us find our purpose-center, smash the walls of dogma, find forgiveness, and defeat fear and anxiety, and, at the end of the day . . . it helps us become better traders on the whole. If you live a life of gratitude, chances are that you are probably living in a state of humbleness as well, and when we are humble, we are open to change.

At the beginning of this chapter you may have been giggling to your-self about gratitude being something necessary in the investment markets, but, hopefully, you now see that it is quite important. In effect, we cannot progress as traders and individuals in life without a solid sense of gratitude that keeps us grounded in every moment that is. Without gratitude, we be-come rigid people who can no longer find it within ourselves to change . . . when change is needed. And if there is one thing we must *all* be certain of in the investment markets, it is that nothing will *ever* stay the same. Change is the *only* inevitable outcome of everything that is, and if we discount it, we will be swept away by its ferocious swirling dervishes. Change is the only thing we can be certain of.

Gratitude Misperceived as Weakness

In the world of trading, there's not much room for anything touchy-feely. And for the most part, any sign of gratitude can often be seen as weakness. Trading floors are tough places, and those who cannot handle the heat generally get tossed out of the kitchen. While we cannot change the minds of all those around us, we can work on ourselves and make the most of every moment, even if it's in the middle of a chaotic scene of trading. Up to this point, we've covered the importance of gratitude, but now we switch directions a bit and cover some of the potential areas of false gratitude that we need to be aware of. Please hang in there and keep reading, and you will see in a moment why this is important to trading.

False gratitude is when:

- We are giving lip service to a person or situation; that is, we really don't mean it.
- Our sense of gratitude comes with a caveat or some other condition. If we attach a condition to gratefulness, we are not truly thankful for what is.
- Our gratefulness comes with an expectation of greater success in the future. This is different from a condition as it implies that we expect a general state of greater well-being, no matter what. True gratitude is accepting the future, even if things don't play out as we would desire.

The problem with exercising a false sense of gratitude is that we are ac-tually only building on resentments or actually creating negative emotions. And it's important to recognize that when we act out this double talk, we are falling far from the emotionally intelligent necessity of healthy emotions that we covered in Chapter 9. See, part of our emotional intelligence is de-pendant on the sincerity of our innermost thoughts. And if we are not true to those around us, how can we ever be true to ourselves? Thus, logic follows that to truly be able to be emotionally aware, we must also be sincere in our gratitude. If we are not, often we are actually presenting gratitude from a stance of egocentricity, and we will thus eventually create walls around our cognizant ability to see situations clearly. What's more, if we act our false gratitude, we may further impair our ability to develop intuition, something extremely desired to proactively see trading opportunities arise. What all of this comes down to is that for all of our emotional health in life (and in trading), we must understand that gratitude is an important part of the cyclical relationship of emotional growth.

Whether you are trading for yourself or for a firm, false gratitude (resentment) can creep up at almost anytime, especially when the market's moving against you and those who share a trading desk around you. It's vitally important for us to recognize it when false gratitude appears and stamp out the negative feelings as soon as they emerge.

The Healing Power of Gratitude

When we finally realize that in every horrendous situation that shakes up our life, there is something incredible to be thankful for, we are able to turn the corner and move in many areas of our personal and trading lives.

If you are experiencing a tough time trading, or just in life, one way to overcome the situation is to count your blessings. At times, this seems hard to do, especially when the world is crumbling around us. In the middle of a hectic trading day, when I am facing losses, I sometimes step away from the market and make a quick list of the things that I am grateful for. In doing so, when I come back to my losing position, I find that often I have a clear head to approach the market with. And having a quiet, calm mind is what we need if we are to trade our way out of a bad day. What's more, when we are in a place of gratitude, our ability to hear our intuition is that much greater. Remember Chapter 10 on intuition when we covered Weber's law? How are you ever going to sense a slight shift in the market when you are focused on negative emotions?

To some, this sounds a little too touchy-feely, but I think if we are all to give it a shot, we will find immediate healing on the days when our trades are falling apart. When we are grateful, we are releasing the negative emotions that cause us to make irrational decisions.

When we find ourselves having trouble being grateful, humor is always a good option. Our thoughts form the reality that we live in. Thus, making light of a situation can help ease the stress of the moment at hand. Sometimes during a trading day where nothing seems to be working, you just have to throw up your hands, and say, "darn it, I just don't know," and then chuckle to yourself about all of the horrible decisions you made that day, while making a mental list of the things you are grateful for at that moment.

It's important to not discount the trades, as we want to learn from our mistakes; however, humoring ourselves for a moment and thinking what we are grateful for . . . can make all the difference in the world.

The market is a constantly shifting paradigm because there are a million different emotions tugging it in different directions each day. However, when we embrace the ever-changing paradigm, and attempt to approach it from a stance of gratitude, the swings that we were not able to predict can be that much more bearable.

Gratitude Is Power

When we approach life and trading from a sense of gratitude, there's a good chance that we will suddenly find ourselves empowered. When we hold strong with a stance of gratitude, chances are that we are also facing our fears directly in the face. When I am in a losing trade and I mention to myself that I am grateful for the day, in essence, I am looking the negative feelings that I am harboring square in the eyes. I am essentially saying to the situation, "this trade has no power over the rest of my day." When we find ourselves emotionally able to handle all events—through gratitude—by looking directly at the situation, we are also living in the moment and the uncertainty of the outcome.

See, if we've just made a bad decision and a trade is falling apart, it's easy to get down. And the problem is that if we're focusing on what happened 15 minutes ago, we're sure not seeing what's happening right now. Thus, gratitude is a vital tool in bringing us back into the moment, when we are stuck somewhere else.

Win or lose, we will learn from the situation, all the while looking our fears directly in the face. And by doing so with gratitude, we stand less of a chance of developing maladaptive fear or anxiety. Really, what it comes down to is that gratitude is one of the most powerful tools of self to combat fear and stress throughout the trading day.

SUMMARY

Gratitude is statistically proven to alter our outlook on life. And based on the empirical data collected by Emmons and McCullough, we'd simply be fools to think any other way.

What's more, by understanding and exercising gratitude, we have a greater chance or furthering our emotional intelligence and emotional awareness, while fending off egocentricity. And all of the aforementioned help combat fear and anxiety, which are two of the trader's worst foes.

Finally, when we trade (and live life) from a stance of gratitude, we also remain humble, while shucking off negative emotions that can keep us from truly positive intuitive thoughts, including that of a larger market shift or potential trade out there via Weber's law.

While I have seen ungrateful traders on the floor, from what I've noticed, not a single one of them is still trading for a living today. Though past performance is never a sure sign of future returns, I can assure one thing: Because of the constant emotional struggle trading brings forward, a sincere lack of ungratefulness only expedites one to burn out or blow up.

Gratitude is the culmination of everything that we've covered so far in this book. Gratitude is our top level of awareness, something that stems from a bold understanding of self, coupled with success. When our trading lives begin to take off, it is because we have an incredible understanding of market knowledge and ourselves. I've never met a successful trader who doesn't have a solid grasp on his or her emotions, and, more often than not, those who finally make it have taken so many hard hits that they exude both intuition and gratitude. But to get there, we must have a solid sense of purpose-center; otherwise we will lack the vital understanding of *why* we are doing *what* we are doing.

Without this essential foundation, all of the things we do on a daily basis can easily become completely overwhelming. However, once we know what our purpose is and understand why we are doing what we are, we can begin to work at a higher level of self within our lives. When we ask, "What's the point?" we have an answer. That answer is our mission statement that we wrote out when we were working on developing our purpose-center.

The next step is developing a deeper understanding of what creates a solid sense of esteem, which helps us recognize where we need to work on ourselves. The destruction of ego through simple self-acceptance will help us avoid making irrational decisions based on momentary machismo or unchecked emotions. This understanding is all part of the larger pursuit of *being* good, not just *looking* good.

When we understand these basic principles in relation to Morita therapy and dogma, we find ourselves in the moment, living from a sense of mindfulness. Morita therapy, the art of living in the reality of the moment, is useless if we cannot emotionally identify what is happening when it is happening. But we know that we are not trying to change the emotion at hand, we simply want to accept it. By doing so, the negative emotions will change themselves. What's more, it is through our understanding of our personal dogma that we find ourselves taking a deeper look into ourselves and the decisions we make each day. When we have a solid sense of esteem that transcends hollow ego, we are able to look beyond conventional thinking of not questioning what's happening around us; identify, acknowledge, and accept our emotions; and then live purely in the reality of the moment at hand. In short, when we seek to destroy personal dogma, we stop making excuses and start getting real. And we challenge the social and market dogmas surrounding us as well. Through this understanding, we also accept that life is a constantly shifting surface of unsteady ground, but we also know that by leaning into the discomfort, we will grow as people and find that we can remain calm, even when the floor is caving in underneath us.

Finally, we must remember that remaining humble is one of the most important aspects of making sure we keep our egos in check. If we live solely on ego, we have fallen into the unconscious trap of not being able to see the emotions that are causing us to make irrational decisions. At this level we are losing the ability to recognize that we have erred and forgive ourselves in a healthy manor. To overcome this debilitating condition, we can simply look into the cause variables of why we are making the decisions that we are, while also using emotional identification to help bring ourselves into the reality of what we are feeling. By doing so, we effect an emotional evolution that will result in greater intuitive capacity.

* * *

Now that we have covered all of the fundamentals of self, in Part II we take a look at some of the more intrinsic items of trading, as in good old-fashioned stress. We will hear from another seasoned trader and a medical doctor, both on the same subject. What's more, we will then move back to the Eastern world to examine some of the principles of relaxation and visualization to, hopefully, help us stay even more calm in the middle of any trading day. Finally, we wrap up Part II with a chapter about self-destructive behavior, which is one of the leading causes of trader blowouts.

Beyond Emotions

Once you've been trading for a while, you'll realize that turning a mediocre trading career into something brilliant has more to with understanding what's happening inside ourselves than with what's happening on Wall Street. We can know all the right things to do, but if our emotions run amok, we will never be able to really trade with a solid sense of purpose and passion. Instead, we will find ourselves trading from a point of irrational emotion. Digging into the problematic emotions that can hinder our trading careers is the only way to move to the next level.

Here's an example of exactly what I mean: While writing this book, I began running an options trading service/newsletter for the Mt. Vernon Options Club. I was very excited at the promise of sharing my knowledge with the subscribers of this service and was elated at the possibility of making other people tons of money. I came out of the gates on fire with several trades that I was sure would be winners. All of my first four trades were devastating losers, and immediately subscribers began to cancel. I know the sales team was working very hard telling the subscribers "This is just a transitional period, hang on," they said, which only added more pressure. At the same time, I had the *worst* trading week of my entire career. The stress was so intense that I took an entire day off (something I rarely ever do) and visited my doctor. I explained to her that I was having panic attacks, and that I wasn't able to sleep at night ... and then we began talking about this book. In the thick of things I realized that I have to walk the walk, and practice what I preach. Deep down I *knew* that my trading skills were good, but the devastating losing streak was causing me to question everything. (You might think that four trades shouldn't qualify as a "losing streak," but I was recommending short-term out-of-the-money options that lose value like lightening when the underlying stock moves away from the strike. And I was feeling the full brunt of the option's time decay.)

In the end, I realized that by taking a day off, I was taking a moment to recognize how stressed out I had become. As a result, I used everything in this book to recenter myself and calm down. But I also realized that even as I write this book about understanding our emotions, even I am not immune to stress or losses. It can sneak up on us when we least expect it. Trading for a living is stressful, and if we don't take the time to understand what stress is, when things get tough, we can be our own worst enemy.

When we cannot see the negative damage that is done, when we face severe losses, or, perhaps, when we sabotage our own trading future when things are going our way, we will remain at an average level, lucky to break even. I've never met a trader who has not sabotaged him- or herself or reacted negatively to a losing position. It's part of what everyone who trades for a living experiences. These difficult moments are part of learning about how we react to the market and how we deal with the decisions we make affecting our trades. In a career where every moment is prompted by a decision that can either make or lose money, stress levels can be far above normal. It's easy to say that in every career every decision can make or lose money, and I agree. But in the world of trading, it's simply much more apparent when you have to watch the greenbacks grow or shrink before your eyes. I experienced some of the worst trading months of my life at the end of 2006, but I knew it would happen from time to time, and with the tools here, I've handled it with integrity ... In my purpose-center, January 2007 proved to be one of my best months ever.

With this in mind, Part II begins by examining stress, including a medical perspective and that of a Wall Street veteran. It continues with discussions of relaxation, affirmation, and visualization, wrapping up with advice about avoiding self-destructive behavior. It is my hope that this part of the book will add some very effective items to your psychological toolbox that will help you trade with passion and purpose, especially when stress is a substantial factor.

CHAPTER 12

Confronting and Defeating Stress

B y definition, stress is "the sum of physical and mental responses to an unacceptable disparity between real or imagined personal experience and personal expectations."[1] One of the fundamental principles of stress management is understanding that we need to make a conscious effort to relax once in a while. But we have to be able to recognize when we're stressed out in the first place. I think at some level, we're all so stressed out about the present moment that in some odd way we think that once we've achieved whatever we're trying to do, we can then finally relax. In short, as a society, we're all so rooted in the outcome that we never stop to consider the journey. Especially for a trader, every ounce of everything is in the outcome. Every trade directly strives to make the most of the outcome, where success is directly measured in dollars. It's a cold, hard reality that, frankly, is stressful. In the trading world, it's hard to enjoy the moment, unless, of course, we've just closed out a tremendously profitable trade. After all, when in the middle of a *huge* trade (especially if it is going against us), it's hard to relax. It's only when we've booked the cash, can we let down our guard. (As a brief side note, I think that, at some level, stress and anxiety go hand in hand; thus, much of what you're reading here should be referenced with Chapter 7.)

Because trading is such a stressful way of life and has various similarities to anxiety, it's no wonder so many traders are alcoholics or drug addicts, or just generally wound up all the time. The only time many traders can let go is after the final bell rings, and they go to the bar. Booze and drugs help many traders check out from the tornado of stress that has surfaced throughout the day. This approach may work for a while, but eventually the destructive things that once helped can completely destroy our lives. Thus, we have to understand that a little stress is good, but too much can take a toll on our greater well-being which is why we must have some tools within ourselves to deal with stress when it begins to consume us.

A LITTLE STRESS IS GOOD

Looking into the cause of our stress, Jan R. Markle, MA, BCIAC, of the Web site, RelaxWithin.com, asserts,

> *Some stress is necessary and desirable to make life interesting. A stress that we relate to as a challenge (within our coping abilities) prompts us to act and we accomplish a goal. But too much stress causes us anxiety and fear and causes us to make mistakes.*
>
> *Our quality of performance is related to our level of stress. Too little stress and we're bored, as retired people or people with unsatisfying jobs might discover. An increase in stress, still within what we are capable of handling, is productive for us and encourages us to perform or accomplish, up to a certain point. That's our "optimum performance range." Actors usually say that a certain amount of nervousness before going on stage is good, because they know that they can turn that stress into a strong performance.*[2]

It is understandable that some of our stress is actually part of the game that allows us to perform at a higher capacity. But our stress is a double-edged sword. While it can help us perform, it can also cause us to make many disastrously wrong decisions when critical moments arise. And if we're not careful, continued stress left unchecked can cause physical health problems as well.

What we need to do is learn to consciously relax in the heat of the moment, and, in a calm state, make the most of the situation at hand. For a trader, this counsel would apply when the entire floor is buckling underneath us and all of our positions are moving in the wrong direction.

When the heat is on during the trading day, relaxing in the middle of a stressful moment is actually a three-part activity. The first part is simply recognizing that stress exists. The second is digging deep within ourselves to make a physical effort to relax (Chapter 14). And the third is to then mentally form a positive sense of the situation (and desired outcome), with affirmations and visualization, which are covered in Chapter 15.

RECOGNIZING STRESS

For many of us, when we've taken on a position that is either working for us or falling apart, we simply accept the situation as part of our job. However, what we need to see is that we have entered a stage of accelerated stress. We're either worried about losing money or simply stressed about how much money we can make, or are afraid to lose if we close out a trade early. We've already covered the proposition that the market is driven by fear and greed. But I'm bringing it up again because it is very, very true. We're either worried about what we're going to lose or about how much we can make, both of which are stressful. Markle tells us that we need to measure our stress when we are feeling out of whack.[3]

Evaluate Your Stress Level

I'm pretty sure most people generally intuitively have a good idea whether they are stressed out . . . but just in case, I've included a brief stress test here (Figure 12.1). Take a few moments to complete this test . . . perhaps just for kicks. But, you never know, you may be surprised by the results.[4]

Remember, stress can be tricky, so there's a good chance the test can help you evaluate your stress level, even if you are not feeling particularly wound up. In addition, the test identifies some of the key symptoms of stress and allows you to identify which factors apply to you. Follow these instructions for taking the test:

1. Rate each of the statements listed on a scale of 1 to 5, where 1 is Never, 2 is Rarely, 3 is Sometimes, 4 is Frequently, and 5 is Always. Put the appropriate number in the blank next to the statement, based on how you feel at this time.
2. Total the points next to each statement to calculate your score.

What your score means:[5]

20–40: Low. You have few stressors in your life or you seem to be managing them quite well.

41–60: Fairly low. You are likely experiencing some negative effects of stress. Depending on the changes and challenges in front of you, you might want to learn ways to deal more effectively with the stressors in your life.

61–80: Moderate. You may be suffering from chronic stress, depending on your ability to deal effectively with the changes in your life. It would be

---

1 = Never, 2 = Rarely, 3 = Sometimes, 4 = Frequently, 5 = Always

_ I have little control or influence over my work.
_ My work interferes with my family/personal life.
_ I have too much work to do and/or unreasonable deadlines.
_ I think there is one right way to do things.
_ I don't receive the recognition I deserve when I do a good job.
_ It's difficult for me to express my thoughts and feelings about my work conditions to my superiors.
_ I am easily irritated and/or upset.
_ I have difficulty exercising.
_ I have witnessed/am aware of bullying (physical or verbal bullying) in my workplace.
_ I keep things inside and don't burden others with my problems.
_ I have difficulty making decisions.
_ I tend to neglect my diet (eat irregularly, eat unhealthy foods, etc.)
_ I try to do everything myself.
_ I rush through the day and have no time left to relax.
_ I make a big deal about everything.
_ I spend a lot of time complaining about the past.
_ I have trouble sleeping and/or sleep too much.
_ I suffer from headaches and migraines.
_ I feel tired/fatigued for no real reason.
_ I feel as if I don't want to get up in the morning.

FIGURE 12.1 A stress test. (Static Stress Test courtesy of Dr. Ervin E. Lambert.)

advantageous to you to learn ways to deal more effectively with change and to minimize the adverse effects of stress.

81–100: High. You are probably suffering from some of the detrimental effects of stress and should seek out resources to help you cope more effectively. Some of the symptoms you may be experiencing include headaches, problems with sleeping (insomnia or sleeping too much), irritability, difficulty concentrating, depression, anxiety, difficulty balancing work and home, and indecision.

Responding to Your Stress

The test gives you a basic read on how stressed out you are in general. I'd be willing to bet that most of us are stressed to some degree. It's just a common fact of life in the 21st century. If you're stressed out in the macropicture, though, your stress level probably rises fivefold when you're in the middle of a trade.

If you take a position and suddenly you catch yourself with sweaty palms, it's important to recognize what's happening. You're either feeling stressed out, are feeling fear, or are having an anxiety-related issue. If you are feeling stressed out in a situation like a losing trade, it's important to recognize and accept that it "is what it is." You're there, in the heat of the moment, things may not be going as planned, and you're stressed. Sometimes when we're really stressed about a trade, we are so involved in the trade, we have trouble stepping back from the situation and seeing just how wound up we've become.

Most of us have an internal alarm that lets us know when we're experiencing stress. If it goes off, *don't* hit the snooze button. When we are able to recognize that we are feeling stressed out, we also have to try to measure the stress level that we're operating at. A little stress is good; it helps trigger our "fight or flight" instincts and can help us perform at a higher level. This is the excitement that many traders enjoy. But there's also another level of stress where our stress can turn into fear or anxiety, and if we're not careful, we can begin making inaccurate, emotional decisions.

To point out how a little stress is good though, Kevin Cuddie mentioned that when he's losing, he trades better because of the pressure (see in Chapter 4). But he also has a "circuit breaker" that signals when he should take a break or stop trading for the day. We have to be able to recognize where this point is for ourselves, because it's usually the area where we start seeing massive losses. Take a moment or two and think about your past trading experiences; identify some of the times you would have been better off if you had gotten up and walked away. What were some of the indications? Were you edgy, sweaty, shaking, or completely numb? Was it after you'd violated some of your most important trading rules? What could you have done to recognize that the stress of the situation had pushed you beyond the point of making rational decisions?

What's most important here is not to think about what you could have done differently in the trade, but to instead think about what you could have done to recognize that you needed to take a step back and calm down in order to look at the situation from an unbiased stance. Only you are in control of you . . . meaning that only you can make yourself take a step back from the situation when things get nuts. If you take the time to look into yourself to find some indications of your personal stress level, you could be much better off in the long run. And once we're able to recognize that we're stressed, we can then begin to use some tools of relaxation to help us see the situation, or trade, more clearly.

MATT McCALL ON STRESS AND INVESTING

Matt McCall is a versatile trader, investor, and money manager who has built his career from the ground up, which is why I've included him here. Matt provides an incredible snapshot into the world of personal drive and the desire to achieve great results. What's more, Matt's money management style leans to holding positions longer than the average trader. Thus, for those who prefer swing trading, Matt's interview holds many gems.

MW: Matt, can you give us a little information about your trading knowledge and how you invest on a daily basis?

MMcC: My trading knowledge is a bit unique and different from most money managers because I focus on both technical and fundamental analysis from a top-down approach. On a daily basis I am constantly analyzing the economic numbers that are released and their effect on the world economy and stock markets. This is the first step in the system my company has been working on for many years. The next stage would be to watch the charts of the major averages on both a daily and weekly chart to determine opportune buy and sell points. From there I will move down to the sectors to uncover any new opportunities, based on both the charts and fundamentals. Finally, in my system, I narrow the search to specific stocks and exchange-traded fund (ETFs). The charts and technical analysis will be the final tool that is used to determine proper entry points for the investments. By going into each trading day with a system, an investor can lower their stress level before the opening bell rings. Over the years I have found many investors do not have a system they follow in determining their investment decisions. By not being prepared, the probability of poor decision making increases and, thus, so does the stress level. Therefore, the first step for any investor should be to develop an investment plan they will use as the map to financial freedom.

MW: What type of pressure do you face each day?

MMcC: The biggest pressure I face on a daily basis has to do with coming up with new money-making ideas. With the competition between money managers and advisors growing each day, it puts the pressure on you to perform. If you miss a high flyer, there will be clients asking why you missed it. After a while, you begin to ask yourself the same question and wonder why you missed the opportunity. Investors need to realize there are nearly 7,000 stocks traded on the three major U.S. exchanges, and unless you buy every one, there will be missed opportunities. If you sit in front of your computer and watch the ticker and say to yourself, "what if," you are hurting your investments twofold. For starters you will be increasing your stress level by coming down on yourself for not buying the stock before the big rally. You will also be wasting time on something you cannot change, and this results in opportunity cost. Instead of focusing your energy in a positive manner toward picking a new investment, the time is wasted on what ifs.

MW: What are some of the techniques you use to calm yourself down and find balance?

MMcC: There are several techniques I use to help calm my emotions. First and foremost is reverting back to my trading system. If you are using a proven strategy that produces solid results over the long term you must realize there will be rough days, weeks, and even years. Once you get out of the stigma that you must make money every day and that you will never take losses, you can become a successful investor. Until you learn to handle your losses and realize it is part of investing, your performance will he handicapped.

Another technique I use involves keeping my emotions to a minimum during both the good and bad times. I find that most successful investors are able to stay on an even keel both when they are making big money and losing hordes. The reason they are so successful is because most emotion-based investment decisions will result in poor judgment and eventually losing trades. I believe uncontrolled emotions are the number one reason investors/traders are not successful in the market.

When you feel your emotions about to take over your investment mind-set there is a good chance your stress level is already too high. There are two simple techniques that can be used in this situation. One involves getting up from your leather chair and walking out of your office and outside for some fresh air. Do not sit back down for at least an hour or until your mind stops thinking about the stock market. If this takes all day, the best thing to do is shut down the computer and take your mind elsewhere. Some may think this is too extreme. However, would you rather end the day with your portfolio where it started and go head first into it tomorrow or would you like to risk taking a large loss?

The second option for emotional investors is to take a step back and analyze what is generating the stress. Whether it be several consecutive losses or missed opportunities, you need to revert back to your investment system. It may be a situation where the market just has not gone your way—that happens to even the best. Or it could be you deviating from your initial plan. Either way you need to find out where the stress is coming from so you can better control your emotions in the future.

MW: Can you give us an example of when you had a whopper of a loser and what you did during and after the trade? Did you recover the lost money in another trade and if so, how?

MMcC: In late 2004 the market was doing well and one of my positions at the time, Aladdin Knowledge System (ALDN), was enjoying the ride. The stock was purchased at $29 and quickly ran up to $32 (10 percent) as it hit a new multiyear high. At that time it was clear the stock was due for a natural pullback of about 5–10 percent. This did occur in the next two weeks, but the stock continued to fall as big volume was building and sellers were taking control of the stock. The initial stop-loss when the position was entered was $27 (7 percent stop-loss). If I would have stayed with my initial parameters and not deviated from my plan, the stock would have been sold at $27, and a small loss of 7 percent would have been locked in. Instead, I held onto the stock—breaking one of my cardinal rules by ignoring the stop-loss—and eventually took a 30 percent hit when I dumped the stock at $20.

This is a perfect example of how stress and natural human emotions took over my investment decision making. The system had generated an initial stop-loss of 7 percent; however, when the time came to sell, my stress level was high because I did not want to take a loss on a stock I felt had potential. The high stress led to my poor decision to hold onto the stock before eventually selling much lower. Unfortunately as humans the only way to learn is to feel the pain firsthand. But believe me, I will not make the same mistake again.

MW: How were you able to get over it?

MMcC: Even though I do look at each trade individually, the portfolio as a whole is how I measure my performance for clients. Therefore, when a losing trade occurs, it is not imperative to run out and make the money back in one stock. As long as I continue to follow my investment system, there will be winners in the future that will make up for the loss. I will remember that trade for a long time, but I'm not going to beat myself up about it. I learned a lesson, and I just have to move on. Investors who are not able to let go of the past losses will continue to hurt their future trading results until they can move on.

MW: What advice would you give an investor or trader who's lost money in the market and is trying to recover their losses?

MMcC: The first piece of advice I would give an investor after losing money in the market is to learn from their losses and use it to make a better decision in the future. If the investor lost a large portion of their portfolio, it's only natural to try and become more aggressive to get the money back they lost. This is the exact wrong action, because it takes the investor out of their risk comfort zone. This type of behavior is why Las Vegas and casinos make large amounts of money. You go from being an investor/trader with a plan to a pure gambler! If you do not learn from your past, it is inevitable you will repeat it.

MW: What advice would you give the investor or trader who is doing very well? What I'm trying to ask is what would you tell a trader who has turned the corner and is beginning to see an ego consummate with his or her bottom line?

MMcC: First and foremost I would say congratulations and then quickly remind them of what got them to where they are. I am sure it involved hard work and discipline. As humans we tend to build egos when we achieve goals that we have set for ourselves. This is fine, but we must set new goals and continue to stay with the investment system that got us to where we are. I personally have had some great quarters and I begin to feel that I can't pick a loser. This leads to buying investments that might fall short of my requirements, but I do it regardless because my ego gets in the way. The key is to control your ego by sticking with what got you there.

Most investors are constantly looking for ways to relieve stress during the decision-making process. This may sound odd, but there needs to be a little stress during the process or investors can become complacent. When things are going well, investors tend to deviate from their system and complacency takes over. To overcome this, investors need to keep a little stress on themselves and increase their investment goals.

MW: When incredibly difficult and stressful moments arise, what would you recommend that an investor do to calm him- or herself, to see the situation clearly?

MMcC: There are times when all investors feel like they cannot do anything right, and every investment they buy goes down immediately. You must know you are not alone; it has happened to all of us (but only a few will admit it). What I have done in the past is taken a step back from the losing trades to reevaluate my position and determine what might have gone wrong. There are two outcomes from this. One, you deviated from your system and made a mistake and you learn from it and get back to work. The other shows that you did exactly what you have done in the past, except this time it did not work.

The majority of the time it is the latter, and as investors we must realize no system is foolproof. If we believe that we will be successful every day, every month, or even every year, we are lying to ourselves. Even the best investors of all time had losing years when they trailed the benchmarks. Once you are able to realize you are human and that your system will produce underperforming results from time to time, you will be able to begin making big money.

Most investors are more stressed when they have a winning position versus a loser. Do not ask me why this is, but over my years I have found most investors feel the loser will come back to breakeven eventually and the winner is bound to give back its gain. This type of pessimistic attitude is not good for your stress level and has to be kept to a minimum to become successful.

An example of a stock that created high levels of stress for my company as well as big profits for our clients is Intuitive Surgical (ISRG). The medical appliance company that creates robots for surgery was one of the best performing stocks in 2005. Throughout the rally the stock had gapped higher on earnings news several times during the year. After each thrust higher, the profits in the position were climbing and my stress level increased because I did not want to give up gains of over 400 percent. To combat the natural emotions of a big winner and selling too early, I reverted back to my company's system that incorporates technical analysis. By using the charts I was able to lower my stress level and determine an appropriate stop-loss price. Eventually the stock was sold and a large gain was booked.

MW: Can you please give some words of wisdom for traders just entering the business and for those who have been around for a while?

MMcC: Traders just entering the business must realize that the lure of big money is not the reason to begin trading. If they enter the trading world only for big money, fast cars, and, houses worthy of MTV's *Cribs*, they will be very disappointed if they do not achieve it in the first couple of years. And for most traders and investors, this is the case. I believe new traders must set realistic goals and be willing to continue to educate themselves everyday . . . only then will they become better traders.

Traders who have been in the business for a while must be doing something right or they wouldn't still be in the market. My advice to those who are just beginning to see profits is to continue what's working, because if it's gotten you this far, something has to be right. Don't forget the basics and, just like the beginning trader, keep educating yourself to be the best you can be.

As far as stress is concerned, a trader just beginning may not have any stress because their emotions have the best of them. However, that can change quickly if the short-term goals are not met. If a new investor is aware of the potential stress generators (losses, missing opportunities), they will be ahead of the curve. The investor who has been successful also needs to keep on top of stress because it can come up to bite you without warning. Always be prepared for any type of market environment, especially in this world we live in.

MW: Lastly, can you please let us know what the three most important traits of successful investors are?

MMcC: The three most important traits of investors are (1) patience, (2) discipline, and (3) hard work.

And, we all get lucky once in a while, but continued success takes time.

* * *

At the end of the day, stress is something that can completely overwhelm us in the world of trading and, as Matt stated, can "bite you without warning." The problem is that we will never be able to defeat stress if we cannot first recognize that it is present in our lives. And the only way to do so is to take a time out and do a sort of self-check to see where we are. As Matt said, if we are aware of stress generators, we can proactively prepare for stress before it ever even begins.

SUMMARY

Throughout this chapter, we took a preliminary look at stress in an attempt to understand why it's vital that we are able to recognize the symptoms of stress. A little stress is good, but too much can cause larger health problems.

In addition, as Matt McCall mentioned, it's important to be aware of our stress generators. Specifically he said, "As far as stress is concerned, a trader just beginning may not have any stress because their emotions have the best of them. However, that can change quickly if the short-term goals are not met. If a new investor is aware of the potential stress generators (losses, missing opportunities), they will be ahead of the curve.... Always be prepared for any type of market environment, especially in this world we live in."

Overall, it's important to take a step back when we're feeling stressed during the trading day, and perhaps go get a cup of coffee. After all, that one moment of taking ourselves out of the situation could be a daily lifeline to profitability.

* * *

In Chapter 13, we look further into stress by examining the medical aspects of the condition and how it can hurt us both mentally and physically if left unchecked. We will hear from Dr. Royce Peterman, who certainly knows her stuff. For any of those who have been battling many stressful trading days lately, this next chapter is for you.

A Medical Evaluation of Stress

The one aspect of trading that we always seem to overlook is that trading *will always be* stressful. We think that each day we're going to walk into the office or onto the trading floor and never have to face the incredible pressure of several positions going against us. And life is much the same too. How often do we wake up in the morning, have something totally sideswipe us during the day, and then feel completely exhausted by the evening? This is just the way it is in our fast-paced society. And if you're in the trading world, you can pretty much guarantee that out-of-the-blue stress will happen on a daily basis.

I remember once right after I graduated from college and had just started trading on a floor; I felt completely unstoppable. I was living my dream. One morning I woke, showered, dressed, and stepped out in the crisp morning ready to take on the world. I specifically remember pulling out of my apartment's parking garage, turning the radio up, and feeling calm, alive, and thrilled to get to work.

By 10:00 a.m. I was sitting on the largest trading loss I'd ever seen, in a trade that I had just opened that morning. I was completely devastated, and as the losses grew, I became more and more lost in the situation. I was a deer standing in headlights. I will never forget that morning for as long as I live. If I was so positive going into the office and ready to take on the world, how was I sideswiped so badly? I remember looking at my P&L, staring at a $20,000 loss, and in complete exasperation, wondering how I got there.

How could I have let a small loser turn into the largest intraday trading loss of my entire life? I've thought about that day over and over and over, and after much mulling, I think I have an answer.

In the book *The 33 Strategies of War*, Robert Greene points out, "Instead of resisting the pull of strategy and the virtues of rational warfare, or imagining that it is beneath you, it is far better to confront its necessity. Mastering the art will only make your life more peaceful and productive in the long run, for you will know how to play the game and win without violence. Ignoring it will lead to a life of endless confusion and defeat."[1] What the author is referring to is that we must approach life—and stress—as warriors. This is not to say we must approach life with violence; we must simply be prepared for the stress of the battle by realizing that we are in the heat of the battle at every moment.

The morning of my great loss, I had failed to see that I was in the middle of a financial battle, and when things got tough, I froze. Trading is a battlefield, and I can assure you that if you don't look at it from some level of competitiveness, you might not last too long. There will be moments when the unexpected will smack you upside the head, and you will find yourself stunned. But like Joe Ritchie pointed out in Chapter 8, when we have built our skills on sensible knowledge, we will intuitively perform when the time comes. However, part of performing with passion and purpose is the subtle realization that we are in the middle of a stressful situation, and the moment of war has arrived. Whether we sink or swim will depend on how well prepared we are to handle the moment, and stress, at hand.

I look back at that morning when everything was falling apart on the trading floor, and I think that if I had stopped for one second to think to myself—"Everything is falling apart, this is a stressful situation. I need to separate myself emotionally and see the situation from afar if I hope to succeed."—I probably would have admitted I was wrong early on and cut my losses quickly. However, with all that was happening and my newness to the floor, I simply didn't have the capacity to make the right call. The stress of the moment was greater than my intuition or experience, and thus I was helpless to stop the events from unfolding as they did. Moreover, my lack of experience created a situation of great stress that was a major contributing factor to my locking up. On that fateful losing day, one of my managers said, "Mark, what you're feeling right now is the difference of how you would like things to be and how they actually are . . . some people just call it stress." And he was right, the trade was going against me, and I was stressed . . . to the max.

I would like to say that my positions came back, but they didn't. Because I was in my first years of trading, I simply didn't have the tools to deal with the losses mounting in my account, or the stress of the situation. I learned some good lessons that day, and one of the most important is that we must be prepared to recognize stress when it sets in. Because if we aren't, when the market or our positions turn against us, we're going to become immobilized in the situation. So learn from my mistake.

This leads us to an interview with Dr. Royce Peterman, who was kind enough to explain the physical attributes of stress, which is essential knowledge if we are ever able to overcome stress mentally.

THE FACTS BEHIND STRESS, FROM DR. ROYCE PETERMAN, MD

Dr. Royce Peterman is currently training as a fellow in cardiology at the University of Colorado Health Sciences Center, focusing on electrophysiology, a subspecialty of cardiology that focuses on the conduction system of the heart and abnormalities that occur within it causing various cardiac arrhythmias. Because of her focus on the heart, she is a great candidate for this book, as stress-related conditions often lead to cardiovascular issues. As traders who wade knee-deep in stress every day, we certainly want to be proactive about any potential problems that could arise in the future.

MW: Dr. Peterman, thanks for sharing your thoughts on the medical aspects of stress, but before we begin, could you please talk a little about your approach to medicine?

RP: First, it's important to understand that osteopathic (DO) medical training is different from allopathic (MD) in a couple of ways. In medical school we learn the same pathology, physiology, and clinical manifestations of disease that allopathic physicians learn. In addition, osteopaths spend a bit more time delving into the anatomy and biomechanics of the body, and we learn several different modalities of manipulative medicine, similar to those strategies used by chiropractors, rolfers, and massage therapists to reestablish structural integrity within the body. I say this as a very simplistic explanation. We have a broad understanding of the interrelationship between physiology and anatomy that these other body workers do not always gain as part of their training. An osteopath learns a different approach to medicine in that we tend to focus on the health within a person's body rather than focusing solely on the disease process. Our fundamental principles teach that the body is a unit, that structure and function are interrelated, and that the body is self-regulating. Basically, what that means is that we believe that problems with the structure of the body, (i.e., the spine, muscles, and fascia) can manifest themselves as systemic diseases and vice versa. We are taught to evaluate and treat structural abnormalities as part of the process of treating systemic illness. One of our key principles teaches that the body has an intrinsic ability to heal itself. I believe that to be true. While many of us do not and will not go on to use a significant amount of manipulative medicine in our practice of treating patients, the philosophies of osteopathy are carried with us throughout our careers. My hope for my personal career is that I will continue to assess my patients with a holistic approach to their cardiac issues and that I will always remember that the heart is only one part of the entire intricate system.

MW: Could you describe the physical attributes of stress?

RP: The body manifests physical and emotional stress in a multitude of ways. In addition, every body is distinctive in how it deals with the stress we put on it. Without doing an extensive literature search on the topic, I would hazard to say that the most common manifestation of stress would be fatigue. With fatigue comes irritability. When we overwork our bodies and our minds, we feel tired. Our bodies are telling us we need to rest. There are, of course, many psychiatric manifestations of emotional stress. There is a condition called conversion disorder in which a person who has undergone extreme emotional stress will actually suffer loss of motor or sensory function of part of their body. For example, after watching the death of a loved one, a patient may lose their vision and become blind, or after being raped a victim may lose complete function of their leg or arm, mimicking a stroke. There are also an endless number of more organic ways in which stress is manifested through medical illness. In hospitalized patients, most notable in intensive-care patients, stress of acute illness can cause gastritis, an inflammation of the stomach lining which can actually lead to significant bleeding from the gastrointestinal tract. As an attempt to prevent this, we actually empirically put patients in the intensive care unit on medications that decrease acid production in the stomach. We have not yet found a good way to eliminate the stress of acute illness. There is also an interesting cardiac diagnosis that is relatively new in the medical community. It is a diagnosis that came out of Japan a few years ago called Takatsubo's cardiomyopathy. It is an extreme dysfunction of the heart that can actually lead to severe heart failure.

The exact pathophysiology has yet to be elucidated, but the current theory is that it results from a catecholamine surge during an emotionally stressful situation. Catecholamines are the hormones responsible for our fight or flight response. The effect they have on the heart is truly dramatic and can be very debilitating. Thankfully it is typically reversible. While we no longer believe that emotional stress will cause someone to suffer a heart attack, there seems to be a clear association between coronary heart disease and Type-A personality. In contrast to Type B individuals, those with Type A personality are twice as likely to develop heart disease and five times more likely to have a heart attack. Many studies have failed to reveal why these competitive, ambitious, stressed-out, often angry and hostile people are more likely to get heart disease. It remains unclear to what degree the hostile behavior is influenced by other factors such as smoking, diet, and alcohol use. However, in some studies the relationship between Type A personality and the development of heart disease persists even after controlling for physiologic, psychosocial, and behavioral risk factors.

More benign symptoms such as nausea and headache can also be mediated by our day-to-day stress. There are many different kinds of headache, but the most common is probably tension headache. Tension headache is caused by spasm in the muscles of our neck and shoulders and those that support our head. Spasm of these muscles can occur as a result of postural problems as well as trauma. However, a very common cause of tension in our neck and spine and, thus, headaches is emotional stress.

We tend to inadvertently clench our jaw muscles and shrug our shoulders as a response to stress or anger. Holding this position for a period of time will result in muscular spasm and thus tension headache. Furthermore, headache is one of the leading medical causes of missed days of work and low productivity in the workplace. This is quite ironic considering it is often our inability to effectively deal with the stress of our jobs that results in the headaches!

MW: When someone is going through a crisis situation—like an investment portfolio falling apart—what's happening to them on a physical level with the stress from the situation?

RP: As I said previously, everybody deals with stress in a different way. Anxiety results in elevated levels of catecholamines within our system. This can lead to high blood pressure, which over time can lead to strokes and heart attacks. It can also result in gastrointestinal upset with nausea and diarrhea. Not to mention the pain that can be associated with muscular tension and loss of structural integrity of the body, which can then lead to further disease within the organ systems of the body. All the while, a person in this situation is most likely not eating properly, sleeping well, or exercising regularly, further perpetuating the physical stress on their body.

MW: What can that person do on a physical or mental level to regain control of themselves?

RP: I don't think it is as much about control as it is about knowing your body and being aware of the effects stress has on it. It is about awareness, not control. It is often the desire to control their environment that finds people in unhealthy situations as a result of their stress. Very often, in medical practice, our patients are unwilling to believe that their headache was caused by how they reacted to the board meeting. People want a quick fix, a pill, or to be told that it is something physically wrong with them rather than simply a response to emotional stress.

Accepting emotional responsibility for our own ailments is very difficult and this idea is met with great resistance. What can a person do? I would like to say, "Avoid stress." But with my profession and Type A personality, I know as well as anybody that is not possible in the world in which we live.

The first step is accepting that emotional stress can and will be manifested in physical ways. Identify situations that cause you stress. Then become familiar with your body and how it deals with stress in physical and emotional ways. This gives you the tools to be prepared for what might come when the portfolio is falling apart.

MW: From a medical perspective, can stress be controlled through positive thinking, a healthy diet, exercise, and breathing techniques?

RP: Again, it is not really about control. Can we learn how to affect the ways in which the stress of our lives manifests itself within our physical body? Absolutely! Different tactics work for different people. There are many techniques used to relieve stress: acupuncture, massage, biofeedback, cognitive therapy, finding a more suitable career, and so on. Our job is to know our limits and to learn what works for us in our attempts to better deal with stress. Don't be too proud to see a therapist. Sometimes we are too in the middle of our lives to see and identify what the problems are.

It is a therapist's job to help us identify our stressors and the impact they have on our lives, behaviors, and relationships, and to help us find ways of coping with our stress that are not destructive. I believe attitude is a huge part of how we deal with life and the stress that it brings us. A balanced diet, regular exercise, and a good night's sleep never hurt anybody either!

MW: In your experience, what are some of the best ways to battle stress on physical and mental levels?

RP: I keep repeating myself, but I believe that the number one way to battle the physical manifestations of stress is to accept and believe that the stress of our lives does, in fact, affect us in a physical way. I cannot say what the best technique for dealing with stress is for everybody. We all have to find that for ourselves. I can tell you what worked for me during medical school and internship, undoubtedly the most stressful times of my life.

In medical school, I maintained my sanity and physical health through yoga. It was a means by which I could meditate and contemplate the effects stress had on my physical and emotional well-being. It allowed me a forum in which to process that information and work out my stress and frustrations in a physical way, which works well for me. I was always more relaxed and able to face the rest of my day and what it had to offer after a good yoga and meditation session. I still am an avid yogi. It continues to be a very valuable tool in assisting me to deal with this hectic world in which I live.

During my internship I learned to believe in a higher power outside myself. I learned that I did not have to be in control of all aspects of my world to be successful or happy, and that the more I tried to control everything, the more frustrated and unhappy I became. I also learned the important lesson that, despite my career as a physician, I am not responsible for the behavior of others or the ways in which they lead their lives. It is a skill to not let other people's actions control our thoughts and emotional well-being—a skill that, when learned, can go a long way in maintaining our emotional and, thus, physical health.

When we are able to finally let go of the misconception that we are somehow responsible for the burdens of the world, it becomes much easier to deal with the stresses of our own lives.

MW: Outside of the questions here, are there any important points that you think are relevant to those battling hefty amounts of stress?

RP: Again, I would just say know your body and its limits, and be open to the idea that emotional stress may manifest itself in physical ways that you may not expect.

MW: Can you give any last words of advice?

RP: Do not look for the magic pill. *You* have the magic. Go inside!

* * *

I would like to repeat one of Dr. Peterman's comments:

It is about awareness, not control. It is often the desire to control their environment that finds people in unhealthy situations as a result of their stress. Very often, in medical practice, our patients are unwilling to believe that their headache was caused by how they reacted to the board meeting. People want a quick fix, a pill, or to be told that it is something physically wrong with them rather than simply a response to emotional stress. Accepting emotional responsibility for our own ailments is very difficult and this idea is met with great resistance. What can a person do? I would like to say, "Avoid stress." But with my profession and Type A personality, I know as well as anybody that is not possible in the world in which we live. The first step is accepting that emotional stress can and will be manifested in physical ways. Identify situations that cause you stress. Then become familiar with your body and how it deals with stress in physical and emotional ways. This gives you the tools to be prepared for what might come when the portfolio is falling apart.

Compare these words of Dr. Peterman to what Greene says in *The 33 Strategies of War:* "But if your mind is armed with the art of war, there is no power that can take that away. In the middle of a crisis, your mind will find its way to the right solution. Having superior strategies at your fingertips will give your maneuvers irresistible force. As Sun-tzu says, 'Being unconquerable lies with yourself.'"[2]

What I'm getting at here is that we have to be informed about what stress is at the most core level, if we are going to succeed in trading for a living. We commonly think that something like stress doesn't have much to do with our ability to make money in the markets. But it does. If we are able to defeat stress at every turn, we only empower ourselves that much more to make calm, cool decisions when the market is a tornado of movement and emotions. And such moments can be some of the most opportune times for making piles of cash. If we're so stressed out that we can't focus on the moment at hand, though, all the opportunity in the world won't matter, because we won't be able recognize that it's there in the first place.

SUMMARY

We have to understand that what we are doing *is* stressful and that we *do* need the tools to calm ourselves in the heart of the battle. Think about it in terms of a carnival sharpshooter. Here's a guy whose job is to make amazing shots with a rifle that most would deem impossible. The situation is stressful, as he has to not only calm himself to take a shot, but is probably dealing with emotions and stress that come with performing in front of a crowd as well. But to do his job, he must have some sort of tool to calm his jitters and put the target deadpan in the scope's crosshairs, and then pull the trigger. And this is almost exactly what seasoned traders do. If you're new to investing, I can assure you when you're starting to feel sweaty palms, there are 100 other guys around the country sitting behind trading screens and feeling cool as a cucumber. And if you let the stress of the moment allow a bad entry, these are the guys waiting to take your money. I know it doesn't sound entirely encouraging, but at the end of the day, it is the truth. Thus, we have to control stress in order to be the best we can be. What's more, stress is an extension of fear and anxiety, which we've already covered, and by understanding that the three all have a codependant relationship, our understanding of each individually, as well as the collective whole, will allow us greater chances of defeating them all.

* * *

With this in mind, Chapters 14, 15, and 16 present some proactive tools and concepts for our stress-battling repertoire to relieve pressure in life and on the trading floor, each and every day. These techniques—relaxation, breathing, visualization, and affirmation—are fundamental in crushing stress, fear, and anxiety. What's more, we will see that when we are able to calm ourselves in the eye of the storm, we also open ourselves up to the psychological tools that make us more intuitive traders, namely, emotional intelligence, emotional awareness, and the ability to disarm ego-centricity. Finally, when we are able to beat stress down, we will remain in the moment, while also allowing ourselves to stay grateful and positive no matter what the market is throwing at us.

CHAPTER 14

The Necessity of Relaxation

iology-online.org defines relaxation as, "A state of relative freedom from both anxiety and skeletal muscle tension."[1] In short, relaxation is when we are in a calm state, feeling peaceful and centered. When we are relaxed, we are free from the tension of the situation. In a peaceful state, we are in the state of affairs at hand, while emotionally removed from the tension of the stress attempting to present itself. We are free from negative emotions attempting to cloud our judgment, and we are able make clear decisions based on the facts at hand. Some will tell you that relaxation is two martinis, and while I can't say I can't completely disagree, we all know that sometimes it's better to just be alert and in the moment. Hence, we have to understand that stress and relaxation go hand in hand, as opposite sides of the trading coin. If we are to combat the stress of the moment, we must learn to relax, no matter what's happening around us.

SIVANANDA PRINCIPLES

Turing to the Eastern world here, we can take a look at the principles of Yoga according to the International Sivananda Yoga Vedanta Centres to help us calm ourselves in tough moments. The centre states, "It may be remembered that in the course of one day, our body usually produces all the substances and energy necessary for the next day. But it often happens that all these substances and energy may be consumed within a few minutes by bad moods, anger, injury or intense irritation. The process of eruption and repression of violent emotions often grows into a regular habit. The result is disastrous, not only for the body, but also for the mind."[2] Thus, in our initial investigation, we look at the three principles of relaxation as defined by the centre:

1. *Physical relaxation.* "We know that every action is the result of thought. Thoughts take form in action, the body reaching to the thought. Just as the mind may send a message to the muscles ordering them to contract, the mind may also send another message to bring the relaxation to the tired muscles."

2. *Mental relaxation.* "When experiencing mental tension, it is advisable to breathe slowly and rhythmically for a few minutes. Soon the mind will become calm. You may experience a kind of floating sensation."

3. *Spiritual relaxation.* "However one may try to relax the mind, all tensions and worries cannot be completely removed until one reaches spiritual relaxation. As long as a person identifies with the body and the mind, there will be worries, sorrows, anxieties, fear and anger. These emotions, in turn, bring tension. Yogis know that unless a person can withdraw from the body/mind idea and separate himself from the ego-consciousness, there is no way of obtaining complete relaxation."

For more information regarding these principles, visit Sivananda.org.

Given the aforementioned, we can see that when we are stressed out in the middle of the trading day, there's more happening than just the tension of the trade. What we can see instead are multiple levels of stressfulness: physical, mental, and spiritual. As we've already discussed, one of the foremost obstacles to dealing with stress is simply recognizing when stress is happening. But once we do, we can implement the necessary tools to bring ourselves back to a sense of centeredness (Chapter 1) and trade at our highest level of unconscious reasoning (Chapter 10), and approach the situation with calm awareness of confident self. One of the best ways to defeat stress is to utilize breathing techniques, something that is proven to help calm us down and aid in bringing us back into the moment.

BREATHING TO DEAL WITH THREE STRESSFUL MOMENTS

Here we cover three breathing techniques that can help in different situations. If you remember the interview in Chapter 2 with Ryan Dempster of the Chicago Cubs, Ryan stated that when the pressure is on, he often takes a step off the mound to calm himself with breathing techniques. Given his level of success, we'd be a little foolish not to at least give breathing exercises a chance. I personally use all three of the breathing exercises I am about to cover—on a regular basis—to calm myself in the middle of almost any hectic situation, or to simply clear my mind and bring myself into the moment before the crazy trading day begins.

The following exercises have been slightly modified because in the middle of a hectic trade we generally don't usually have the luxury of taking significant time to relax, as many breathing experts suggest. I've modified the breathing techniques into a sort of by-the-moment toolbox to help relieve the particular type of stress each moment dictates.

Sometimes we're lucky enough to have an epiphany that we're beginning to see things heat up around us. We're just entering into a moment when everything is beginning to go berserk, and somehow we've been insightful enough to see it coming. Such a moment can occur before a huge trade ensues, before a big meeting, or right before almost any stressful situation. I call this the "Uh oh! Things are heating up!" stressful moment.

Then there are days when the entire world is on our shoulders, and we feel completely out of sorts. These are the moments when compete chaos is unfolding around us, and we can barely keep our head above water. I call this the, "I'm totally in over my head!" stressful moment. In these moments, we are standing in the middle of a hurricane and no matter what we seem to do, nothing seems to work. When we are feeling this level of stress, we are in the heart of the storm.

A third type of stressful moment is the endless tornado or life storm that never seems to end. You know the type; it's just one thing after another. And then you have to get up and do it all over again. But the problem is that you're so stressed out before you ever even get started, that it's almost impossible to think clearly as everything unfolds around you. I call this the "Forget it all!" stressful moment . . . it's usually when we cuddle up with three or four martinis.

1. Uh Oh! Things Are Heating Up!

If you find yourself thinking, "What the heck am I getting myself into?" Rejoice. Why? You've been lucky enough to be cognizant of the moment and the stress that is beginning to build. What's happening is that you have been perceptive enough to see that things are heating up. You may have heard the cliché twist, "The light at the end of tunnel is really only an oncoming train." And that's perhaps what your subconscious is telling you in this type of moment. But here's the thing: because you've recognized the stress of the situation, you can make the outcome unfold in any way you like. You have a chance to proactively alter the situation because while things are heating up, they're not totally out of control yet.

After significant research, I think there's one breathing technique that works especially well in this situation. And after we make an effort to consciously use this technique for a while, it eventually becomes second nature. After practicing something for a while, it can eventually become ingrained in us, just like an athletic skill. Much like Barry Bonds is able to step up to the plate and crank out home run after home run—regardless of the pressure—we can learn to calm ourselves (almost unconsciously) time and time again, no matter how hectic the situation is.

The technique I'm referring to is called the Hakalau Technique, and it comes from The Harley Street Stress Management Clinic in London, England. When you recognize that you are entering a stressful situation, inhale a few big breaths, from deep in your stomach. (As a side note, deep breathing, also known as stomach or abdominal breathing, "comes from the abdomen and uses the diaphragm rather than the chest muscles to draw air deeper into the lungs."[3]) Then, looking forward, pick something slightly above your normal eye line to focus on. It might be the top of someone's head, the wall, the header of a doorway, or a trading screen in the distance. While you are doing this, remember to keep your eyes open (which is great, so if you're on the trading floor, in the middle of a crowd, no one around you will know what you're doing.) Next, start feeling your scope of vision being to broaden while you slowly become aware of the things happening in your peripheral vision.

While taking slow, deep breaths, your only goal is to become aware of absolutely everything happening in the space you are in. In your mind's eye, feel that you can see 360 degrees around your head. As you breathe deeply, become completely aware of everything happening all around your body. Feel the moment, listen to the sounds, and see the people moving. Observe all that is.

Your goal here is to become aware of the chaos that is at hand; however, what should happen is that when you begin to see everything unfolding, you will find a relaxed sense of self. Many times, we begin feeling stressed because we simply can't take in everything happening at that very moment. Thus, if we can separate ourselves from the situation, if only briefly, we are then able to put ourselves back into the situation, slightly less stressed, a little removed, but alert and ready to make whatever incredible decision is essential at that very moment.

When you begin to feel stressed, try this technique for 30 seconds and you may very well find that you're able to return to your center and trade like you've never traded before. This exercise can bring you into the moment so you can focus all of your attention on the events at hand.

2. I'm Totally in Over My Head!

Wow, do I ever know how this feels! Sometimes you stop for a moment and say to yourself, "Things are nuts right now. I don't know how I'm going to get out of this." At this point, you're in the middle of hurricane and there's probably no time to take a coffee break. This exercise will allow you to stay completely focused on the moment and continue trading, while standing in the eye of the storm.

Here's how it works: Breathe in through your nose while counting to 10. Then hold the breath deep in your stomach while you count to 15 (if you're a heavy smoker, or are going to sue me for having a heart attack because I told you to hold your breath so long, please only count to 3). Then quietly exhale through your mouth—to a point where you have absolutely *no* air in your lungs whatsoever. Repeat.

Personally, when I'm *really* stressed, I'm lucky if I can do this exercise more than five times in a row, but I noticed that doing so definitely helps calm my nerves. On the occasions that I've sat and breathed like this for a few minutes (and used the affirmations and visualization described in Chapter 15), I've walked back into the storm cool as a cucumber and done some of my best trading. I firmly stand behind this breathing exercise and believe that it can help calm any of us down when things around us are a tornado.

With this technique in mind, sometimes when I'm trading, and I have a chaotic set of circumstances that I feel like I have absolutely no control of—like one of those days where everything I do is wrong—I make it a point to go get a cup of coffee, sit down, and then do this exercise. Here's why: When interacting with the coffee machine, or the barista, I have to at least kind of pay attention to the coffee maker or the person I'm buying the coffee from. That redirected attention helps us out of our own head, if only for a moment.

After I've got a cup of joe, I sit down somewhere and then kind of look at the table or my cup of coffee. I try to let my vision drift away, not focusing on anything. (Just to let you know, when I first started doing this, I usually closed my eyes to find calmness in the cool darkness of letting my eyelids fall for a moment. In doing so, I found that as I let my head hang a little; my entire body relaxed a little. It's really quite amazing.) Then, I would do the breathing exercise while simply trying to not think of the events at hand. Focusing our mind's eye on a tranquil thought or remembering something pleasant in our past can help us to step outside of the situation. The object of this mental refocusing is known as an anchor. I've found that taking the time to sit down, anchor myself, close my eyes, and do this breathing exercise is generally the most effective way to completely bring myself back to center. However, everyone is different and you will need to simply take the time to see what works for you.

I've done this on the floor, while behind my computer, in a meeting, and even in an all-out argument with my significant other. I don't make a spectacle of it, and I've found that I can politely (and unnoticeably) do it while someone else is talking. And it seems that while utilizing this technique, I also hear every word being spoken more clearly, without my emotive opinion.

Sometimes we are so wound up that we fail to see things clearly . . . like the simple fact that our position is not coming back. I once heard an incredible trader say, "When you truly understand the market, you know to close a losing position and turn it the other way." While this statement has much more to do with our understanding of order flow and momentum, the one thing that should hit home is that it's much harder to turn a potential disaster into something positive if we can't see the situation calmly and clearly.

Really, when we are able to calm ourselves in the middle of a storm, we are able to do almost anything. No matter who you are, the breathing exercise I've just described is an amazing asset to calm yourself when things get rough.

3. Forget It All!

When I first heard of this breathing technique, I have to tell you that I thought to myself, "Okay, no way can this really help!" But it does. Quite often, we can find ourselves under the thumb of the world and almost nothing seems possible. It can happen at the end of a long trading day or when we are simply on our way to work . . . dreading the day ahead. The issue is that in all of our lives (and even more so in our trading lives), we are intricately part of an anxiety-ridden society that continually pushes us to our limit. Seemingly, there is no end. What happens is that we can find ourselves feeling like we just want to "forget it all." However, there's an amazing breathing technique that can help us in these foggy moments of frustration, sadness, and anxiety. And if you're waiting for the opening bell, and you find yourself having trouble seeing the day in a positive light, this exercise can help dramatically.

According to Dennis Lewis, the author of *The Tao of Natural Breathing*, some of our anxiety is attributed to the fact that we simply aren't breathing right.[4] Lewis (and other medical experts) argues that part of our anxiety and stress is related to the simple fact that most of us, in a constantly hectic state of trying to accomplish everything, create a type of self-inflicted hyperventilation.

Because of our wound-up lifestyles, many of us breathe in a rapid, short manner that reduces the level of carbon dioxide in our body. When we breathe like this, we are actually triggering the fight or flight reflex of our anatomy, something that we don't need all day, every day. If we live in a constant state of fight or flight, we become tense, anxious, and irritable. While this reflex can help trigger adrenaline in the short term, it can hurt us both mentally and physically after long periods of time. Lewis also states that because we are depriving our bodies of oxygen, we can have difficulty thinking clearly, thus finding ourselves at the mercy of our emotions.

Lewis is alluding to the fact that we need to retrain ourselves how to breathe in order to reduce our anxiety and stress. Have you ever noticed that when you make a deep sigh, you suddenly feel more relaxed? This is no coincidence; it's your body telling you that you need to calm down, by exhaling and then taking in more air. When you catch yourself making a deep sigh, your body is unconsciously trying to fight hyperventilation. It's a warning sign that you are tense, anxious, or stressed.

And the breathing technique to overcome our self-induced hyperventilation is as simple as our sighs. That's it . . . just sigh. Sigh, taking deep breaths in and exhaling deeply out. This is going to sound a little corny, but when you sigh, imagine that you are letting all of your problems and anxiety go with that breath you are exhaling. Imagine the bad trade escaping your body with the air leaving your lungs. Then, take a big, deep breath in, and repeat.

* * *

There are other complicated relaxation methods that involve lying down on your back and combining this type of breathing with meditation; however, in the busy life of a trader, you probably don't have time to do so. And, you might feel a little awkward lying down in the middle of the floor at work.

Many experts believe that while we are consciously breathing, if we think of all the things we are grateful for, we are able to expel additional stress and find ourselves peaceful in the moment. This is as simple as repeating to ourselves all the things we are grateful for, even the most simple things, like having shoes on our feet. If you remember in the chapter on gratitude, it's proven that grateful people are happy people. Thus, while breathing deeply, remember to think about all of the things you are thankful for. Through breathing and gratitude, when we are having a rough moment, we can change our perception of the entire situation at hand. Gratitude coupled with deep breathing can produce tremendous results of relaxation and help us come back to center. I think this is something that all traders could use a little more of.

SUMMARY

Taking the time to slow down and simply breathe when we feel stressed out can make all the difference in the world and bring us back to the moment. And if your positions are moving away from you, or you are frozen and not sure what to do with your winners, it's vital to have some additional tools that will help you clear your head to make the most profitable decision possible.

Breathing is more than something that simply helps us calm down physically . . . it actually can help us regain the mental prowess we need to overcome any situation.

What's more, at the end of a long day, the breathing techniques described in this chapter can actually help us feel refreshed, so that we may go the extra mile, and put in the research needed after the closing bell rings. If we take a few moments before the opening bell clangs each morning and practice the aforementioned exercises, while simultaneously going over the things that we are grateful for, chances are we will enter our day in a state of mindfulness (Chapter 1) and have a much better chance of staying in the moment, no matter what happens. Really, breathing combined with gratitude is one of the most powerful tools to help us steer clear of negative emotions that can pop up at any moment in the trading day.

CHAPTER 15

Affirmation and Visualization

A ll great traders have a plan...and they can see it each and every day. What I have just mentioned is an elevated concept of visualization, something that all the greats I have met on Wall Street have in common. Remember Chapter 4 with Kevin Cuddie, who hasn't had a losing month in over five years? Kevin mentioned that he uses visualization as a regular part of his trading. And given his track record, it's obvious that what he does works.

With Kevin in mind, throughout this chapter we discuss how affirmation and visualization can actually help us not only trade better, but also defeat stress and help us to become stronger, more confident people at the same time. Admittedly, the subjects of affirmation and visualization can be a little tough to really embrace at first, but for those who do, the results commonly seem very positive.

AFFIRMING OURSELVES

Personally, I've had a little trouble with the subject of affirmation for many years. When I first began looking into ways to improve my trading outside of market-related factors, I initially found affirmations somewhat silly. However, affirmations are a form of meditation and visualization and can help us to see our true potential. Affirmations are vitally important to become successful in all areas of our lives. I now believe that almost every successful person has some sort of affirmation tool that they use on a daily basis, even if they don't call it an "affirmation."

Affirmations are a pep talk of self-esteem help to keep stress in check, allow us greater emotional intelligence and awareness, and ultimately result in a healthy ego.

Affirmations Explained

To explain affirmations, I would like to reference the work, *Thinking Body, Dancing Mind*, by Chungliang Haung and Jerry Lynch. The authors use the principles of the Tao and I Ching to bring forth "Extraordinary Performance in Athletics, Business and Life." In the book they assert:

> *Affirmations are very important tools for awakening the Tao and living with its forces. They are strong, positive statements about something that is already true. If you're having a hard day, for instance, tell yourself, "I am calm, happy and in the moment." Just by being open to this thought and saying it to yourself, you will allow yourself to become nearer to this positive state of mind and even become calm and happy. To replace the random, endless, negative, or positive chatter that filters into your mind each moment of the day, affirmations are conscious preplanned, positive thoughts to direct your actions and behaviors in a positive way.*[1]

Affirmations come into play in the trader's day when things are becoming a little too hectic, and we recognize that stress has begun to rear its ugly head. The problem is that we will have no power to combat a stressful situation if we cannot identify that we are feeling anxious in the first place. But if we can train ourselves to see stress poking us in the side, we can begin to defeat the negativity hidden in the back of our minds.

We have to remember that whatever we dream *can* come true, and, thus, we must believe in our affirmations. If we are affirming that we are the best trader in the entire world, then we have to believe that such is true, or, at least, that we have the potential to be the best.

Affirmations will not work if we don't have confidence in what we are saying. Or, at least, the affirmation will not work if we don't have confidence in ourselves. Believing in ourselves is the core of positive self-talk. Here's the kicker, though: At times, we all question ourselves in our minds. When a difficult situation arises, we can either tune it out entirely or begin to speak to ourselves in a negative manner that is harmful and self-defeating. Thus, to use affirmations in a positive way, we must be able to recognize when they are needed the most—when we are down on ourselves and we are struggling to make sense of things.

When you begin to feel the stress of a trade (or life) weigh on your shoulders, recognize that is exactly the moment when you need to lift yourself up, affirming that you believe in yourself. For example, if you are in the middle of a losing trade, and the entire world is extremely hectic, take a moment to say, "I am quiet and calm, and this situation will unfold as I have already drawn."

Or, "With spirit and soul, the stress on my shoulders will now unfold."

Or, "This is only one trade; I will not let my commitment to success fade."

What's more, going all the way back to Chapter 1 where we covered our mission statement and our purpose-center, we will find the roots for some of our most amazing affirmations. If you are struggling with a string of bad trades, affirm your mission statement to yourself in your mind. By doing so, you are reinforcing what you desire, your commitment to why you are doing what you are, and letting go of the negative self-talk that can drag you down.

By repeating a positive affirmation quietly to yourself while utilizing breathing techniques (covered in Chapter 14), you can recover your center . . . and see the situation clearly. In trading, there are times when we can actually get too caught up in the moment, which is a dichotomy from much of the "we want to stay in the moment" talk so far in this book. What's important, though, is that if we get so caught up in the moment that we are microfocused on one small detail, we will unconsciously put on blinders, keeping us from trading intuitively. And if we get caught up in the emotions of the moment, we will not be able to effectively see that we've let our feelings get the best of us, and, thus we fall victim to knee-jerk trading reactions that turn our day into nothing but a crap shoot.

Life Application

Imagine that you are stuck in rush hour traffic or jammed in the subway after a long hard day. These moments are the perfect time to practice quieting our mind by breathing deeply and then repeating several affirmations to ourselves. For example, if you are completely crammed in a subway car— a stinky, loud, uncomfortable New York subway car—close your eyes for one moment (perhaps while keeping your hand on your wallet in your coat pocket) and say to yourself, "Thank you for this day; I am calm in every way." Quietly giving gratitude to the world through affirmations is one of the best ways to center ourselves in the moment. By doing so we are able to remove ourselves from the frustration of the situation.

In the day-to-day life of a trader, almost every situation is stressful, and with every trade we can often question our understanding of the markets. At these exact moments of self-doubt, when the entire ceiling seems like it's crashing down on our heads, is when we need to remember that we are incredibly strong and have worked hard enough to triumph over any situation. It's not always easy to do, especially when we feel the market or life has taken the wind out of our sails. However, a few simple affirmations can do wonders (coupled with some deep breaths) to help us regain our confidence and tackle the moment.

Most traders question everything at one point or another; thus it's essential that we affirm our greatness to ourselves to endure the stress of everything at hand.

VISUALIZING SUCCESS

Our minds are extraordinarily powerful. I'm constantly fascinated by our capacity to create imaginative movies in our heads. Because our minds are so remarkable, we are able to "see" a situation unfold—all in a flash—before it happens. It's really pretty amazing.

What I'm talking about here is visualization, the mind's ability to think in pictures. We see the outcome in our minds, before it ever actually occurs. But there's more to the story. For some, the act of visualization is simply a ho-hum experience, not to be taken seriously. But to be the best we can be, we need to challenge this line of thinking. Visualization is actually a significant part of training our subconscious to create the behaviors we need to achieve the success we desire. For example, many athletes use visualization on a regular basis, not only to train, but also to perform at their peak level during competition.

The way visualization works is to create a picture in your mind of exactly how you want a scene to unfold. Basically, you are seeing yourself in action, performing at your personal peak level, to create a desired outcome.

There's a very important distinction to be aware of though. To effectively use visualization, we cannot simply "see" the outcome or the end. Instead, we must picture, as clearly as possible, all of our actions that will make the goal come true.

Let me give you examples of incorrect and correct visualization.

Incorrect Visualization

Recently I was playing pool with some friends and was in the position where I needed to shoot in the eight ball to win the game. In my minds eye, I visualized the eight ball dropping in the pocket and then, of course, the excitement of the win. I visualized the ball dropping over and over. Finally, I took the shot . . . and I missed. What went wrong? Of course, my pool game needs some work—I don't want to overvalue my skill level—but some of the problem was that I was only seeing the *outcome*. I had visualized the ball dropping, and the victory, but I did not take the time to visualize myself actually shooting the ball. I wasn't seeing myself completely calm, with impeccable form, focusing on the ball. I wasn't visualizing the form of my stroke or the motion of the cue ball striking the eight ball. I forgot that the actual mechanics of the shot were the most important part of the eight ball dropping in the pocket, and I had not visualized the entire picture of what was to happen. We can visualize the win all we want, but if we don't visualize the actions we need to take in order to get where we want to go, we're probably not going to succeed.

Of course, even with visualization, there's always the chance of physical error, but with proper visualization, our chances of victory are much grater.

Using Visualization Correctly

To use visualization correctly, first of all, make a clear decision of what you want the outcome to be. You have to know how the situation will end before you can envision the events needed to make it happen.

Once you've clearly defined the outcome, picture yourself in the situation, exactly as you think it will happen. See what you are wearing, how you look, how you are feeling, the look on your face...perhaps even the shoes you are wearing. Next, see yourself in action from beginning to end. If you're in a sporting event, you will see your incredible form and technique while you execute the task at hand. If you are trading, you might see your screens, as well as yourself. See yourself taking in all of the information at hand, leaving no stone unturned. In addition, you must see your mood in the situation, along with the details of how the events will unfold. And if you are able to envision these details while utilizing a breathing technique, either preceded or followed by an affirmation, your chances of success will be that much greater.

At the end of the day, visualization is one of the most important facets of success that we can utilize. If we can see ourselves triumphing, we already know the actions we must take to do so. It's a type of mental plan, and given that many professional athletes use it, I'd have to say it works.

SUMMARY

Affirmations and visualization are two very strong tools not only to defeat stress and negativity, but also to help carry us in an even more positive direction when things are going our way. And for the trader, the simple use of his or her mission statement as an affirmation can make all the difference in the world if times seem a little rough.

Overall, it's easy to shuck off affirmations and visualization as items that are too touchy-feely for gritty traders. But, as I stated at the beginning of this chapter, every truly great trader I've *ever* met uses them both.

Finally, it's important to understand that like almost anything there's a right way and a wrong way to use affirmations and visualizations. For affirmations, if we catch ourselves with a false gratitude (Chapter 11) approach, we may never actually reap any of the gains the tool provides. What's more, for visualization, we must see ourselves in the process of making the foreseen event transpire, remembering that the journey is what creates the destination. Visualization without seeing ourselves utilizing the proper mechanics, knowledge, money management, and so on will only lead us to disappointment if the desired outcome is not achieved. Regardless, even if you experience a setback with either of these tools in the beginning, keep using them. It won't be long until you see the intrinsic benefits of both.

CHAPTER 16

Avoiding Self-Destructive Behavior

O n trading floors, I commonly see one thing... when a string of great trades surfaces, it's exactly the moment the guy who just made a ton of money begins to tear himself down. I constantly try to understand this behavioral self-destruction because I see it constantly in traders.

Self-destruction can be said to be something that causes self-implosion if certain variables are met.[1] Sounds about right. If you're a trader, you've probably got a Mr. Self-destruct-o in you, which you may utilize more often than you like to admit. Really, in the world of trading, to tear ourselves down seems almost human nature. At this point, we need to stop and ask ourselves three very important questions:

1. Why do we self-destruct?
2. How can we recognize when the self-destruct mode is in operation?
3. How do we thwart this seemingly inevitable occurrence?

Finding the answers is a tall order, and I'm sure several doctoral papers have tried to do so. However, I do think a few simple answers can help us.

UNDERSTANDING WHY WE BLOW UP LEADS TO RECOGNITION

Self-destruction can be rooted deep in our psyche, sometimes as a result of experiences from our childhood. At some levels, the only thing that will help overcome a tendency to self-destruct is professional therapy. But in less severe cases, it's possible for us to thwart destructive thinking simply by understanding what it is.

After much research, I came upon Ben Oofana, a guy who seems to really have a penchant for understanding the self-destructive nature of people. Ben Oofana is a healer who received training from a medicine man in the Kiowa tribe, Horac Daukei.[2] The Kiowa are Native Americans who are characterized as nomadic people of the plains. Today, most of the members live in southwestern Oklahoma. Oofana asserts,

> *The thoughts, feelings and emotions that we experience in response to the events of our lives need to go through a process in which they can be resolved. We're meant to digest our internal responses. When this doesn't happen, the conflicted or painful thoughts and feelings drop out of our conscious awareness. As they descend into our subconscious, they become more deeply embedded. Over time they become part of the fabric of our personality. These conflicted dynamics become hardwired into us.*
>
> *When patterns of thought descend into the subconscious, they become much more powerful and take on a greater permanence as they transform into beliefs. These beliefs act as filters or structures that have a major impact in determining how we think, feel and respond to the world there after.*[3]

What it really comes down to is that because we suppress our feelings and emotions, we are not able to transcend to the next level of greatness that we truly deserve.

Somewhere in the back of our minds, we have some type of emotional holdup that we have yet to recognize. From the viewpoint of Morita therapy, we are not able to live in the moment because we are not able to acknowledge the emotions that we are feeling. And by not accepting the bold emotions that come with trading, we can fall apart and never even know why. For traders, this holdup may simply be a fear of success, derived from some sort of negative experience of our past. (Again, professional therapy could be needed to truly assist with the issue.) On a lighter level, though, if we can recognize that we are entering an emotionally destructive phase— when it begins—we can attempt to defeat the negative nature of ourselves. By admitting to ourselves that we are feeling destructive, we are essentially taking the first step to overcoming the negative battle within ourselves.

Traders (and sometimes any of us in life) often begin to question themselves when things go their way based on deeply engrained self-told pseudotruths that we think are real. Case in point: Once in a while, when a novice trader is making a killing, I see a look on their face that is something like, "It can't be this easy!" And then, more often than not, I see them begin to fall apart. To add icing on the cake, if there's an older trader who's taken some hard licks in the market telling the kid not to get too cocky, it's generally just a matter of time before a whopper of a loss ensues.

Life and the markets are a complicated business and it's human nature for us to question whether what we're doing is working. I sometimes hear guys on the trading floor say things like, "You're never smarter than the market," which is exactly the kind of self-told pseudotruth I'm talking about. We sometimes begin to think the collective whole is always smarter than we are, and that we certainly cannot prosper forever. But we can. It's exactly at this moment when we have to realize that we are strong people who have worked hard to get to where we are. And, in doing so, we take the first step of overcoming self-destructive behaviors that appear from time to time.

THWARTING SELF-DESTRUCTION AND CLEANING UP THE MESS

In figuring out how to avoid self-destruction, I would like to go back to Oofana, whose resolution of the issue holds that we need to "digest" the thoughts, emotions, and events of our lives. We need to clean up our lives by healing the emotions that cause us to defeat ourselves at every turn. At some level, the cycles of subconscious self-destructive actions can only come to an end when we grow so tired of inadequate results that we resolve to free ourselves. Remember in the Introduction when we talked about Sisyphus, who pushed a boulder up a hill over and over, for all of eternity, only to see it roll back down every time it got to the top? That story is a perfect example of the self-destructive thinking that can block our success.

Have you ever asked yourself any of the following questions?

- How can I be smarter than the market?
- There's too much information out there; how can I ever understand it all?
- How can I beat the insiders when they have all the information?
- Why haven't I had a loser recently?
- Things have been going great lately; I wonder when the next unexpected event that kills my stocks will appear out of the blue?

These kinds of questions hit every trader sooner or later. While we may not be able to stop these questions from rising, we can positively put them to rest when they do. Here's an example.

How can I be smarter than the market?

Answer: Because I've done my research, and I am confident in myself. I may not be smarter than the entire market, but I am aware of what's happening around me, and I have given myself all the tools I need to succeed. More importantly, I believe in myself and I believe in what I am doing.

The next time one of these questions comes up, simply answer it as if you are answering someone who is asking you something ridiculous. Answer yourself, and affirm to yourself that you're damn good at what you do. And then get on with it, and trade like you know you can!

I think at some level, after we've all had some big winners in the market, many of us stop to ponder why our trades are doing so well. At times we might feel that we are just reading the market correctly, or simply that the information we may have received was right on target. But somewhere in this mode of thought, we are looking for a chink in the armor and are thinking, "Nothing lasts forever." My point here is that when we begin to go down this road, we are looking for something wrong and we open the door for failure. In the end, we could be trying to find something that will help us justify a loss, should it appear, but in doing so, we're only inviting trouble.

And it is in this last statement that we find some significant answers. We often feel we have to justify everything—including our losses. Thus, by inventing destructive thoughts, we will have some sort of justified answer when things fall apart. But we can just let go. We simply need to recognize when we are beginning to enter this phase and affirm to ourselves, "I am great; I believe success is part of my fate."

As Ryan Dempster stated in Chapter 2, one of the worst things we can do is "doubt." And with this in mind, we must work hard to rid ourselves of self-doubt. We must remember that we know what we know, and what we know is there because we've worked hard to know it.

Buckminster Fuller, the famous inventor said, "Given the resources on Earth, every man, woman, and child should be a millionaire many times over."[4] I would like to add that many, many of these resources are in us. We must simply lay our negative self-talk down and walk boldly into the future we have visualized.

Much of what our self-destructive thoughts come down to is a form of obsessive thinking that leads us to create the reality we fear. When we worry too much, we open the door to ruin. Thus, in our worries, it's important to recognize that the motivator behind the thoughts at hand is really just fear. And fear can ruin everything. Don't get me wrong, a little bit of fear can keep us from doing really stupid things, but if we fear too much, it can tear us down. And, as we covered in Chapter 6, fear is a slippery slope that, if not kept in check, can quickly manifest itself into something that keeps us from living to our highest potential.

But we can defeat fear at every turn, and in doing so, we will also refute some of our self-destructive self-talk that holds us back. In trading, one of the simplest ways to overcome our fear is to utilize trading stops. If we have precise stop-loss points, or trailing stops on winning positions, we can essentially let go of the situation. We know exactly where the end is, or in, terms of trailing stops, know roughly where the end will be should things turn around. If we just put in some circuit breakers that are completely unemotional, then we have a much harder time letting our fears and doubts get the best of us.

Finally, remember the concept of 'egocentricity' that we covered in Chapter 9? Well, I'm here to tell you that egocentric behavior is the number one killer of traders. I hear it out loud all the time; some guy will say something like, "I can't buy a break" or "I'm the kiss of death on any stock," or "you might as well use me as a contrarian indicator," or even, "that market maker just took the stock down just to get my stop." These are egocentric excuses for our own lack of knowledge and personal understanding. And for those who think this way when things are going against them, when things are good, all it takes is one little losing trade to set them in a negative self-talk downward spiral. The only way out of this is to (1) be positive and (2) realize that if we ever think the market is revolving around us, we are regressing to about age 11. I've been guilty of this type of behavior before, and actually don't know many who trade for a living that haven't . . . but it is a bad trait and will only set us up for a self-destruct-o moment in the future. And when we're in self-destruct mode, we sure as heck can't see any profitable opportunities surfacing around us.

SUMMARY

I want to mention that after many years of trading, I am guilty of all of the destructive behaviors mentioned in this chapter. So if you find yourself identifying with any of the aforementioned, don't feel bad . . . they are a normal part of learning to trade for a living. Self-destructive thoughts come when we have not yet built our repertoire of knowledge and confidence to a point where we are operating at a high level of efficacy. And sometimes a higher sense of value can only come after we've taken a couple of licks. It's kind of like a rite of passage to the markets. The important thing to remember is that even if you haven't been around the markets for too long, it's crucial to work extremely hard at self-honesty in order to be able to recognize self-destructive patterns when they surface. Often, even if we know negative feelings are looming, we are helpless to keep them at bay . . . purely because we don't want to believe that we are capable of tearing ourselves down. Believe it though, because I've yet to meet someone who trades for a living that hasn't taken a loss or two due to self-destructive behavior.

Lastly, if you catch yourself letting self-destructive thoughts into your trading, it may be a good idea to just take some time off. See, if we're already feeling that something bad is going to happen, we are in self-destruct-o mode. But if we do not make the necessary changes to thwart our own behavior and then we have a big loser, our inner subconscious may start saying things like, "See, I told you so." And when we begin this cycle, we are on the road to maladaptive fear and anxiety. Thus, sometimes the best thing to do is simply to save ourselves from ourselves by taking a day or two off. Every second that you are trading, much is at risk . . . don't play when your own deck is loaded against you.

* * *

Kevin Cuddie (Chapter 4) stated that when he's having a bad trading day, the elevated emotions can help him trade better. We know there is an elevated sense of stress that can help us perform at a higher level. But there's a point when no matter how hard we try, we just can't seem to make the right decisions. Part of avoiding self-destructive behavior is to know where this point is and ensure that we have a circuit breaker that keeps us from completely blowing up. And having a circuit breaker plan is as simple as knowing our trading plans and risk tolerance, both of which we cover in Chapters 17 and 18.

PART III

Developing Your Game Plan

So far, we've covered all the touchy-feely aspects of trading psychology, including fear, anxiety, stress, relaxation, affirmation, and visualization, as well as avoidance of self-destructive behavior. Now we take a close look utilizing these concepts to help develop a workable game plan for success. What's more, we cover putting together a risk management plan, while also taking a look at the constant of change in the market and within ourselves. These items may seem immaterial and frivolous at first, but they are vitally necessary for our attempt to consciously recognize if we are to ever be the best traders we know we can be.

Importantly, many traders *do* take time to develop a trading plan but never stop to consider the importance of a risk plan in terms of our own boundaries. If we know where our personal risk tolerances are, we can open the gates up further when we are underperforming and put the brakes on when things are moving against us. It's essential that each and every one of us have trading and risk plans, as without these two vital items, our trading will become nothing more than a stray arrow launched into the night sky or a rowboat in the middle of the ocean without any oars.

CHAPTER 17

Creating a Trading Plan

Take calculated risks. That is quite different from being rash.
                    —George S. Patton

The first step in developing our trading plan is to establish a sincere level of honesty of dedication within ourselves. And while focusing on honesty and dedication may not seem like a really important part of the trading plan, it is. In fact, the self-establishment of honesty and dedication are the framing that holds a roof up. Without them, the shingles might as well be lying in the front yard.

You have to stop and ask yourself, "Am I really putting in the time?" Many traders are available during market hours, but really only so in a trading capacity. Have you ever been on the floor of the Chicago Board of Options Exchange (CBOE) at 4:15 p.m. EST, fifteen minutes after the market closes? The place is a ghost town. Some traders return to their offices to work at their computers, but most desks are empty an hour after the close. I've seen it firsthand. More often than not, the foosball table in the lobby gets more attention than the day's activity sheets. Or plans are being made for happy hour or for later in the evening. After you've lived the battle of the trading day, who really wants to rehash it? I know I usually don't. The only guys who really want to talk about it are those who are new to the field.

But as traders or at-home investors, we cannot have pride in ourselves, or our research if we are not putting in the time. And without pride, which requires self-honesty to do the work, we will not have the esteem necessary to make rational decisions when the time comes.

If you lie to yourself, you're finished. And if you're not putting in the time, you're lying to yourself. I remember in my first year of trading, I would do a little research at night, which seemed like more than most of the guys, so I kept telling myself that I was doing the work. But because I was comparing my little bit of work to the nothingness of some of the other traders, I was really just lying to myself, benchmarking my own halfhearted efforts on the nothingness of others. At the end of the day, I just wasn't putting in the time. And after I took a few hits over the first year, I began to ask what was wrong with my trading plan. It took me a long time to figure it out. What I discovered was that because I hadn't made the commitment to being honest with myself and to remain as dedicated as possible (regardless of what the other traders were doing), my trading plan was just a piece of paper sitting on a desk. Without honesty and dedication, the trading plan (and everything else we hope to achieve in the markets) is a sham.

THE PLAN

In the beginning of the book, we covered what it means to know your purpose in terms of trading. Now I would like to take the sense of self that we uncovered in discovering our purpose-center one step further. Not only do we need to know our purpose, but we also need to have a plan to go with it. Not having plan is like running into a battle with your uniform on, but without a weapon. You're dressed for the part, but, really, ya got nuttin'. We must sit down and honestly decide what and how we are going to trade. I think the best traders in the world not only know *why* they trade, but also know *what* they are going to trade and *how* they are going to trade it. And they not only know these things, they have written out their plans, just so they have no doubt in their own minds as to what they are doing. In everyday life, we call it a business plan or, on a microlevel, a mission statement.

If you do not have clear and honest plan that you have written down on paper—the more detail, the better—you will fall victim to the opportunistic gambling of another trader's machismo calls. How do I know? Because I've never seen a trader not jump on someone else's call at one or two random moments in his or her career. It's just that way ... especially when things are slow. If you're standing there (or are in a chat room on your computer) and all of a sudden someone pumps a stock, we all have a tendency to want to piggyback the hyped call. Why? I don't know, but darn it, we just do. But if you have a trading plan in place, and you also know your trading purpose, your chances of shrugging off the irrationality of the situation are much greater.

So how do you put together a trading plan? In her book, *Divine Intuition*, Lynn A. Robinson suggests that the problem with finding answers is that sometimes we can never see them because we don't know what the questions are.[1] However, when we finally figure out the questions, we are then open to finding the answers. So if you aren't sure what your trading plan is, then here's a question-based exercise to help. Sit down and write out one or two paragraphs about what you enjoy in the market by answering the following questions:

- What type of trading do you prefer?
- Do you like to trade arbitrage, technicals, fundamentals, or order flow?
- What is it that moves you?

After you finish writing your answers, sum them up in one question. Here's an example:

I enjoy trading statistical arbitrage. I like to use basic descriptive statistics to identify entry points. I think there are some identifiable correlations in the market, where two or more stocks generally trade together and produce opportunities for me to make money. I believe that the statistical relationships also show the emotion of traders, as when a pair reaches three standard deviations from the mean, it seems that the pair reconverges as the market infers the stocks are trading too far from one another. I think at some level, Wall Street infers the relationship between two highly correlated stocks, and with fundamental and technicals in mind, creates the self-fulfilling prophecy.

Question to myself:

How can I learn more about pairs trading and develop all of the skills necessary to be the best trader I can be?

In the preceding, I have identified what type of trading I prefer and have opened the door to recognizing what I must do to become the best pairs trader I can be. Once I have brought myself to this level of clarification, I can then begin to build a more detailed trading plan. Here's a brief example:

My trading plan is to trade statistical arbitrage, or pairs trading. I will use basic descriptive statistics to identify entry points, and I will keep my strategy simple. Once I have found a plausible trade, I will then use fundamental and technical analysis to further identify whether the position is really tradable. No matter whether I am using statistics or not, I promise myself that I will always look at fundamental and technical analysis—and all earnings and news—before ever entering a position.

I will not trade a convergence pair unless it is trading at or within 10% of the third standard deviation. I will never take a loss larger than 5% of my total account. I will honor my stops, which are predetermined, before I ever enter a trade. I will not trade hype stocks, technology, biotech, or the housing sector.

Summary: I will trade stat arb, while utilizing fundamental, technical, and news analysis as secondary filters, and will not step outside of my predetermined boundaries or stop losses . . . and will never piggyback someone else's random calls.

Voila. I have voiced myself to myself and set up some very defined ground rules for my trading style. This information, along with a clearly identified purpose, is essential in helping to keep things together when tough times appear. I have found my purpose, centered myself, built a foundation, and created a trading plan. What's more, in the back of my mind, I've consciously told myself that there will be times when everything falls apart, and, at those moments, I will do my best to calm myself in the storm. In recognizing such, I will make every effort to step outside of myself, and do my best to work harder and smarter to reverse the losses in my account (and life). However, I recognize that I will be able to do so effectively only if I forgive myself for all that is.

When we strive to be great, we must remind ourselves to move through each and every trading day (and life) with a plan that allows us to recognize our strengths and shortcomings, and applaud ourselves for approaching our mistakes with forgiveness, and, of course, a little bit of humor. What's more, we must have integrity in our trading and in ourselves, if we are to avoid the negative emotions that can trigger things like egocentricity and self-destructiveness. Despite the public's opinion of Wall Street, integrity is actually very important in trading.

TRADING PLAN INTEGRITY THROUGH PHILOSOPHY

"Integrity" is a complicated word because all of our beliefs are different; what some of us perceive as integrity, others do not. However, for the sake of this text, I would like to reference the philosopher Plato who believed that men should follow a higher guide of morality in order to escape the trappings of self-interest.[2] What I am getting at is that if we are to escape the trappings of self-interest, our morality must first begin with integrity, a basic building block of ethics. It's not bad to pursue self-interest, but it is a negative thing to let our own desires maliciously attempt to hinder another for our own benefit. Thus, to proceed with perceived self-interest that is not harmful to others, we must operate from a moral stance of high integrity. I'm bringing this up here because the integrity that you put into your actions on the floor and in your trading plan will likely determine how well you are able to emotionally adapt to the stress of trading.

Before I get too far, I would like to insert that in today's society, we cannot confuse our understanding of integrity with lifestyle. While one person's choice of life might contradict yours, it doesn't necessarily make it wrong. With this in mind, I would argue that integrity is living kindly, helping others, and being careful of how we can potentially hurt others. In addition, trading (and living) with integrity is being proud of what we've accomplished because we've worked hard. Thus, in our trading careers, it is important to approach all of our failures and successes with integrity. Integrity is found in reflection, and goes hand in hand with pride. Living and trading with integrity gives us a sense of pride, which only helps boost our self-esteem. What it comes down to is that by living and trading with integrity, we are laying a foundation of success.

And here's where integrity in our trading plan comes in. The success coach Vinny Roazzi contends that we need to think of success as not only physical and even mental, but as spiritual as well. He says, "Success is not in the doing, it's in the being."[3] Thus, when we incorporate integrity into our trading plan as one of the items by which we expect to move through our trading day, we are actually creating a positive sense of self (and spirituality for some) that will help us trade with passion and purpose every day.

And, here's where we come back to Plato's principles. While you may be infinitely strong in your ability to make money in the market, integrity on a Platonic level also means treating those around you with respect and helping to pass on your knowledge. And it goes without saying that illegal activities such as insider trading and front running should be beyond our boundaries of integrity. But the main point here is that when we incorporate integrity into our trading plan, and do so from a stance of desiring to help others, we keep ourselves flowing with the ideas of the world and abundant in success.

When you have articulated a purpose and a trading plan, you have stated exactly what you will be doing, and you know why you are doing it. Basically, you have created a sense of integrity for what you hope to accomplish. And in having a trading plan with predefined rules, your stops and circuit breakers will (hopefully) keep you from having your entire account turned upside down.

There's another type of integrity that I would like to address: integrity in the things we say. Here's an example: When I first began trading, there was a guy on our floor that would pump a stock every time his position would begin to move against him. I think that somewhere in his mind he felt that pumping the position might trigger enough volume to move the stock enough for him to get out. The funny thing was that even if the surrounding traders had taken positions, it probably wouldn't have made a difference anyway. However, he felt that if he could get more traders behind the position, not only would the stock go up, but also, I think in his subconscious he was trying to not have to deal with the fact that he was wrong. Over time, most of the traders around him got pretty tired of his calls. The stock picks were purely self-motivated and had no integrity.

On the other end of the spectrum, I know a trader who shared his insights on a fair and even level when he thought a stock had potential. And before he ever began, he would let you know whether he already had a position. The guy had integrity, and because of that, when he spoke, everyone listened.

* * *

When we sum up the pieces, we see that by building a trading plan, we are also building a sense of integrity in ourselves. Basically, we are giving ourselves the best possible tool for success by having a road map of how we are going to get where we want to go. But developing a trading plan takes time and hard work. And, for many of us, our trading plans can change as our market knowledge grows. Thus, even when we do have a trading plan, it's important to remember that it's never too late to switch up and change our plan if the market demands so. Trading is about change, and if we are to succeed, we have to be able to roll with the punches, even if it means staying late and coming up with a new plan.

SUMMARY

It's important to keep in mind that integrity is actually a tool in our trading plan that we can use to do the best job we can to help others, and to keep ourselves in line with ourselves . . . especially when times get tough. I want to clarify that I'm certainly not talking about being perfect; certainly none of us are. But we do want to try to hold ourselves to a high level of integrity whenever possible. And if we falter from our trading plan or the integrity in our life, no big deal. We just forgive ourselves and get back up again.

* * *

Having come this far, the next step is to solidify the other side of the trading plan, the risk plan, which is often overlooked. The risk plan attempts to help us become very honest with ourselves so we know exactly what we are willing to put on the line every day. It's funny, I hear of people going to Vegas, saying that they will only risk a certain amount before they stop gambling. But the funny thing is that many don't have the same approach to the market, which can be even more unforgiving than the poker tables in sin city. The idea here is to know what we're getting into before we ever stick a toe in the water. The market is about taking risks, and sometimes when they don't work out, we have to laugh at ourselves a little. But with a plan, as described in Chapter 18, we can keep going.

Understanding Risk

J ust by taking the time to understand risk, we can take a huge bite out of our stress and not only learn to live with passion and purpose, but trade with it as well. At its core, risk is the potential for losses derived from any decision we make to act. Some calculate risk in terms of probability, while others look at it purely as a subjective element. Regardless, risk is involved in every bit of our lives. Everything we do involves some degree of risk. In investing, however, we often do not look at the term *risk* by itself, but instead use the term *risk management*.

Risk management is central to investing, and there are professionals completely dedicated to the subject. I believe, however, that everything we do as traders involves risk management. We not only have to manage our risk in terms of dollars, but we also have to manage, in a sense, the risk to ourselves. We have to know when we are hitting a critical level and when we are about to crumble.

MANAGING THE BIG PICTURE

Once we understand that risk is inherent in the game of life (and trading), we are able to move beyond the term and push ourselves further and harder than we ever knew possible. To do so, we must assess the potential risks at hand and consider the outcomes. Thus, as a trader, it's a good idea to sit down and write out what all of our risks are and then consider what our reaction will be should both unexpected and anticipated events unfold. At some level, by doing this risk inventory, we at least know how far we are willing to go to achieve our dreams. I always chuckle a little when I hear the motto of the rap star 50 Cent, who titled one of his albums, *Get Rich, or Die Try'n*. Wow. Now this guy put it all on the line, and what's more, he put his money where his mouth is, literally. Given that he made the firm declaration to himself of what he wanted to achieve, it's no wonder he's reached the level of success he has. He was willing to die for it.

Not every trader thinks the same way, and I'm certainly not insinuating that we have to risk our lives for success, but we do need to know what we are risking and how far we're willing to go. With this in mind, one way to know this is to write out a risk sheet, which is a list of what we hope to achieve and what we're willing to risk to achieve it. Here's my imagined risk sheet for 50-Cent:

Dream: To get rich, and I mean filthy, bling bling rich.

What I'm willing to risk to get it:

1. Be willing to die.
2. Be willing to work hard to do it.
3. Produce music that might be criticized.
4. Taking an occasional bullet.

What I'm not willing to risk:

1. Nuttin.

Okay, so humor aside, here's another example. This is my list:

Dream: To get rich, and I mean filthy, bling bling rich, so I can enjoy the rest of my life, help my family and others, paint, write, and simply live without financial worries.

What I'm willing to risk in terms of trading and writing to get it:

1. All of my finances, as long as I do not have a family to directly take care of.
2. Time, because my dream isn't going to come true overnight, and as I once heard, it takes 15 years to become an overnight success.
3. Living an easy, nonstressed life. Trading is stressful and to make my dreams come true, I know there will be some tough times.
4. The outcome. I can't determine whether everything will work out, but I can work as hard as I can to make it happen. Like Ryan Dempster said,

don't ask what if it isn't going to happen, only ask, "what if I don't work hard enough?" Regardless, I risk the fact that I might not make it.

5. The potential that my trading ideas won't work.

6. Until I'm 40, settling down and starting a family. Right now I know because I work 24/7 trading and writing, these things may not come true, but I'm willing to take the risk.

7. Potentially being shunned by my family and peers for failing. If I lose everything, chances are they will say, "Geez, why didn't you just take a safer route? You're so irresponsible!" But I am willing to risk not being accepted if things fall apart, just to consider the possibility of my dreams coming true.

8. Putting my ideas and writing out there . . . and having them criticized. It's human nature for many to try to tear down what they don't like, agree with, or deem beneath them. I have looked deeply at this risk and accept that I might receive poor reviews.

9. My future. I understand that by trading for a living, at some level, I am living dangerously; I accept the risk inherent with my choices.

10. My own health by pushing myself as hard as I can.

What I'm not willing to risk to achieve my dreams:

1. The health and well-being of my friends and family.

2. The chances of going to jail by doing something illegal.

That about sums it up. I completely understand where I want to go, and while this list doesn't clearly define how I'm going to get there, I at least know what I am willing to do to make things happen. And if things do fall apart, my only course of action will be to look at my list, recognize that risk was my plan, and instead of sobbing about why things didn't work out, to get up and do it again and again.

When we completely understand the risks we are willing to take, we are free to launch ourselves into our dreams.

In terms of trading, it's important that we have a risk plan in place as well. The list can be the same as the two preceding examples, but instead of our personal risks, the list would contain what risks our trading plan outlines for us. As an example, a few of our "What I'm willing to risk" entries might be something like:

1. No more than 5% of my total account value on any one trade.

2. No more than 10% of the capital in an open trade.

3. Trying a new style of investing, as long as the losses never exceed 5% of my account value.

What you can see is that by writing down our trading risk plan, we have clearly defined what our risk tolerances are. Really, creating a risk plan is all about forming a sense of self that layers directly on top of the mission statement we covered in Chapter 1. Understanding risk is synonymous with clearly identifying our personal, trading, and overall account stop-loss points. And when we understand our risk plan, we have a solid sense of purpose-center that will keep us calm when the markets are a tornado around us.

Realize, too, that if we are not willing to risk much, then we probably won't receive anything extraordinarily grand either. Taking a trading application and applying it to the concept of our risk plan, we can use the risk-to-reward ratio. The risk-to-reward ratio is a great barometer in any potential trade that measures what we are willing to lose versus what we hope to gain. For many, when the risk-to-reward ratio exceeds their tolerance for potential losses versus gains, there simply is no trade. Thus, if you make your risk plan and you then lay the items you are willing to risk side by side with that which you are not willing to lose, and the risk side looks discouragingly overwhelming, it may be a good idea to take some time to do a little soul searching. What's more, if the risks far outweigh the rewards, you may want to think about rebalancing the risk items.

If you lay the risk items next to what you are not willing to give up and see that the risks far outweigh the potential rewards, you might decide that you are completely okay with all potential outcomes. Then you at least know that there's not much on the risk side of your life standing in the way of your success, except perhaps your ability to learn, execute, and, most important, apply the concepts in this book to yourself to transcend the average psychology of the ordinary trader. Trading is risk, there's no other way to look at it. But for each and every one of us, somewhere in there is a delicate balance between risk and the dreams that we hope to achieve.

IN CLOSING

I would like to point out two things that Mike Palumbo and Ryan Dempster each said, which I think relate to risk as well.

Mike said that he plans to keep trading, and no matter what happens, if he loses everything, he has incredible children and great friends. Even with all of Mike's money, he clearly understands the risks involved and has identified what is truly important in his life.

Finally, Ryan Dempster, of the Chicago Cubs, said, "And remember, nobody's perfect. Part of the fun of life is to have failures and learn from those failures. More often than not, with this in mind, you're going to succeed. If you look in the mirror the morning after something went against you, and you can honestly say I did everything to prepare, and I did my best . . . you have no reason to be mad." Ryan also understands what the risks are, and he knows that even when he's worked as hard as he possibly can, there might be moments when not every thing works out. But if we've done all that we can, we have no reason to be upset. We simply pick ourselves up, dust ourselves off, and start over again.

SUMMARY

Though this chapter on our risk plan was admittedly a short one, it was one of the most important. To be successful in the markets, we must have a bold understanding of exactly what we are willing to lay on the line every day, including the aspects of our personal lives such as time spent with friends and family. Only when we clearly identify what we are willing to give up are we able to lean completely into our dreams.

* * *

The final key to developing a successful game plan is understanding that change is constant, which is the topic of Chapter 19.

CHAPTER 19

Change Is Constant

F inancial markets are like rivers that constantly flow though our lives. No matter who you are, your life is somehow affected by the never-ending ebb and flow of money. The question at hand is whether you actually help determine the direction of the rivers or whether you are simply at the mercy of the currents. What we have to remember is—no matter what—at least you're in the river. You're in the motion of things, trying to forge forward, every day!

Sometimes things are a little rougher than usual, and everything around us seems to crumble. Occasionally we find ourselves afflicted by bad luck, but more often than not, we're simply the recipients of the situation we've created. Regardless, when everything crumbles, we find ourselves upset, angry, frustrated, humiliated, and humbled. But tough times and feeling bad are part of life and a big part of learning our way in the trading world as well. These disenchanting emotions are tough when they're sitting on our shoulders, but we have to remember that when everything is buckling, we're learning and seeing things that we may have not been open to otherwise. It helps to remind ourselves that things *will* change. And it's crucial to keep in mind that change is what creates movement in the market, which provides us as traders with the opportunity for profit. In essence, change is something that we can certainly count on day in and day out in the markets.

CHANGE IS THE ONLY CONSTANT WE CAN COUNT ON

When examining life and the markets, we need to always remember that *everything* is constantly changing, and that *nothing* will *ever* remain the same. As the Buddhist nun Pema Chodron asserts, "Life is a constant shift of ground, things are always on the move, and as soon as we finally understand that the only constant that we can truly count on is that: things will always change."[1] In short, life (and investing) is filled with discomfort because the outcomes can easily shift from our initial expectations, changing from what we first anticipated. The discomfort brought on by change cannot be avoided. Indeed, as Chodron says, "The point is to lean toward the discomfort of life and see it clearly rather than protect ourselves from it."[2]

Taking Chodron's words to heart, we see that leaning into the discomfort of the markets is key to our success in trading. And to put some of what we've already read in perspective, in Chapter 1 we covered centeredness and in Chapter 3 we investigated our egos and esteems. What I'm hoping to have brought forth from Chapters 1 and 3 and our current conversation about change is that once we know ourselves, by leaning into our pain when things begin to go wrong, we find ourselves at a place of honesty, emotional intelligence, gratitude, and intuitiveness. In other words, leaning into the discomfort of the situation forces us to look at it with completely open eyes and question what's happening.

Sometimes though, we can be completely humiliated by the situation and may have trouble facing even ourselves. But when this happens, we have to remember to retain our sense of humor. It's actually pretty funny that most who trade for a living think they're pretty darn smart, but even the greatest traders of all time can't see every heart-wrenching market move coming, even when it's right there in front of them. But then, when we're completely broadsided by our own credulity, we suddenly find ourselves searching for answers...something we may have never done otherwise.

If we go through a period of ego-based behavior, sometimes the best thing possible is to have to endure a rough time or two. When we're down, the sense of humbleness that we feel can truly open new doors that were previously locked by the bolstered sense of artificial self that had somehow grown out of control. When we are wounded, we retreat to a place of modesty that may actually be our greatest stepping stone to becoming great traders and people, something that could never happen without the constant of change.

Let me give you an example: Recently, while trading a client's account, I had a spread trade open where I was short CH Robinson (Nasdaq: CHRW) and long Arkansas Best Trucking (Nasdaq: ABFS). The position continued to pull in the wrong direction throughout an entire year, and yet, for some reason, I kept it open. I'm not sure why—except that by leaving the position open and not looking at it each day, I was able to live in denial. I was able to pretend that the position was not negative and would come back at any moment. After about six months, I looked again at the position and realized that it had drawn down the account about 7 percent. My position stops are generally at 5 percent of total account value, and in this trade I had broken my rule by 2 percent. It doesn't sound like much, but when you're trading hundreds of thousands of dollars, little percentages add up to big bucks.

> *Nothing is as frightening as ignorance in action.*
> —Goethe

For six months I turned my cheek, trying to bury my head in the sand. However, after six months, I couldn't ignore the problem one moment longer. I leaned completely into the pain of the situation, humbled myself, had a long talk with my client, and told him of my plan to resolve the loss. What I told him was, "Look, the account is down, and I've been living in denial. However, what I would like to do is keep part of the position open, and continue trading. Here's exactly where our loss point is . . . I believe in the position and am going to have to do a little trading to pull the position into better shape, and utilize some option strategies. What I'm going to do is not without risk, but I need you to know exactly what's happening and agree to the plan at hand." My client thought about it for about five seconds, and said, "I can't believe you've held on this long. I know the risks here, and you know I know, so now keep doing what we both know you can do."

The words were like instant relief to a painful case of poison ivy. Not only did I relieve my own personal torment for looking the other way, but also my client agreed that the position should stay alive. I was honest with myself and with my client, and let him know that what I was doing was outside of my normal trading plan. And in an effort to remain honest, I informed him of the strategy I had planned and how I would execute it in the market. Everything worked out in the end.

Amazingly, once we have accepted defeat and let ourselves mentally realize a loss, we clear our own minds and consciousness to make an intellect-based informed decision potentially with intuition in the most critical of times. But to do so, we have to humbly accept the humility of the situation at hand. It's a type of rock bottom that forces us to take inventory of what we are doing, why we are doing it, what we know, and where we want to be. A business that doesn't take inventory on a regular basis doesn't stay in business for long. For the life of me, I can't seem to understand why we think our personal and trading lives are so much different.

I wish it hadn't taken me six months to learn the lesson, but sometimes you just have to learn the hard way.

At the end of the trading day, what we have to understand is that change is not only constant, but also a great evolutionary tool for us as people and traders. For example, when we take a position, the reasons for the position can quickly shift. We need to understand that our thinking and the position must change. Similarly, when things begin to change, if we do nothing at all, we are equally missing out on what could be the greatest opportunity of our lives. By allowing ourselves to openly accept change, we have the best chance to make incredible decisions when everything is going our way, or completely trading against us.

The point is that it's what we do with change that determines whether we will become superstar traders or fade away.

To recap what we've just covered, investing is a river, and often you're going to get caught in a whirlpool or find yourself tumbling over a waterfall. The facts are that because you decided to play in the river in the first place, sooner or later you're going to have a moment when it feels like you're about to drown. We must accept that there will be moments in trading when we're dragged to the bottom of the river and we'll consider caving in. But if we humbly look at the complete situation for all that it truly is, we will be able to clearly find a solution to swim back to the top again

Life is a river.

Investing is a river.

We swim in the water because there's no other place to be more alive.

Finally, genius is jumping into the middle of a roaring river and surviving. Stupidity is jumping into the middle of a roaring river and drowning. C'est la vie of the trader.

WHEN LIFE BLOWS UP, MAKE A CHANGE

Unfortunately, regardless of our planning, sometimes we simply get caught on the wrong end of a trade. Equally, in life, sometimes things just go haywire out of the blue. At these moments we need to pull together all of the tools we've collected to try to regain some sense of the situation. First and foremost, as I asserted in Chapter 1, if we have a clear sense of why we are doing what we are doing, these moments of difficulty can be a little less hectic. This is the fundamental grounding in our trading, and it will help keep us centered when the market has us by the toes.

The difficult part of being a trader is that at times, regardless of our efforts to stay sane, we can come unglued if our positions move against us in a big way. And, at some of these times, none of the tips we discussed so far can help. It's easy to practice breathing and visualization when the pressure isn't on, but when we have to focus, sometimes there just isn't time. At these moments of insane stress, one thing that we can do as traders is simply close out half of the winning or losing position. In doing so, we are able to take off a little pressure so we can then take a step back from the situation. I've heard great traders say time and time again, "Don't let a little loss turn into a big one." And this is exactly what can happen if the stress of the situation overtakes our ability to think rationally. I've personally had to learn this the hard way, but I'm not the only one who has. As an example, I offer the following story about the French war with Prussia in 1806 as described by Robert Greene in *The 33 Strategies of War*.[3]

Hoping to unseat Napoleon as emperor and restore Prussia to its previous glory, the king of Prussia declared war on France with a six-week time frame to prepare. He consulted his generals who inevitably argued with one another about style and strategy, but finally agreed to a military marching parade battlefield technique derived from Frederick the Great. However, Napoleon already had his troops on the move with nothing more than armory and backpacks, having shed the typical heavy wagons and other slow-moving equipment often found in large armies of the day. As a result, his troops were able to enter Prussia before the king ever had a chance to properly organize his glorified "parade" of troops.

Near the town of Jena, the French troops waged a vicious battle on one of Prussia's youngest generals, a man by the name of Hohenlohe. The Prussian troops were glorious in their precise marching tactics in the middle of an open field, something the most seasoned war enthusiast would love to see. However, Napoleon's troops never showed in a line. Instead they fired from behind trees and from rooftops, all the while running to and fro with almost no organization. In the end, the French were utilizing guerilla warfare . . . and Prussia's outdated "don't we look pretty" strategy exposed its troops to a massive barrage of bullets coming from everywhere and nowhere at the same time. Prussia was quickly defeated in the battle of Jena, and the entire country and army fell quickly after.

My father once told me, "A street fight, is a street fight, is a street fight." And from what I can tell, Napoleon knew this, as do most successful traders. With this in mind, here's where it comes together. In the first few chapters we talked about centering ourselves and creating a foundation of knowledge, which is absolutely essential for our longevity in the world of trading. But we also need to know when to put on our brass knuckles and start swinging. It sounds rough, and it is.

In stressful moments, after calming yourself, if you see that the only way to effectively trade your way out of a situation is to start swinging madly (e.g., with short scalp-oriented trades); then do it. Do what you must, but only do it if you have quieted yourself and your instincts are screaming for you to take action. And of course, only take brazen action if you have made the rational decision that this is what the situation requires.

Sometimes, when all else fails, guerilla warfare is the only thing that will prevail. Trust yourself.

There's another lesson in the story of Napoleon and Prussia, though, and that's of aged and obsolete tactics. Prussia was defeated because the old generals failed to see that things had changed.

As time passes, it's inevitable that things around us change. No matter how much most of us like things the way they were, they *never* stay the same. To paraphrase Chodron, the only thing we can count on in life is the never-ending instability because everything is constantly changing. The sooner we realize this truth, the better off we are. It's fairly safe to say that most trading styles only stick around for a year or two before some larger macrochange in the market causes the style to err. This fundamental principle is why most black-box systems get killed after a while. Black-box systems generally cannot read emotion and, thus, cannot see a paradigm shift while it is unfolding. But you can.

It's vitally important to realize that if your trading is not working or if you are having some serious emotional issues, you need to reevaluate what you're doing. You need to declare guerrilla warfare on your own mind and attack yourself from every angle. Dig deep, quiet the inner chatter of your mind, and seek the problem that's causing so much stress. Is it your trading style or the way you are approaching your trading mentality? Are your fundamentals lacking?

If you cannot honestly answer some of these questions, I can assure you that there are going to be some tough times ahead. I know because I've been there. While some of this chapter is a reiteration of Chapter 3, it is vitally important for each and every one of us to look at ourselves with unbridled honesty and do everything we can to effect positive change. Of course, this is where forgiveness comes in, but fret not, because if you've made it this far, you're certainly on your way to great things.

THE LAW OF FLOTATION WASN'T BASED ON THE CONTEMPLATION OF SINKING THINGS

I first heard about the "law of flotation... [being] discovered by thinking about things that float naturally" from Wayne Dyer, the renowned Christian

Scientist speaker. I have to say that it took me a little while to completely get it. What this statement means is that when the first theories of flotation were investigated we used materials that floated, such as wood, to build ships. However, as time went on, we began to see that flotation had more to do with water displacement and the entrapment of air than with items that just naturally floated. Hence, the eventual arrival of metal and concrete ships.

Sometimes natural logic keeps us from thinking beyond what we see and from seeing change on the horizon. To be successful traders, we need to understand that the market always changes because new paradigms continually surface and the dynamics of the markets change.

What we have to remember in life and in trading is that while something might seem impossible at first, we may have just not completely grasped the concept to make it a reality. And then, like discovering that concrete and steel can float, we find something stronger and more brilliant than anything we have ever known. When we simply embrace the concept that absurdity may simply be something we just don't understand yet, we at least are leaving ourselves open to see changes when they do arrive, even if we don't completely understand them.

At first, we don't understand why some things happen, and we think that the "wood" of the market should be what floats. However, the *best* investors of any age find some way to refute what the broader public thinks. Warren Buffett is a great example. When everyone else is selling, he is looking for buys. When the masses are buying, he patiently sits on the sidelines.

But there's more to the story. In understanding the theory of flotation, we see that somewhere within ourselves we eventually find a sense of strength that perhaps we never ever knew we had. And this amazing feat usually only comes from the experience, knowledge, and dedication to not only see change in the markets, but within ourselves as well. However, change usually lurks in the one corner that we've yet to look . . . or at least never think possible to look. One of the best traders I've ever known—a guy by the name of Adam Jones—once told me, "The key to trading is waiting for someone to leave a pile of money in a corner somewhere . . . and then when the rest of the world isn't looking, just walk over and pick it up." And he was so right. However, finding that "pile" of money (the change) is something that only comes with experience. Weather the tough storms—even when everything feels like it's falling apart—and you will eventually find your way to recognizing the piles of money hidden in change that the masses have overlooked.

SUMMARY

Throughout this chapter, we looked into change as a potential profit center when we are personally able to see and recognize that change is transpiring.

What's more, we also reminded ourselves that change is constant and is something that we should always expect. Finally, when we go through periods where we have not been able to recognize change and are suffering because of such, when we are finally honest with ourselves, we will come back to a humble sense of centered self that can open the door to new ideas that will only help us in the future.

Last Words

If you're not already exhausted from my rhetoric, I'm thrilled to still have you with me. Here's where I get to tell you all of the things that I haven't yet said. I would like to start by mentioning that I firmly believe in everything that you have just read. Everything in this book (except the lives of the people in the interviews, of course) is something that I have personally lived through and discovered (more often than not) the hard way.

Of note, I strongly feel one of the most important facets of success in trading, and in our business and personal lives, is to learn to laugh at ourselves. We *have* to take life with a grain of salt. If everything were easy, it really wouldn't be that interesting would it?

What I'm really saying is, please, no matter what happens; please don't lose your sense of humor, because sometimes it's all we have. I look back on the past 10 years, and I've done so many things that I'm embarrassed about that I can barely even believe some are true.

If having a little dirt on your hands is a sign of humbleness, then let me tell you, I've found humility many times over. We're all only human, and while we expect ourselves and the other people in our lives to never slip up, we do. For many of us, we fall down in our trading and personal lives quite often. If we never made mistakes, how would we ever have compassion for others or learn new things?

I believe that compassion is one of the most important keys to life. Without compassion for ourselves and others, we walk a rigid line of "self-riotousness" that will only shut us off from experiencing all of the things that this great world has to offer.

As one example, I'm amazed when I hear people (especially in the financial community) talk about collecting art. Here are people with tons of money who chatter about, uphold, and gawk at the brilliance of those who are long gone. But from what I've seen, these same people would have *never* associated with the actual artists in their own lives.

We scorn those whom we see as different, but yet, when the actual person can no longer actually invade our space, we hold them up with high regard. In some way, this is how it was for Jessie Livermore, the great trader, who I'm sure met considerable resistance in his lifetime. Yet today we hold him up as a market genius, even tough he died broke and insane.

Personally, I would rather die expelled from society, having lived fully, rather than having meandered though life without seeing, feeling, and experiencing as much as possible.

On a similar note, in the earlier chapter about integrity, I again reiterate that understanding the veracity of ourselves is laudable only if we are able to live with grace and understanding, not only for ourselves, but also for those around us. I continually find myself at a complete dead end in attempting to understand people who profess a spiritual faith, yet have absolutely no ability or desire to extend grace to those around them. It's important to remember that even Jesus walked with thieves, liars, taxmen, and the scorned. In fact, if I'm not mistaken, he preferred their company.

When we become so righteous that we cannot see that judging our peers has become a regular part of our life, we are living in a manner where much of what we are doing goes against what we preach.

Really, what I'm getting at is that no matter if we are judging someone on the trading floor or in our regular lives, we are not living to our full capacity simply because somehow judging others is in our spectrum of acceptable behaviors. If, in terms of religions and many philosophies from East to West, forgiveness is the key to greatness, then why do many of us never quite live this principle to its fullness?

Again, I'm not just talking about the way we view others, but the way we see ourselves as well. Look, we've all made mistakes, and for some reason it's engrained in our American society that retribution and repayment are the only answers. But they are not. In many Eastern and Western religions, the only retribution needed is our personal regret and honesty of the situation.

So with this I say, please let it all go. We all have axes that we've been grinding for years, and many of us have come to a point that we don't even know why. Perhaps we do it simply to have something to hang on to, because if we were to truly let go, then we wouldn't have anyone to blame for not living the dream we are capable of.

I know that some personal issues are much greater than others and require a great deal of professional help, but at some level, no matter who we are or what we've been through, greatness is only achieved by our courageous first step to effect change and let go of the things that are holding us down.

With all of this in mind, there's a trading term that sticks out in my mind that directly relates to what I'm talking about. The term is *turning the corner.* For so many traders, it's a struggle to soak up everything to a point where we understand the markets and ourselves well enough to become profitable. And much of turning the corner also has to do with understanding how we react to the events at hand. The point is, when we are finally able to "take a step to the next level," we are suddenly able to take everything that we've learned and apply it almost unconsciously. What it comes down to is "unconscious reasoning," or in another word: intuition.

With all that I've just mentioned, if we work hard to make sure that we turn the corner from a stance of grace, we are simply letting go of the thought that we know it all. Only when we surrender are we able to perform at our pinnacle of greatness.

In the end, I hope that we can all turn the corner and live happy, healthy lives, filled with incredible love, profitability, and hope for everything great that the future could possibly hold.

Lastly, I learned so much putting this book together. It made me realize that I, too, still have so much to live and learn.

And, by the way, I just want to add to you, the reader . . . thank you.

About the Interviewees

Kevin Cuddie is currently the managing director at Fox River Execution Technology in Geneva, Illinois. At Fox River, Kevin is responsible for creating and improving the trading logic within the algorithms to maximize execution quality for its clients.

. Previous to Fox River, Kevin owned a proprietary trading firm in Denver, Colorado. He has consulted and trained thousands of equity traders around the world. His most recent consulting job brought him to Shenyang, China, where he trained hundreds of equity traders specializing in NYSE stocks. Since the initial training period, the team has not had a losing month, echoing Kevin's own track record of maintaining a period of more than five years without a losing month.

Ryan Dempster began his baseball career with the Florida Marlins in 1998, making 121 starts in four years. In 2002 he was traded to the Cincinnati Reds. In 2003, he underwent the infamous and so-called Tommy John elbow surgery and was traded to the Chicago Cubs. Because of unprecedented dedication, his recovery was astonishing, and he quickly came back to pitch in the last half of the 2005 season. In a matter of months, he earned 33 of 25 saves, giving him the best save percentage in the league. Of note, Ryan was a National League All Star in 2000 and in 2006 was selected by the Cubs for major league baseball's Roberto Clemente Award.

Ryan is extremely active in charitable work, and in the 2001 season, was given the All Heart Award by the Florida chapter of the Baseball Writers' Association of America for being a positive role model for the community.

The Reverend Dr. Michael Eckelkamp has served as a parish pastor for 17 years. He has served in a variety of roles in the Lutheran Church Missouri Synod and currently serves on the Healthy Ministries Task Force of the Rocky Mountain District. He completed his Master of Divinity and Master of Sacred Theology at Concordia Seminary and his doctorate at Westminster Theological Seminary. He has served short-term missionary efforts in India and Kyrgystan. In addition, he leads tours in the Holy Land. He is currently considering the publication of his doctoral dissertation titled: Pastor Care to Families Affected by Chemical Idolatry.

Vic Frierson, as executive director of Park Heights Community Health (PHCH), coordinates every phase of a grassroots initiative in which health care providers, businesses, residents, and government interests collaborate toward the accomplishment of various short- and long-range public health goals. Under his direction, in 2006 PHCH completed construction of a $4.5 million community-based, community-managed health/multipurpose center.

Additionally, Vic has worked in several youth-serving capacities for more than 25 years. His most notable youth services accomplishments include founding, in 1994, and currently directing the PEACE Project, Inc., a performing arts, violence prevention, and risk-reduction initiative for high-risk youths. (See at www.PeaceProjectBaltimore.org.)

In 2001, he founded the Malcolm X Youth Center, which provides an array of remedial education, job readiness, development, and placement services in a one-stop location for out-of-school youths of ages 16 to 21, where he currently serves as director.

Vic is also the coauthor of *Prevention Tools: Building Strong Communities* (1996).

He graduated from the University of Louisville (Kentucky), where he earned a Bachelor of Science degree in counseling and guidance.

Julia Guth has been the executive director of The Oxford Club (a private club specializing in investment education and opportunities) for 14 years. For students of Investment U and members of The Oxford Club, she is a tireless advocate for attaining their respective goals and values. Ms. Guth holds an MBA from Thunderbird, The American Graduate School of International Management. A former specialist for Maryland's Office of International Trade, she was also an investment-services representative for one of the country's leading financial-services firms. Ms. Guth has written many reports on real estate in the Yucatan (Mexico) and Nicaragua. In addition, she has lived in countries like Spain and Brazil, and was part of the original team that arrived at what is now Rancho Santana, Nicaragua, on horseback, in 1998.

Matt McCall is the president of Penn Financial Group, LLC, an investment advisory firm offering personalized money management. Matt is also the editor of The PFG Letter, a semimonthly newsletter that concentrates on the PFG top-down approach to investing along with technical analysis. Before founding PFG, Matt was the chief technical analyst at Winning on Wall Street. There he built a reputation as a straight shooter as the cohost of a nationally syndicated radio show and at his investment seminars throughout the country

Sue Myers, PhD, APRN, BC, has had extensive clinical experience in hospital, community, and outpatient settings. She has practiced as a pediatric nurse practitioner since 1985 in primary care settings, including pediatric oncology, public health, and community health. While studying for her doctoral nursing degree, Dr. Myers was a nursing instructor at George Mason University. She is a member of Sigma Theta Tau, Inc., and is certified by the ANCC as a pediatric nurse practitioner.

In Dr. Myers's recently defended dissertation in 2002, she inducted a theory of problem solving by low-income parents about their children's health care. Her publications include an article on childhood obesity and clinical assessment of harsh childhood discipline strategies.

Her areas of expertise include all aspects of pediatric health care, with special emphasis on development and adolescent health. In addition to part-time faculty duties, Dr. Myers works half time as a research nurse with Partners Telemedicine in a home telemetry clinical trial.

Mike Palumbo was born in Chicago, Illinois, in 1966, and adopted by two fantastic parents. He earned his bachelor's degree at the Illinois Institute of Technology, and his MBA from Northwestern. Mike's trading career began at Susquehanna Investment Group, where he moved from clerk to trader in only six months, a record at the time. After moving to JSS Investments, Mike was able to earn enough trading capital to found Third Millennium Securities with $250,000.

By 1998, the firm had grown to over $6 million, but in August of the same year, when the Dow dropped almost 20 percent, Third Millennium lost $5 million. Mike states, "Being undercapitalized for the amount of risk I had, the clearinghouse suspended our operation until the risk was lowered (by the positions expiring) and I received a check from the IRS for overpayment of taxes for $1 million. It was the hardest time of my life. My marriage became unraveled and my wife and I were separated and subsequently divorced. But by April 1999, TMT was up and running again and my upstairs operation combined with a couple of floor traders made close to $10 million that year."

By 2000, Mike single-handedly pulled in more than $40 million out of the market, and TMT was the talk of the CBOE. As of 2006, Third Millennium is valued at $150 million and is now considering evolving into a hedge fund. Mike was named one of the top 100 proprietary traders in the world by *TraderMonthly* magazine and has also appeared live on CNBC's *Power Lunch* with Bill Griffith.

Dr. Royce Lee Peterman grew up in rural central Michigan and completed her undergraduate training in biology at Michigan State University.

She worked as a medical technician for a couple years after college until 1995 when she moved to Denver. She did basic science research at the University of Colorado Health Sciences Center until 1998, at which time she moved to San Francisco for medical school at Touro University. She spent her third-year clerkships primarily in Las Vegas, Nevada, and her last year of medical school training at several places around the country. She spent time in remote areas of Alaska, at the Mayo Clinic, the Cleveland Clinic, and the University of Cincinnati, to name a few. After she received her degree in osteopathic medicine in 2002, she spent her first year of internship at Henry Ford Hospital in Detroit. She moved back to Denver where she completed three years of internal medicine residency and currently is training as a fellow in cardiology at the University of Colorado Health Sciences Center. She plans to pursue further training in electrophysiology, a subspecialty of cardiology that focuses on the conduction system of the heart and abnormalities that occur within it causing various cardiac arrhythmias.

Joe Ritchie is the infamous founder of Chicago Research and Trading (CRT), which he sold to NationsBanc in 1993 for $225 million.

After his windfall success with CRT, Ritchie founded JD Dialog, which spawned scores of companies in the United States, employing over 5,000 people nationwide. JD Dialog has funded several computer-related ventures in post–cold war Russia, while also creating several new service-oriented companies in Japan. In 2003, Ritchie was introduced to Paul Kagame and his key staff and was so astounded by their character that he joined their ranks. Shortly after, Ritchie was instrumental in bringing Rwanda to the attention of Rick Warren, the author of *The Purpose-Driven Life* (Zondervan, 2002). Warren and Ritchie are currently aiding Project Rwanda, a nonprofit dedicated to furthering "the economic development of Rwanda."

Outside of his charitable works, Ritchie headed Steve Fossett's mission control for his world-record attempts at being the first man to blow around the world—solo—in a hot air balloon. Ritchie has also served as Fossett's recovery director and chase-plane pilot. On his own, Joe set five verified speed records in his Avanti P180 turboprop plane in 2003.

Currently, Joe is the CEO of Fox River, a multimillion dollar Chicago firm that specializes in execution systems, which, according to the independent firm Elkins McSherr, ranks in the top 5 percent in execution quality for all of Wall Street.

Bob Williams is a financial professional and a lifelong resident of Baltimore, Maryland. As a proud and active member of his local community, Bob completed his undergraduate studies at Towson University in north Baltimore and earned a Master of Science degree in finance from the University of Baltimore's Robert Merrick School of Business.

In 2002 Bob walked away from his role as lead financial analyst at a $3 billion private corporation to pursue his interests in trading financial markets. His knowledge of corporate finance and the tools he developed trading full time have brought him to the Oxford Club, a private financial organization headquartered in Baltimore, Maryland, offering a variety of wealth-building and premium trading services to its members. Bob currently serves as the Oxford Club's financial researcher.

Notes

Chapter 1   Finding Your Purpose-Center

1. The Todo Institute, Morita Therapy, accessed January 2007, http://www.todoinstitute.org/morita.html.

2. Dictionary.com, Dogma, accessed August 2006, http://dictionary.reference.com/browse/dogma.

3. TangoUK.com, Proprioception and Tango, accessed September 2006, http://www.tangouk.co.uk/proprioception.htm.

4. Learner.org, History of Psychology, Discovering Psychology, accessed August 2006, http://www.learner.org/discoveringpsychology/history/history_nonflash.html.

Chapter 3   Self-Honesty and Self-Esteem

1. Pema Chodron, *When Things Fall Apart, Heart Advice for Difficult Times*, Boston: Shambhala Publications, 1997, page 17.

2. Spencer Johnson, *Who Moved My Cheese?* New York: G.P. Putnam's Sons, 2002, page 71.

3. Nick Leeson, *Coping with Stress*, Virgin Books, 2005. Author comment: I have not used any specific excerpts from Leeson's book in *Trade with Passion and Purpose*, but I would like to recommend it as a great read.

4. Sun Tzu, *The Art of War*, Special Edition, El Norte Press, 2005, page 61.

5. Charles P. Kindleberger, *Manias, Panics, and Crashes*, Hoboken, New Jersey: John Wiley & Sons, 2005, page 81.

6. Nathaniel Branden, *Honoring the Self and Personal Transformation*, Los Angeles: Bantam, 1985, page 22.

7. Dictionary.com, Self-esteem defined, accessed July 2006, http://dictionary.reference.com/search?r=2&q=self-esteem.

8. Branden, *Honoring the Self*, page 19.

9. James Neil, *Definitions of Various Self Constructs*, 2005, accessed June 2006, http://www.wilderdom.com/self/.

Chapter 4   The Balance of Humbleness

1. Victoria Weinberg, "Big-Picture Player" *TraderMonthly* (February/March 2006), page 54. Only the "5 secrets" were reprinted in this extract. Reprinted with gracious permission of TraderMonthly Magazine and Doubledown Media, LLC.

Chapter 5   Be Courageous, Be Forgiving

1. Catherine Ponder, *The Dynamic Laws of Prosperity*, Camarillo, California: DeVorss Publications, 1984.
2. Richard Healey, The Metaphysics of Emptiness: Excerpt, 1998. Accessed September 2006, http://web.arizona.edu/~phil/faculty/rhealey.htm.
3. "This Quantum World," Thisquantumworld.com, accessed January 2007, http://thisquantumworld.com/ht/index.php.
4. "A Short History of Vacuum Terminology and Technology," McAllister Technical Services, accessed January 2007, http://www.mcallister.com/vacuum.html.
5. Ponder, *Dynamic Laws*, page 41.
6. Ibid., page 46.

Chapter 6   An Investigation of Fear

1. "Fear," *Merriam-Webster Online Dictionary*, 2004, accessed January 2006, http://www.merriam-webster.com.
2. "Fear, Fearing and Fears," Answers.com, accessed February 2006, http://www.answers.com.
3. Laurel Duphiney Edmundson, *The Neurobiology of Fear*, 2002, accessed March 2006, http://serendip.brynmawr.edu/bb/neuro/neuro00/web2/Edmundson.html.
4. Harvard College, Brain protein may play role in innate and learned fear, November 2005, accessed July 2006, http://www.researchmatters.harvard.edu/story.php?article_id=989.
5. McLean Hospital/Harvard College press release, Brain protein may play role in innate and learned fear, November 17, 2005, accessed June 2006, http://www.mclean.harvard.edu/news/press/current.php?id=88.
6. J. Panksepp, *Affective Neuroscience: The Foundations of Human and Animal Emotions*, New York Oxford: Oxford University Press, 1998.
7. Esther Jean Bay, *Fear and Anxiety: A Simultaneous Concept Analysis*, accessed August 2006, http://www.findarticles.com/p/articles/mi_qa3836/is_1999 07/ai_n8875265/print.
8. Kerstin Ackerl, Michaela Atzmueller, and Karl Grammer, *The Scent of Fear*, Ludwig-Boltzmann-Institute for Urban Ethology at the Institute of Anthropology/University of Vienna, 2002.
9. LeDoux, Joseph, *The Emotional Brain: The Mysterious Underpinnings of Emotional Life*, Simon & Schuster: New York, 1997.

10. Pavlov, I. P., *Conditioned Reflexes: An Investigation of the Physiological Activity of the Cerebral Cortex* (translated by G. V. Anrep), London: Oxford University Press, 1927.

11. Simon Ungar, *Environmental Perception, Cognition and Appraisal*, Glasgow: Caledonian University, 1999.

12. Panksepp, *Affective Neuroscience.*

13. Zevin, B. D., ed., *Nothing to Fear: The Selected Addresses of Franklin Delano Roosevelt*, 1932–1945.

14. "Greed," MSN Encarta, accessed January 2007, http://encarta.msn.com/dictionary_1861615261/greed.html.

15. Ibid.

16. "Collective Unconscious," MSN Encarta, accessed January 2007, http://encarta.msn.com/dictionary_collective%2520unconscious.html.

17. Ibid.

18. Tolman, E.C., "Cognitive Maps in Rats and Man," *Psychological Review* 55: 189–208, 1948.

Chapter 7   Overcoming Adversity and Anxiety

1. Pema Chodron, *When Things Fall Apart, Heart Advice for Difficult Times*, Boston: Shambhala Publications, 1997, page 17.

2. Seligman, M.E.P., Walker, E.F. & Rosenhan, D.L., *Abnormal Psychology* (4th ed.), New York: W.W. Norton & Company, 2001.

Chapter 8   Cause and Effect

1. "The Nizkor Project," TheNizkorProject.org, accessed January 2007, http://www.nizkor.org/.

2. "Causation," Dictionary of the History of Ideas, accessed January 2007, http://etext.lib.virginia.edu/DicHist/dict.html.

3. "False Dilemma," ChangingMinds.org, accessed January 2007, http://changingminds.org/disciplines/argument/fallacies/false_dilemma.htm.

4. Dharma Singh Khalsa, *The End of Karma*, New York: Hay House, 2005.

5. Jack Schwager, *The New Market Wizards*. New York: Harper Business, HarperCollins Publishers, 1992, pages 342–362.

6. G. K. Chesterton, *Orthodoxy*. San Francisco, Ignatius Press, 1995, pages 18–34.

Chapter 9   Emotional Intelligence: The Intuition Wild Card

1. Hein, Steve, *Introduction to Emotional Intelligence*, EQI.org, accessed January 2007, http://eqi.org/history.htm.

2. The term *emotional intelligence* was originally coined by Keith Beasley in 1987. Ibid.

3. Reinemeyer, Erika, *Edward Lee Thorndike*, Muskingum College, accessed January 2007, http://www.muskingum.edu/~psych/psycweb/history/thorndike .htm.

4. W. L. Payne, A Study of Emotion: Developing Emotional Intelligence; Self-Integration; Relating to Fear, Pain and Desire (Theory, Structure of Reality, Problem-Solving, Contraction/Expansion, Tuning In/Coming Out/Letting Go), page 1. Doctoral dissertation, Cincinnati, Ohio: The Union For Experimenting Colleges and Universities (now The Union Institute). Abstract available at http:// eqi.org/payne.htm.

5. Howard Gardener, *The Shattered Mind*, New York: Random House, 1975.

6. Biography: Daniel Goleman, Ph.D., The Consortium for Research on Emotional Intelligence in Organizations, accessed January 2007, http://www.eiconsortium .org/members/goleman.htm.

7. P. Salovey and J. D. Mayer, "Emotional Intelligence," *Imagination, Cognition, and Personality* 9 (1990): 185–211.

8. Bob Hoffman, *The Negative Love Syndrome and the Quadrinity Model: A Path to Personal Freedom and Love: The Hoffman Process*, accessed November 2006, https://www.hoffmaninstitute.org/process/negative-love/4.html.

9. John Snarley and George E. Vaillant, *How Fathers Care for The Next Generation: A Four-Decade Study*. Boston: Harvard University Press, 2002.

10. Dalip Singh, *Emotional Intelligence at Work: A Professional Guide*. London: Sage Publications, 2001.

11. Richard T. Allen, *Beyond Liberalism. A Study of the Political Thought of L. von Mises, K. Popper, F. A. Hayek and M. Polanyi, with an Appendix on A. Kolnai*, Chapter 14., accessed November 2006, http:// www.kfki.hu/chemonet/polanyi/ 9601/chap14.html.

12. Max Scheler, *Formalism in Ethics and Non-Formal Ethics of Values: A New Attempt Toward the Foundation of an Ethical Personalism*, trans. M. S. Frings and R. L. Funk, Evanston, Illinois: Northwestern University Press, 1973.

13. Max Scheler, *The Nature of Sympathy*, trans. Peter Heath, New Haven, Connecticut: Yale University Press, 1954.

Chapter 10   Developing Intuition

1. "MBTI® Basics," Myers and Briggs Foundation, accessed January 2007, http:// www.myersbriggs.org/my%2Dmbti%2Dpersonality%2Dtype/mbti%2Dbasics/.

2. Karol G. Ross, Ph.D., Gary A. Klein, Ph.D., Peter Thunholm, Ph.D., John F. Schmitt, and Holly C. Baxter, Ph.D., "The Recognition-Primed Decision Model," *Military Review*, July–August 2004, accessed January 2007, http://www.au.af.mil/ au/awc/awcgate/milreview/ross.pdf.

3. "Myers-Briggs Type Indicator."

4. Lynn A. Robinson, *Divine Intuition*, London: DK Adult, Dorling Kindersley Limited, 2001.

5. Paul Budnik, Jr., Mountain Math Software, promotional content for book, accessed November 2006, http://www.mtnmath.com/willbe.html.

6. Paul P. Budnik, Jr., *What Is and What Will Be: Integrating Spirituality and Science*, Los Gatos, California: Mountain Math Software, 2006.

7. Paul P. Budnik, Jr., "Einstein's Intuition," in *What Is and What Will Be: Integrating Spirituality and Science*, Los Gatos, California: Mountain Math Software, 2006, accessed November 2006, http://www.mtnmath.com/whatrh/node107 .html.

8. Paul P. Budnik, Jr., "Developing Intuition," in *What Is and What Will Be: Integrating Spirituality and Science*, Los Gatos, California: Mountain Math Software, 2006, accessed November 2006, http://www.mtnmath.com/book/node40 .html.

9. Edwin Lefevre and Roger Lowenstein, *Reminiscences of a Stock Operator*, Chicago: Wiley Investment Classics, 2006.

Chapter 11   Expressing Gratitude

1. R. A. Emmons and M. E. McCullough, "Counting Blessings Versus Burdens: Experimental Studies of Gratitude and Subjective Well-Being in Daily Life," *Journal of Personality and Social Psychology* 84 (2003): 377–389.

2. Robert A. Emmons and Michael E. McCullough, *Dimensions and Perspectives of Gratitude; Highlights from the Research Project on Gratitude and Thankfulness*, University of California, Davis, accessed September 2006, http:// psychology.ucdavis.edu/labs/emmons/.

3. Emmons and McCullough, "Counting Blessings . . . ," page 378.

4. Ibid.

5. Ibid., page 377.

6. B. Weiner, "An Attributional Theory of Achievement Motivation and Emotion," *Psychological Review* 92 (1985): 548–573.

7. Emmons and McCullough, "Counting Blessings . . . ," page 378.

8. L. J. Walker and R. C. Pitts, "Naturalistic Conceptions of Moral Maturity, *Developmental Psychology* 34 (1998): 403–419.

9. Emmons and McCullough, "Counting Blessings . . . ," page 381.

10. Ibid., page 388.

Chapter 12   Confronting and Defeating Stress

1. "Stress," MedicineNet, Inc., accessed January 2007, http://www.medterms.com/ script/main/art.asp?articlekey=20104.

2. Jan R. Markle, MA, BCIAC, Relaxwithin.com, accessed September 2006, http://www.relaxwithin.com/mneed.htm.

3. Ibid.

4. Dr. Ervin E. Lambert, "Static Stress Test," accessed June 2006, http://www.About.com.

5. Ibid.

Chapter 13   A Medical Evaluation of Stress

1. Robert Greene, *The 33 Strategies of War*, London: Viking Adult, 2006, page xviii.

2. Ibid., xix.

Chapter 14   The Necessity of Relaxation

1. "Relaxation," Biology-online.org, accessed September 2006, http://www.biology-online.org/dictionary/Relaxation.

2. "Proper Relaxation," International Sivananda Yoga Vedanta Centres, accessed June 2006, http://www.sivananda.org/.

3. *Abdominal Breathing*, University of California, Los Angeles, accessed June 2006, http://www.thecenter.ucla.edu/stress.html.

4. Dennis Lewis, *The Tao of Natural Breathing*, Berkeley, California: Rodmell Press, 2006.

Chapter 15   Affirmation and Visualization

1. Chungliang Huang and Jerry Lynch, *Thinking Body, Dancing Mind*, New York: Bantam Trade (paperback edition), 1994.

Chapter 16   Avoiding Self-Destructive Behavior

1. Messina, James J., Ph.D, *Stop Self-Destructive Anger Responses*, Coping.org, accessed January 2007, http://www.coping.org/anger/selfdest.htm.

2. Ben Oofana, Biography, accessed June 2006, http://www.doiohm.com/bio.htm.

3. Ben Oofana, *Understanding Dysfunctional Life Patterns*, accessed June 2006, http://www.doiohm.com/hardwired.htm.

4. Frederick Mann, The Millionaire's Secret (I) (1997), Accessed August 2006, http://www.mind-trek.com/milliona/tl13a.htm.

Chapter 17   Creating a Trading Plan

1. Lynn A. Robinson, *Divine Intuition*, London: DK Adult, Dorling Kindersley Limited, 2001.

2. Damian Cox, Marguerite La Caze, and Michael Levine, "Integrity," Stanford Encyclopedia of Philosophy, 2005, accessed August 2006, http://plato.stanford.edu/entries/integrity/.

3. Vinny Roazzi, *Get Rich with Integrity*, accessed September 2006, http://www.pioneerthinking.com/ara-success.html.

Chapter 19   Change Is Constant

1. Pema Chodron, *When Things Fall Apart, Heart Advice for Difficult Times*, Boston, Massachusts: Shambhala Publications, 1997.

2. Ibid.

3. Robert Greene, *The 33 Strategies of War*, London: Viking Adult, 2006.

Bibliography

Ackerl, Kerstin, Michaela Atzmueller, and Karl Grammer. *The Scent of Fear.* Vienna: Ludwig-Boltzman-Institute for Urban Ethology at the Institute of Anthropology/University of Vienna, 2002.

Allen, Richard T. *Beyond Liberalism. A Study of the Political Thought of L. von Mises, K. Popper, F.A. Hayek and M. Polanyi, with an Appendix on A. Kolnai.* Accessed November 2006. http://www.kfki.hu/chemonet/polanyi/9601/chap14.html

Bay, Esther Jean. *Fear and Anxiety: A Simultaneous Concept Analysis.* Accessed September 2006. http://www.findarticles.com/p/articles/mi_qa3836/is_199907/ai_n88 75265/print.

Benartzi, Shlomo, and Richard H. Thaler. "Myopic Loss Aversion and the Equity Premium Puzzle." NBER Working Paper No. W4369 (May 1993). Available at: ssrn: http://ssrn.com/abstract=227015.

Biology-online.org. Accessed September 2006. http://www.biology-online.org/ dictionary/Relaxation.

Bourke, Joanna. *Fear: A Cultural History.* Emeryville, CA: Shoemaker & Hoard, 2006.

Branden, Nathaniel. *Honoring the Self and Personal Transformation.* Los Angeles: Bantam, 1985.

Budnik, Paul, Jr. Mountain Math Software. Accessed November 2006. http://www. mtnmath.com/willbe.html.

Budnik, Paul P., Jr. *What Is and What Will Be: Integrating Spirituality and Science.* Los Gatos, California: Mountain Math Software, 2006.

Camerer, C., G. Loewenstein, and R. Rabin, eds. *Advances in Behavioral Economics.* Princeton, NJ: Princeton University Press, 2003.

Campbell, Joseph. *The Portable Jung.* New York: Penguin Books, 1971.

Chesterton, G. K., *Orthodoxy.* San Francisco, Ignatius Press, 1995.

Chodron, Pema. *When Things Fall Apart, Heart Advice for Difficult Times.* Boston: Shambhala Publications, 1997.

Cox, Damian, Marguerite La Caze, and Michael Levine. "Integrity." *Stanford Encyclopedia of Philosophy,* 2005. Accessed August 2006. http://plato.stanford. edu/entries/integrity/.

Cunningham, Lawrence A. "Behavioral Finance and Investor Governance." *Washington & Lee Law Review* (2002): Vol. 59, p. 767. DOI: 10.2139/ssrn.255778.

Dictionary.com. Accessed July 2006. http://www.dictionary.com.

Edmundson, Laurel Duphiney. *The Neurobiology of Fear.* Accessed January 2007. http://serendip.brynmawr.edu/bb/neuro00/web2/edmunson.html.

Emmons, R. A., and M. E. McCullough. (2003). "Counting Blessings Versus Burdens: Experimental Studies of Gratitude and Subjective Well-Being in Daily Life." *Journal of Personality and Social Psychology* 84 (2003): 377–389.

Emmons, Robert A., and Michael E. McCullough. *Dimensions and Perspectives of Gratitude; Highlights from the Research Project on Gratitude and Thankfulness.* University of California, Davis. Accessed September 2006. http://psychology.ucdavis.edu/labs/emmons/.

Gardener, Howard. *The Shattered Mind.* New York: Random House, 1975.

Goleman, Daniel. *Emotional Intelligence: Why It Can Matter More Than IQ.* New York: Bantam Books, 1995.

Gray, John. *Mars and Venus Starting Over: A Practical Guide for Finding Love Again After a Painful Breakup, Divorce, or the Loss of a Loved One.* New York: Harper Paperbacks (reprint edition), 2002.

Greene, Robert. *The 33 Strategies of War.* London, Viking Adult. 2006.

Harvard College, Brain protein may play role in innate and learned fear, November 2005. Accessed January 2007. http://mclean.harvard.edu/news/press/current.php?ID=88.

Healey, Richard. The Metaphysics of Emptiness: Excerpt, 1998. Accessed September 2006. http://web.arizona.edu/~phil/faculty/rhealey.htm.

Hoffman, Bob. *The Negative Love Syndrome and the Quadrinity Model: A Path to Personal Freedom and Love.* The Hoffman Process. Accessed November 2006. https://www.hoffmaninstitute.org/process/negative-love/4.html.

Huang, Chungliang, and Jerry Lynch. *Thinking Body, Dancing Mind.* New York: Bantam Trade (paperback edition), 1994.

International Sivananda Yoga Vedanta Centres, Accessed June 2006. http://www.sivananda.org/.

James, Neil. *Definitions of Various Self Constructs.* Available at http://www.wilderdom.com/self/.

Johnson, Spencer. *Who Moved My Cheese?* New York: Putnam, 2002.

Kahneman, D., and A. Tversky. "Prospect Theory: An Analysis of Decision Under Risk." *Econometrica* XVLII (1979): 263–291.

Khalsa, Dharma Singh. *The End of Karma.* New York: Hay House, 2005.

Kindleberger, Charles P. *Manias, Panics, and Crashes.* Hoboken, New Jersey: John Wiley & Sons, 2005.

Lambert, Ervin E. Static Stress Test. Accessed June 2006. http://www.About.com.

Leeson, Nick. *Coping with Stress.* New York: Virgin Books, 2005.

Leeson, Nick. *Rogue Trader: How I Brought Down Barings Bank and Shook the Financial World.* New York: Little Brown and Company, 1996.

Lefevre, Edwin, and Roger Lowenstein. *Reminiscences of a Stock Operator.* Chicago: Wiley Investment Classics, 2006.

Lewis, Dennis. *The Tao of Natural Breathing.* Berkeley, California: Rodmell Press, 2006.

Mann, Frederick. The Millionaire's Secret (I) (1997). Accessed August 2006. http://www.mind-trek.com/milliona/tl13a.htm.

Market Psychology Consulting. http://www.marketpsych.com.

Markle, Jan R., MA, BCIAC. Relaxwithin.com. Accessed September 2006. http://www.relaxwithin.com/mneed.htm.

McLean Hospital/Harvard College press release, *Brain Protein May Play Role in Innate and Learned Fear,* November 17, 2005.

Oofana, Ben. *Understanding Dysfunctional Life Patterns.* Accessed June 2006. http://www.doiohm.com/.

Panskepp, J. *Affective Neuroscience: The Foundations of Human and Animal Emotions.* New York, Oxford: Oxford University Press, 1998.

Payne, Wayne Leon. *A Study of Emotion, Developing Emotional Intelligence, 1985.* The Union for Experimenting Colleges and Universities. Accessed September 2006. http://eqi.org/payne.htm#The%20original%20abstract.

Ponder, Catherine. *The Dynamic Laws of Prosperity.* Camarillo, California: DeVorss Publications, 1984.

Rabin, Matthew. "Psychology and Economics." *Journal of Economic Literature* 36, no. 1 (March 1998): 11–46.

Robin, Corey. *Fear: The History of a Political Idea.* Oxford: Oxford University Press, 2004.

Roazzi, Vinny. *Get Rich with Integrity.* Accessed September 2006. http://www.pioneerthinking.com/ara-success.html.

Robinson, Lynn A. *Divine Intuition.* London: DK Adult, Dorling Kindersley Limited, 2001.

Salovey, P., and J. D. Mayer. "Emotional Intelligence." *Imagination, Cognition, and Personality* (1990): 185–211.

Scheler, Max. *The Nature of Sympathy,* trans. Peter Heath, W. Stark, Bernan Wand. New Haven, Connecticut: Yale University Press, 1954: pp. Liv. 274.

Scheler, Max. *The Philosophical Review,* Vol. 64, No. 4 (October 1955), pp. 671–673, DOI: 10.2307/2182652. *Formalism in Ethics and Non-Formal Ethics of Values: A New Attempt Toward the Foundation of an Ethical Personalism,* trans. M. S. Frings and R. L. Funk. Evanston, Illinois: Northwestern University Press, 1973.

Schwager, Jack. *The New Market Wizards.* New York: Harper Business, Harper-Collins Publishers, 1992.

Seligman, M.E.P., E. F. Walker, and D. L. Rosenhan. *Abnormal Psychology,* 4th ed. New York: W.W. Norton & Company, 2001.

Shefrin, Hersh. *Beyond Greed and Fear: Understanding Behavioral Finance and the Psychology of Investing.* Oxford: Oxford University Press, 2002.

Shleifer, Andrei. *Inefficient Markets: An Introduction to Behavioral Finance.* Oxford: Oxford University Press, 2003.

Singh, Dalip. Emotional Intelligence at Work: A Professional Guide. London: Sage Publications, 2001.

Snarley John, and George E. Vaillant. *How Fathers Care for The Next Generation: A Four-Decade Study.* Boston: Harvard University Press, 2002.

Spielrein, Sabina. "Destruction as Cause of Becoming [1912]," trans. *Journal of Analytical Psychology* 39 (1994): 155–186.

StockCharts.com. Accessed November 2006. http://www.stockcharts.com.

Strachey, James. *The Ego and the Id* (The Standard Edition of the Complete Works of Sigmund Freud). New York: W.W. Norton & Company, 1960.

Sun Tzu. *The Art of War,* Special Edition. El Paso: El Paso Norte Press, 2005.

The ToDo Institute. *Morita Therapy.* Accessed June 2006. http://www.todoinstitute.org/morita.html.

Ungar, Simon. *Environmental Perception, Cognition and Appraisal.* Glasgow: Caledonian University, 1999.

University of California, Los Angeles. Accessed June 2006. http://www.thecenter.ucla.edu/stress.html.

Weinberg, Victoria. "Big-Picture Player." *TraderMonthly* (February/March 2006): p. 54.

Zald, D. H., and J. V. Pardo. "Emotion, Olfaction, and the Human Amygdala: Amygdala Activation During Aversive Olfactory Stimulation." *Proceedings, National Academy of Sciences (USA)* 94 (April 1997): 4119–4124.

About the Author

Mark Whistler is the author of the recently released book *Trading Pairs* (John Wiley & Sons, 2004) and is one of two creators of PairsTrader.com and TradeWithPassionandPurpose.com. He is also a regular columnist for *TraderMonthly* magazine and TraderDaily.com as well as for the educational investment Web site, Investopedia.com. In addition, Mark is the editor for the trading/newsletter service, The Volatility Trader, found at www.mtvernonoptionsclub.com and is a regular contributor to the Accelerated Profits Report and the Smart Options Report (www.SmartOptionsReport.com). Just a few of his other writing credentials include *Investment U, The Motley Fool, Active Trader* magazine, BullMarket.com, OptionInvestor.com, and Stock and Commodities.

Mark's trading specialties are statistical arbitrage, in-the-money option reversals, and small cap fundamental analysis. Mark also writes and conducts research for The Oxford Club and is an investment panelist on the executive committee for the Mt. Vernon Options Club.

In his spare time, Mark is an avid painter with a particular inclination towards the neoclassical and surrealist styles, "because," he says, "life is truly that bizarre."

Index